MILTON STUDIES
XLVI

MILTON STUDIES

XLVI ❧ *Edited by*

Albert C. Labriola

UNIVERSITY OF PITTSBURGH PRESS

MILTON STUDIES

is published annually by the University of Pittsburgh Press as a forum for Milton scholarship and criticism. Articles submitted for publication may be biographical; they may interpret some aspect of Milton's writings; or they may define literary, intellectual, or historical contexts—by studying the work of his contemporaries, the traditions that affected his thought and art, contemporary political and religious movements, his influence on other writers, or the history of critical response to his work.

Manuscripts should be upward of 3,000 words in length and should conform to *The Chicago Manual of Style*. Manuscripts and editorial correspondence should be addressed to Albert C. Labriola, Department of English, Duquesne University, Pittsburgh, Pa., 15282–1703. Manuscripts should be accompanied by a self-addressed envelope and sufficient unattached postage.

Milton Studies does not review books.

Within the United States, *Milton Studies* may be ordered from the University of Pittsburgh Press, c/o Chicago Distribution Center, 11030 South Langley Avenue, Chicago, Ill., 60628, 1-800-621-2736.

Published by the University of Pittsburgh Press, Pittsburgh, Pa. 15260

Copyright © 2006, University of Pittsburgh Press

Manufactured in the United States of America

Printed on acid-free paper

10 9 8 7 6 5 4 3 2 1

ISBN 0-8229-4289-5

CONTENTS

OBEDIENCE IN *OF EDUCATION* AND *PARADISE LOST*

Jeffrey Gore

IN *OF EDUCATION*, John Milton offered a curriculum based on the classical trivium and physical exercises, and he believed that such an education would address a larger moral concern: "The end then of learning is to repair the ruins of our first parents by regaining to know God aright, and out of that knowledge to love him, to imitate him, to be like him."[1] Humanist claims that language-based education serves a greater moral purpose were commonplace in the early modern period: Roger Ascham argues in *The Scholemaster* that his humanist curriculum serves "God, our Prince, and our whole countrie," and Erasmus argues in *De Pueris Instituendis* that the ultimate goal of education is to provide a person with the means to virtue through learning a language.[2] Classical touchstones for such humanist beliefs in education's promise include Quintilian's argument in *Institutio Oratio* for the development of the *vir bonus peritus dicendi* [the good man experienced in speaking] and Plato's argument in the *Meno* that the end of knowledge is virtue, dependent upon our understanding the Good.[3] But today, such educational prerogatives seem distant from us in terms of both their means and their ends; we no longer organize education around a cohesive training in grammar, rhetoric, and logic, and apart from the occasional call for national service (as we have recently experienced with the teaching of foreign languages), we rarely conceive of education as a means to a unified ideological or moral goal.[4]

Although there are numerous studies that draw connections between early modern education and its classical antecedents, one of the most under-theorized questions is this relationship between teaching languages and the perceived moral good.[5] Given the relationship today between education and the marketplace, it is not terribly difficult for us to read early modern educational documents and to conceive how training in certain skills prepares a person for a particular career. Thus, we can recognize easily how training in rhetoric under a curriculum like Milton's would prepare students for "pub-like offices" (YP 2:379) or how training in wrestling and the "exact use of their

1

weapon" (YP 2:409) would prepare students for the "offices of war" (YP 2:377–79). But how would learning classical languages and rhetoric—and in the curricula of Milton and many of his contemporaries, practical skills like husbandry and the treatment of a "crudity"—serve to strengthen or "repair" one's relationship with God?

The answer to this question may lie in paradise. The central problem of *Paradise Lost* is the possibility of obedience; obedience is the foundation upon which Milton conceives both life in the garden and his curriculum to be organized. Although this essay explores first how obedience works within Milton's curriculum, I wish to make some initial comments about how it works in *Paradise Lost*. The failure of Adam and Eve in *Paradise Lost* might seem to revolve around a fairly uncontroversial, legalistic definition of obedience: their failure to follow a rule given by a higher power to govern their existence. Certainly, Adam and Eve's transgression of this rule does form the dramatic and theological center of the poem, but under this definition of obedience, readers in the tradition of William Empson might be entirely justified in considering that God acts as a repressive force outside human existence, the "Uncle Joe Stalin" who orders Adam and Eve's submission to an arguably arbitrary rule.[6] Without an additional understanding of obedience, a reader might be left filling in the gap between fear of punishment and love of God in a manner that, under the current analysis, would be unnecessarily mystified. This uncontroversial notion of obedience would provide the reader little to understand how both the creation and development of Adam's and Eve's characters, or *ethos*, made them "sufficient to have stood, though free to fall."[7]

I. Discipline and "Audible Harmony"

The discipline that comes from learning the rules of grammar and rhetoric provides coherence to Milton's whole curriculum. Obedience and discipline for Milton, however, do not only include our decisions to follow rules. Rather, through discipline the Miltonic cosmos is ordered, and this very discipline allows us to respond to the world. In *The Reason of Church-Government*, Milton considers discipline to be the unity of what allows us to make certain ordering decisions with the very factors that enable us to recognize order and divinity: "And certainly discipline is not only the removall of disorder, but if any visible shape can be given to divine things, the very visible shape and image of vertue, whereby she is not only seene in the regular gestures and motions of her heavenly paces as she walkes, but also makes the harmony of her voice *audible to mortall ears*" (YP 1:751–52; emphasis mine). Indeed, obedience has its etymological root in the audible ("to obey" equals *ob-*

audire, to hear toward or before another). In Milton's thought, discipline and obedience make heavenly and earthly form audible, and comprehension has a moral, theological, and disciplinary aspect. Milton's curriculum displays a different attitude toward discipline than we might hold and it boasts a fairly bold claim about education. In our own liberal society, which values so very highly the intellectual, cultural, and economic freedoms of "limited government," discipline is often perceived negatively. However, for Milton, obedience is less a submission to external rules and more the very potential for relation among human beings, God, and cosmos. And because he views discipline positively, it is my argument that as much as *Of Education* might teach a set of skills, its primary lesson is in obedience. Through discipline students achieve a greater sense of obedience and of what allows them to "repair the ruins" between themselves and God. I do not think we have to assert that this process of "repair," which notably comes from postlapsarian education through largely secular texts, would ever have to be complete. However, the following reading proceeds upon the assumption that Milton draws from humanist traditions certain methods of teaching Latin grammar and classical imitation in order to create in learners a "natural" obedient tendency. The resulting habits of thought and invention would be comparable to the tendencies of Adam in *Paradise Lost,* who had an "obedient tongue" from the moment of his creation: his "tongue obeyed and readily could name / Whate'er [he] saw" (*PL* 8.272–73). From the standpoint of the ideals of contemporary liberal education, nothing could seem more pedantic and restraining than Renaissance imitation. However, when understood as a matter of organizing both language education and ideology under Christian humanism, the training in obedience that imitation provides makes perfect sense. One could argue that the importance to Milton of this synergistic relationship between learning languages and moral training prohibits him from fully joining in the reform efforts of his contemporaries, the "many modern *Janua's* and *Didactics*" he claims not to have read (YP 2:364).

Like many of his contemporaries, Milton was involved in the reformation of education, but his proposed reforms still remain true to classical humanism. For one thing, he was intent upon improving the inefficient practices of teaching Latin grammar. In the introduction to his own Latin grammar text, *Accedence Commenc't Grammar,* he notes, "It hath been long a general complaint, not without cause, in the bringing up of Youth, and still is, that the tenth part of mans life, ordinarily extended, is taken up learning, and that very scarcely, the Latin Tongue" (YP 8:86). Lily's grammar, with its two sections in English and Latin devoted to the same grammatical lessons, was made the official grammar text of English schools by a royal mandate from Henry VIII in 1540, but a century later it had become the source of much debate and reform attempts. However, insofar as Milton may have shared in the spirit of correcting certain inefficiencies with other reformers of his day, such as Comenius and Samuel Hartlib (to whom *Of Education* is addressed), his curriculum remains essentially humanist. Gauri Viswanathan states, "[Milton] took from classical humanist educators . . . a belief in the character-strengthening function provided by Greek and Latin and combined it with the restorative purposes of moral agency."[8] The underlying emphasis in Comenius's work was to make the products of culture more accessible to a larger group of students: his methods of teaching placed much less stress on correct Latin than did humanists from Erasmus to Milton, and Comenius's projected Pansophic encyclopedia was supposed to draw together all the world's useful knowledge.[9] Under the humanist tradition, however, students gain moral agency not by the possession of a cultural product but through the socialization process of learning the culture.

Whereas one learns this sense of agency in *Of Education,* and it is innate in *Paradise Lost,* in both works this agency is based upon one's obedience to one's created nature. Once the student has walked in the schoolroom door, this obedience is not a matter of voluntarism; there is no choice of whether they obey specific commands.[10] Certainly, the student could leave the school, but once there, his choice is whether to be "a part of something," to exist in an environment and have something to do. A student's participation in the humanist educational experience is an "apprehensive" activity comparable to Adam's when he named the animals ("I named them, as they passed, and understood / Their nature, with such knowledge God endued / My sudden *apprehension*" [*PL* 8.352–54; emphasis mine]). Adam addresses here the dynamic of moral and linguistic agency. On the one hand, understanding requires an acceptance of the "givens" of language and nature: "I named them . . . and understood their nature, *with such knowledge God endued*" (emphasis mine). On the other hand, one actively "takes command" through apprehension. Words such as *apprehension* and *comprehension* contain the Latin base *prehendere:* to grasp, to seize, to take by surprise. This etymological history resonates in Milton's assumption—common among educators from Vives to Comenius—of the progression from rudimentary to higher-level understanding: the "knowledge of God and things invisible [begins] by orderly conning over the visible and inferior creature" (YP 2:368–69). (Had Milton leaned in this passage toward the Latin-based rather than the Germanic term, he might have opted for "apprehension of" rather than "conning over.")

For the grammar school student, obedience begins through the apprehensive activity of memorizing certain qualities of language. The stress in Milton's curriculum is upon language as a rule-governed system, with obedience to its rules the primary consideration from the very beginning.[11] Under Milton's curriculum, students would begin with the most material studies of the Latin language, focusing on "distinct and cleer pronuntiation" and becoming "expert in the usefullest points of grammar" (YP 2:383). Learning grammar is a process of memorizing rules, which requires obedience while it also exercises a person in the act of obeying. Milton's student would obey the demand to learn the rule and would obey the rule by employing the part of speech correctly in writing and speech. He would internalize the demand and the rule as he recognizes and remembers the nature of this rule for its correct use.

Milton's insistence upon the importance of the rules of grammar is consistent with the rule-governed nature of participation in the humanities. Gregor Reisch's 1503 encyclopedia, the *Margarita Philosophica,* contains a woodcut drawing of the schoolboy's entry into the "Tower of Knowledge," which illustrates the "two-fold" nature of grammar's relationship to the humanities as a whole. On the one hand, grammar is a key held by a female figure who invites the young scholar to the tower. On the other hand, grammar is the "foundation" of the whole tower: the first two floors of the tower are classrooms led by Donatus and Priscian, writers of Latin grammars widely used in the Middle Ages (figures representing the trivium, quadrivium, and natural and moral sciences occupy the next four levels).[12] Grammar is not simply the key, in the sense that one must learn Latin grammar to begin the "real reading." Rather, I suggest that the rule-governed reasoning that is so clearly part of learning grammar would be the foundation that supports the entire system in the same way that the bottom two floors in Reisch's illustration do. Grammar allows for rhetoric, logic, and more advanced studies, in addition to the various practical activities—also rule-governed—that Milton and many of his contemporaries began to include in their curricula. Seen as the ontological architecture of the entire system, the rule-governed nature of grammatical learning makes obedience not only the necessary initial step; it is there in every step that counts.

The reading I am here proposing, with its emphasis on grammar and rules, is certainly controversial.[13] Milton stresses the importance of not focusing too long on grammar, and he spends relatively little time on the subject in his treatise. But even though it was at times common practice among schoolteachers—in what would have been the beginning of mass literacy—to teach the "forms"[14] (YP 2:373) separate from their use, there is nothing really new among educational theorists for Milton to stress this point. At least since Erasmus, educators had been noting the inefficiency of simply memorizing grammatical rules separate from their application. Notably, Erasmus was one of the founders of St. Paul's, which Milton attended as an adolescent, and his

A schoolboy's entry into the "Tower of Knowledge," from Gregor Reisch, *Margarita Philosophica* (1503). Courtesy of Newberry Library, Chicago.

influence is widely recognized in studies of education in the period. Milton suggests in the Erasmian tradition that students begin "conversing among pure Authors digested" as soon as possible.[15] But it is clear that this "conversing" will not abandon previous training in grammar: throughout *Of Education,* Milton prescribes practices that reinforce grammatical learning, such as the common practices of collecting (usually in a commonplace book) *exempla* of rules of grammar to be found in "maxims" and "copious invention" (YP 2:372). The latter phrase is almost certainly referring to Erasmus's practice of having students write *copia,* or "inventive" variations on a sentence, a writing exercise that requires and reinforces one's understanding of grammar.[16] No matter how quickly one moves from formal grammatical studies into reading, we have to remember that reading itself is a matter of reinforcing one's obedience to grammatical rules; there is no reading without obedience to grammatical rules, something true for all languages but obvious to anyone studying Latin. Aubrey confirms the importance for Milton of brevity in grammatical study: "in a years time [Milton] made [his nine- and ten-year-old nephews] capable of interpreting a Latin author at sight."[17] However, my very point is that we should not overlook all that might have occurred in this year, all that it might have meant to his students in the formation of a relationship with their teacher and the language he is teaching them.

Certainly, there is the possibility that we could read such passages as "language is but the instrument convaying to us things usefull to be known" (YP 2:369) and assume that Milton is suggesting that language is entirely utilitarian, and we might conclude that little good is seen to come from grammatical study. But Milton's statement needs to be considered within its historical context, which is very different from our own, in which foreign language learning does not form the foundation of our curricula. Medieval grammar teaching emphasized learning grammatical rules abstractly, for better understanding how language works. (Directly after asserting the instrumentalism of language, Milton confronts such pedagogical assumptions: "if [a linguist] have not studied the solid things in [languages] as well as the words and lexicons, he were nothing so much to be esteem'd a learned man" [YP 2:369–70]). Humanist learning since Erasmus still emphasized rules, but for a purpose: to aid the student in reading, writing, and speaking a foreign language. In a certain sense, grammar was more important in the Renaissance than in the Middle Ages, for its rules were "embodied," that is, incorporated into the eyes, mouth, and hand of the learner for practical application. In *Crisis of the Aristocracy,* Lawrence Stone considers how this incorporation process served to create a small, literate public and to generate middle-class mobility. By Milton's time, the instrumentalism of rhetorical training had reached such a critical mass that a new stage of instrumentalism was beginning in the wake of Francis Bacon's promise in the *Advancement of Learning* to "teach men how to raise and make theire fortune." As David Cressy remarks, the proposed reforms of Hartlib and Comenius were consistent with this general trend.[18] Although Milton's language here is possibly responding to this instrumentalist thinking, the kind of humanist teaching necessary for his cultural agenda—"repairing the ruines"—still required teaching grammar and rhetoric in a patient, restrained, and ultimately correct fashion. The question of which curricula—Milton's or those of the Hartlib circle—would actually be more effective at teaching functional Latin is almost beside the point of my reading. I argue that the most important feature of Milton's pedagogy is that it gives students something to obey and exercises their "sufficiency" to do so.

When we consider Milton's emphasis on the need of precise grammar and pronunciation, his criticism against grammatical teaching is really against the *prolonged* study of grammar as a set of rules separate from their use. He argues, rather, for a progression from "sensible things . . . to the knowledge of God and things invisible" (YP 2:368–69). I wish to assert the importance in Milton's curriculum of rudimentary knowledge, of the "lowly wisdom" Raphael suggests—"Be lowly wise" (*PL* 8.173). Like scales and arpeggios for a classical pianist, the rules of grammar are always present in even our most complex expressions, and our use of language is a continued affirmation of the importance of this most rudimentary knowledge. Both Erasmus and Ascham write, "In manhood we remember nothing so well as the truths which we imbibed in our youth."[19] Because Milton's entire curriculum is based on foreign language texts, the socialization that Walter Ong suggests accompanied the teaching of grammar would be foundational to the lessons and stages that follow the teacher-student relationship.[20]

Having learned the rules of grammar, Milton's student would still be restrained from employing them too quickly. Two of Milton's major complaints in the educational treatise are with curricula that do not recognize a sense of restraint in the student's progression. First, he complains that students are thrust too quickly into complex questions: "in stead of beginning with Arts most easie, and those be such as are most obvious to the sence, they present their young unmatriculated novices at first comming with the most intellective abstractions of Logick and metaphysicks" (YP 2:374). Second, Milton complains that these curricula lead students into composition too quickly: "forcing the empty wits of children to compose Theams, verses and Orations, which are the acts of ripest judgment and the finall work of a head fill'd by long reading, and observing, with elegant maxims, and copious invention" (YP 2:372). He calls for a sense of pedagogical restraint that would not have always coincided with other reformers of his day. For instance, under

Comenius's curriculum, students would learn only the most basic rudiments of Latin before beginning to employ them in speech and reading, with less regard for correct employment or models to imitate.[21] Under Milton's curriculum, however, students work to acquire grammatically correct Latin and imitate models and incorporate rhetorical techniques before being given the pressure of creative compositions or thinking in complex forms of logic. Through this process of "filling the head," the student also exercises his disciplined sense of obedience.

For readers most interested in the individualism or antinomialism of Milton, the poet who was "rusticated" from Cambridge and would one day advocate beheading the king, it should be clear that I am suggesting that his writings on education present us an alternative view. One could certainly plot a trajectory that includes these rebellious incidents from Milton's life, the oppositional tone of many of his prose writings (beginning with *Prolusions*), and the emphasis on liberty in writings such as *Areopagitica* and argue that I have overlooked the essential emphasis in Milton. To be sure, we know that the force of much of his thought is against the *tout court* acceptance of conventions, even those based on seemingly transparent statements in the Bible, as we see in *The Doctrine and Discipline of Divorce*.[22] Along such lines, he makes explicit statements that would lead us to consider his ambivalence toward rules in *The Reason of Church-Government*, where he casts doubt upon whether "the rules of Aristotle . . . are strictly to be kept." But, if we look further into this passage, we see that he is suggesting that the use of "judgement," which might lead to breaking the Aristotelian rules of poetry, "is no transgression, but an inriching of art" (YP 1:813).[23] In *Of Education*, we encounter the Milton who is most interested in socializing schoolboys to have this potential for judgment (which might one day exceed convention or the status quo).[24] Similarly, in *Defensio Secunda*, Milton argues for the importance that liberty be grounded upon virtue: "You, therefore, who wish to remain free . . . learn to obey right reason, to master yourselves" (YP 4:684). Liberty may, in fact, be the "nurse of all great wits" (YP 2:559); however, *Of Education* is more directed at cultivating the "great wits." The distinction I am drawing here, by bracketing off liberty momentarily, is really based upon a question of what kind of learning is appropriate for adolescents and what kind might be more appropriate for other communities, such as the mature community of scholars and lawmakers considered in *Areopagitica*. Although Milton's "fit reader" lives by such Christian liberty, the curriculum in *Of Education* serves to socialize such a reader in a process of self-mastery during his adolescent years.

In "Milton and the Hartlib Circle," Barbara Lewalski overstresses the individualism of Milton's educational project at the expense of considering more fully how a training in convention, consistent with humanism, provides Milton a framework for his curriculum (or, in other words, how this training in pagan classics, farming, and wrestling would allow him to argue that he is "repairing" a relationship with God).[25] Lewalski's aim, after the manner of Ernest Sirluck's introduction to the Yale collection,[26] is to distance Milton's treatise from the work of the Hartlib circle: "[Milton] took some care to associate his treatise with ancient classical and humanist programs and to dissociate it from the Comenian texts that were seminal for the Hartlib Circle's educational schemes." The emphasis in her discussion of the work of Comenius, Hartlib, and John Dury is upon how the comprehensive, systematic nature of their plans for universal education would allow for little "diversity of opinion." She argues, however, that "Milton's deepest conviction . . . is that genuine education . . . must be largely self-motivated and self-directed."[27] I believe that Lewalski is correct in her distinction: there is a level of "self-direction" that would be needed from the student reading primary texts under Milton's curriculum that might not be necessary for the student reading Comenius's proposed encyclopedias with their "useful knowledge" already systematized. But the force of Lewalski's argument—for Miltonic liberty in opposition to Comenian conformity—causes her to stress liberty as the foundation of Milton's educational treatise in a way that would make it incompatible with the humanism with which she claims Milton is associated.[28] Liberty, or free will, may be a necessary condition in both religious and educational life; we could certainly agree that such is the case with Milton. However, liberty is not, in itself, a sufficient condition for either. (Pedagogically, no one is educated *by* freedom; theologically, humans were not "sufficient to have stood" *because* they were "free to fall.") Lewalski stresses liberty as the distinction between Milton and the Hartlib circle, but it is at the expense of recognizing the intense discipline necessary for Latin education to help create the "self-mastery" discussed above. In other words, Lewalski's concern with liberty is consistent with many of Milton's writings; in a humanist curriculum for adolescent boys, however, she has put the cart before the horse.

Memory is key to leading students to gain this obedient sensibility further.[29] Exercises in imitation will follow the memorization of the rules of grammar. In *John Milton at St. Paul's School*, Donald Clark reminds us that imitation was the long-preferred method for offering students the material and means for invention. Along with memorizing the rules of grammar, students under Milton's curriculum memorized various texts that embodied these rules. Memorization was a common practice throughout Milton's own education, as were practices of parsing, double translation, and paraphrase. Certainly, all of these activities involve forms of "creative" interpretation (for one makes word choices in parsing, translation, and paraphrase). However, as

Clark reminds us, whether a student is analyzing the employment of rules by a text deemed excellent or writing a composition that imitates an excellent text (also known as *genesis*), the student is involved in a practice of imitation.[30]

The primary text on early and premodern memory is Frances Yates's *Art of Memory*. Yates's scope is tremendous, extending from the Latin writers on rhetoric and memory, through the medieval period, up to Francis Bacon and Descartes. At first blush, much of her system might seem little related to *Of Education,* but a few introductory words are in order to establish the actual connection. Central to writings on memory since Cicero, Quintilian, and the unknown author of *Ad Herennium* is the distinction between natural and artificial memory. Natural memory is our ability to remember without benefit of a learned mnemonic system. Artificial memory comes from learning a formalized system of "places" of rhetoric (topoi, loci), which can then be organized in the memory to correspond to familiar, physical structures. For example, one might imagine that the expected parts, or places, of an argument correspond to the architectural features of a room or auditorium where a speech will be given, so when one glances around the room, one remembers the different parts of arguments.[31] Most significant here is how this training in memory relates to ethical training. In *De inventione,* Cicero considers memory as an aspect of virtue. Virtue for Cicero is a "habit of mind in harmony with reason and the order of nature" (note the similarity between this definition and Milton's definition of discipline from *The Reason of Church-Government* cited above). Virtue has four parts—Prudence, Justice, Fortitude, and Temperance—and Memory is a part of Prudence.[32] Because there was little need in the Middle Ages to train orators, Aquinas and other readers during this time highlighted these virtues when reading *De inventione,* but they deemphasized their relationship with rhetoric or memory by translating them into the four cardinal virtues of Catholic piety. Of course, it would be extremely problematic to align Milton with either Aquinas's Catholicism or the kind of classicism it supports. Furthermore, both Ramus and Bacon had presented deep challenges to the "art of memory" as a system of knowledge and had essentially only left intact a very pragmatic set of mnemonic techniques, without much of the ontological heritage, which for Yates is essential to the art of memory. What is most noteworthy about Yates's history and Aquinas's moment within it is how they illustrate the long, varied history of the relationship between memory and virtue. For Milton, virtue comes from the discipline of the learning experience, which is essentially a memorization process, be it memorizing statements or incorporating certain habits. Discipline, as he conceives it, is not a thing that is taught or a skill that is possessed. It is a state of being, of living within, where a student is taught to "appreciate" a world (again) by redirecting his or her tendencies to what that world provides. It is discipline that "makes heavenly form audible to mortal ears," and it is discipline that exercises the ability to become more obedient.

These memory drills served as a kind of digestion process of a culture, from its most rudimentary level toward the gradual recognition of this culture as a single, unified body of knowledge: "In which methodicall course it is so suppos'd they must proceed by the steddy pace of learning onward, as at convenient times for memories sake to retire back into the middle ward, and sometimes into the rear of what they have been taught, untill they have confirm'd and solidly united the whole body of their perfected knowledge" (YP 2:406–7). Teachers had the responsibility to direct students, over the course of many years, to recognize continuities within this memorized body of knowledge. These exercises in memory are so important in Milton's plan of study because, through memorization, the objects that form the system of culture are inscribed upon the person.[33] (The most apt illustration of this principle may come from the recurring metaphor in Yates's history of memory of the arrangement of letters on wax tablets.[34]) As the student grows within this system, the system serves to create the very personhood of the student. The acquisition of this Latinate humanist culture is, as Pierre Bourdieu writes, a "slow process of co-option and initiation which is equivalent to a second birth."[35]

Inscribing on a student this cultural unity serves to create a state of devotion to the cultural unity (that is, to its particular texts and languages), but also to inculcate obedience itself as a quality of the student's character. After focusing primarily on these rules, students studied Greek and Latin books of education: "But here the main skill and groundwork will be, to temper them such lectures and explanations upon every opportunity, as may lead and draw them in willing obedience, enflam'd with the study of learning, and the admiration of vertue; stirr'd up with high hopes of living to be brave men, and worthy patriots, dear to God, and famous to all ages" (YP 2:384–85). The goal of teaching books on education is not only to offer students an awareness of educational principles (as if they were studying for careers in teaching) but also "to draw them in willing obedience." The result of years of exercising within the rule-governed structures of language would be the growing appreciation of what it means to participate in a culture.

We can recognize in the passage above a progression from means to ends: tempering lectures creates willing obedience that causes students to become "enflam'd" with learning and virtue, with this virtue allowing one to be dear to God, and so on. Certainly, there is a progressive structure in Milton's program, from the most "sensible things . . . to the knowledge of God and things invisible" (YP 2:368–69). However, it is more startling if we stand back from the program as a sequence of instruments for obtaining certain ends and consider that the goal of the program, being dear to God, for Milton is a matter of obedience. As the most rudimentary virtue in this progression, obedience is the necessary factor throughout. (Thus, obedience is comparable to grammar, as the architectural foundation in my discussion of Gregor Reisch's illustration above.) The student obeys to become obedient, to *become himself*, the "true Poem" Milton discusses in *An Apology to Smectymnuus*. Through years of this kind of education, the student would "have in himselfe the experience and the practice of all that is praise-worthy," and consistent with the synergistic relationship between language learning and sensibility, this student would become a "composition, and patterne of the best and honourablest things" (YP 1:890). Notably, the relationship between practice and experience acts for Milton as an unquestioned assumption of education's promise: "Ere halfe these Authors be read, which will soon be with plying hard, and dayly, they cannot choose but be masters of any ordinary prose" (YP 2:389).

The certainty of Milton's rhetoric here is worth noting: by following this plan of study, students could not choose but to become masters of its goods. Under the current reading, they could not, in turn, choose but to *become* its goods. (Thus, the "goods" are not simply goods, per se, but more the foundations of experience and selfhood.) Viswanathan, however, is unconvinced: "[Milton's curriculum] is too programmatic, arbitrary, and idiosyncratic, and its principles of organization are too unscientific. For instance, Milton never clarifies how the study of agriculture and natural history leads one to discriminate between good and evil. Nor does he relate the practical sciences to the classical course of studies that he believes prerequisite to full participation in matters of state."[36] I would like to offer, *pace* Viswanathan, that what she refers to as its "unscientific" nature is, in fact, the virtue of this curriculum. She criticizes Milton's program because she does not recognize a correlation between its subject matter ("agriculture and natural history") and its proposed outcomes. Her very critique seems to work from the (also unquestioned) assumption that education would be the acquisition of either a set of cultural goods (comparable to some of the "Great Books" arguments of our time) or a set of standardized instruments (akin to the "skills" argument of education). Milton's program, on the other hand, is designed to inculcate a sense of obedience through practice and experience.

II. Milton's Monism

By considering Milton's material monism, we can better understand the synergistic educational possibilities of his regimen of seemingly very different physical and intellectual exercises. Stephen Fallon explains monism:

"Instead of being trapped in an ontologically alien body, the soul is one with the body. Spirit and matter become for Milton two modes of the same substance: spirit is rarefied matter, and matter is dense spirit."[37] In the preface to the second edition of *Surprised by Sin,* Stanley Fish argues that *Paradise Lost* is based upon an "ontology of monism."[38] My reading below of Milton's epic is consistent with Fish's position, but I wish to stress how monism is not just a poetic illustration of a theological position for Milton. Milton's humanist curriculum was an institutional expression of this belief. From an ontological perspective, schooling can always be understood as monistic: it grounds its students in a world and provides them with a means to cope with this world through habit-forming exercises where spirit is formed through art by the organization of matter. Of course, our understanding of education does not have to be ontological or monistic; we can bracket off the physical or choose to ignore how activity forms us as beings. In our analysis of a curriculum, we can, for instance, consider only the subject matter, the "reading list," and ignore how this reading list and the activities we perform with these readings serve to form our relationship with the corpus and our general habits of thought or the nature of our being. But for Fish's argument about *Paradise Lost* to stand, one has to accept that this materialist ontology is an intentional aspect of the poem. Similarly, I argue that *Of Education* is organized to ground its learners within such a monistic ontology: it intentionally teaches obedient habits of thought through synergistic physical and mental exercises.

Throughout Milton's treatise, both material and intellectual concerns contribute to the same character-building program. He begins his description of the school with its most material foundation: "First to finde out a spatious house and ground about it for an *Academy*" (YP 2:379). He provides for the possibility that the school building would be a significant place for a memorable experience to occur and not simply an arbitrary point in space for the exchange of knowledge as an object or tool. Milton's curriculum does not simply focus on traditional intellectual concerns but also includes more clearly materialistic activities such as studies of agriculture, physical exercise, and music, and even offers instructions for the limitations of students going abroad. The important thing to keep in mind with all of these studies is that they occur in the same environment, the same academy where the student began with the rule-governed elements of grammar. Agriculture, games, music, and warfare all share with the language-based exercises a respect for the rules that allow the student to participate in activities (for example, a person cannot grow a garden without respecting the "rules" of nature that govern the growth of plants).[39]

Richard J. DuRocher argues that we read *Of Education* with the greatest emphasis on these material activities: "In contrast with the standard grammar school curriculum built around the trivium of grammar, logic, and rhetoric, Milton's program emphasizes *res* instead of *verba*, things rather than words. . . . For the seventeenth century, Milton's reading program devoted unprecedented attention to practical matters."[40] DuRocher reads Milton's educational treatise in the context of Latin authors like Varro, Manilius, and Vitruvius, who wrote on agriculture, astronomy, and architecture, respectively. In the treatise and in Milton's own teaching, these traditional Latin texts on practical activities form the foundation of his students' reading once they have learned the rudiments of grammar.[41] DuRocher argues that in this Latin tradition, labor, and particularly the labor of farming, is part of an unfallen life that brings humans into material contact with the nature of which they are a part and "cultivates communities as well as individual souls."[42] Most notably, he contrasts this tradition of writings on practical activities intent upon building communities with writings that support more destructive practices like mining and papal and Roman imperialism. I wish to place the emphasis more upon the grammatical aspects of the traditional trivium than DuRocher does, but I would argue that for Milton the two are the same. *Verba* are a form of *res* with which humans may perform various violent activities like building empires or cultivating communities and individual souls. It is through the experience of laboring with language, which is thoroughly material insofar as it involves bodily habits, that the self is composed as part of a larger, potentially peaceful world of culture.

As much as DuRocher leads us to consider practical activities as part of a tradition of peaceful community building, we must recognize, too, that Milton advises teaching students "the exact use of their weapon; to guard and to strike safely with edge, or point" (YP 2:409), and he gives advice for their progression from learning to be foot soldiers to the skills of military horsemanship. Robert Fallon argues that Milton's inclusion of such activities in his teaching was part of his support of training an army for the Puritan cause.[43] Although DuRocher's and Fallon's positions are contrary, they need not be contradictory as long as one recognizes that warfare might have a limited place within a largely peaceful community that is not a militaristic empire. While Milton's training might teach young men to become "renowned and perfect Commanders in the service of their country," training in the martial arts can also be directed primarily at teaching students to have a sense of "just and wise discipline" (YP 2:412). For Milton, the greatest purpose of this training is the growth of a connected body and spirit: "This [exercise] will keep them healthy, nimble, strong, and well in breath, [and] is also the likeliest means to make them grow large, and tall, and to inspire them with a gallant and fearlesse courage, which being temper'd with seasonable lectures and precepts to them of true fortitude, and patience, will turn into a native and heroick valour, and make them hate the cowardise of doing wrong" (YP 2:409). Most notably, this training in the martial arts must be "tempered with seasonable lectures" to ensure that there is a connection between intellectual and physical training and that this training reinforces a sense of moral good, in "true fortitude and patience." Although Michael Lieb argues that Milton's academy "might well be looked upon as an officer-cadet school for Cromwell's New Model Army," his emphasis, which is consistent with my own, is upon how military training is part of a classical gymnastic training of an "inextricably united" body and soul.[44]

English civil war publications—such as *The Souldiers Pocket Bible* (1643) and *The Souldiers Catechisme* (1645)—attest to the clearly religious sense of purpose in military action.[45] For the Puritans, military training was a foundational means of expressing and cultivating a Puritan sensibility. Boyd Berry writes, "[The] puritans prized military drill and the ordered deployment of massed troops . . . and no doubt the preachers . . . had to tackle the problem that non-combatant drill is drudgery [with sermons that] explicitly exhorted them to develop harmony within their ranks." Through drills, Puritan soldiers "could express an inner, spiritual state of faithfulness."[46] Again, we see the same monistic continuity assumed between inner and outer: through drills (that is, the regular form of bodily practice designed to create a soldier as a trustworthy member of a group), soldiers could express their faithfulness, their trust in God and each other. Soldiers obey so as to express obedience. At this point, a formula for education emerges: by practicing X (in its most rudimentary form), one expresses X (in and toward its more complex forms). As with the Puritan soldier, the nature of the devotional drill with students is to inculcate obedience. By considering Milton's monism, then, of spirit and matter acting as two modes of the same substance, it is possible to see how material labor, both in the active and contemplative sense, can create a state of obedience that will allow students to have the mature, initiated frame of mind necessary to consider difficult questions, such as the difference between good and evil, which Viswanathan mentions above.

To emphasize further the learned nature of obedience in *Of Education*, we might consider the importance of Latin rather than English being taught as the foundation of Milton's curriculum. Milton's curriculum—which progresses from the most rudimentary rules of a culture to a more complex experience with this culture—is comparable to the learning experience of every human who has progressed from the infantile learning of the rudiments of language and hygiene to more complex activities.[47] By beginning with Latin, however, Milton is proposing a curriculum that offers a controlled, learned cultural unity that we can distinguish from what might seem natural or inherited, in part because it is based on a foreign language. The emphasis is, thus, upon a person's process of initiation into a longstanding tradition of teaching outside the vernacular that goes back to the Romans, who, as Clark reminds us, were originally not taught in Latin, but in Greek.[48] Ong emphasizes that a foreign language is important in establishing the school as a "marginal environment" in which such an initiation process can occur.[49] By teaching in a language foreign to its students, teachers can control the rate at which students begin to employ the rules of its grammar in more complex exercises. The very "inefficiency" of teaching in a foreign tongue allows teachers to maintain an environment where learning the language also exercises an obedient sensibility.

III. Education and Obedience in *Paradise Lost*

From the perspective of theological history, it might seem that the potential of education to "repair the ruines" of our postlapsarian world in *Of Education* might best be compared to the educational process described in Books Eleven and Twelve, the postlapsarian section of Milton's epic. Michael's lesson begins with the promise to impart to Adam certain information he does not already know: "I am sent / To show thee what shall come in future days" (*PL* 11.356–57). He states clearly the conflict he will illustrate: "good with bad / . . . supernal grace contending / With sinfulness of men" (*PL* 11.358–60). He even tells his fallen student the desired pedagogical outcome of this lesson:

> To learn
> True patience, and to temper joy with fear
> And pious sorrow, equally inured
> By moderation either state to bear,
> Prosperous or adverse.   (PL 11.360–64)

Michael then proceeds to illustrate this conflict of "good with bad" by showing Adam, Cain, and Abel, and illustrates the "supernal grace" of a succession of men, Noah, Abraham, and Moses, who contend with the "sinfulness of men." Within each of these illustrations, Michael prepares his student with "shadowy types" (*PL* 12.303) for the ultimate "truth" of grace, the arrival of the Messiah. With his clearly illustrated concepts and openly revealed pedagogical techniques—which would certainly receive the approval of Viswanathan—Michael succeeds in teaching Adam, who declares at the end of the lesson his adherence to the key concept of this essay: "Henceforth, I learn that to obey is best" (*PL* 12.561). Further affirmation of the success of Michael's pedagogy is the fact that he instructs Adam to summarize an appropriate version of this lesson to Eve: "thou at season fit / Let her with thee partake what thou hast heard, / Chiefly what may concern her Faith to know" (*PL* 12.597–99).

From a pedagogical perspective, however, the learning process described in Books Eleven and Twelve is precisely not the one I have been describing in *Of Education*. I initially questioned how learning classical languages and rhetoric and practical skills like husbandry and the treatment of a "crudity" would serve to strengthen or repair one's relationship with God. While Books Eleven and Twelve tell a history of human folly that thoroughly illustrates the need for a messiah, almost entirely absent from *Of Education* is any serious attempt to teach texts with Christian content. This absence is what leads to Viswanathan's valid (but underinformed) question. The difference between the approach to obedience found in the final books of *Paradise Lost* and that found in *Of Education* is the difference between an informed, rational decision to obey and an obedient tendency. The first word in Adam's statement, "Henceforth, I learn that to obey is best," is a clear signal of a deliberate, committed decision, based upon overwhelming evidence from the various scenes Michael has shown Adam. (Similarly, Jameela Lares argues that Michael's presentation of various episodes in providential history is more similar to preaching than it is to pedagogical activity.[50]) But *Of Education* does not really provide scenes or summarizable content. Rather, I have attempted to demonstrate that through exercises in language and other rule-governed systems, *Of Education* exercises its student in an obedient tendency. It might best be described by Ong as an example of "Erasmus' ideal of an education terminating not in philosophy and science but in language and literary study, with theology itself cast in a grammatical rather than a philosophical mold."[51] Training in the rhetorical arts begins with an assumption of the special nature of the human capacity to speak, which can be both deliberate and automatic (that is, we can consider our words carefully, but most often we do not). As a socialization process, the domestication of this capacity can also regulate other capacities for coping with the world, such as our moral behavior, which can also be both deliberate and automatic.

In contrast to this controlled, gradual teaching in *Of Education,* God creates Adam in a state of obedience from the beginning in *Paradise Lost.* As soon as Adam becomes conscious after his creation, he begins to look for his "great maker" so as to know and adore him (*PL* 8.278–80). But even before finding this great maker, as an "object" for his obedience, Adam reveals that he is fully aware that obedience is the factor uniting his body and soul. When Adam first tries to speak, his "tongue obeyed and readily could name / Whate'er [he] saw" (*PL* 8.272–73). While Milton's educator gradually inculcates obedience through the process of teaching a foreign tongue, Adam is created obedient with a tongue that inherently obeys. Because this sense of obedience exists before Adam even encounters God, obedience here is not really the submission to an exterior, repressive force or law. Rather, obedience is the name Adam uses for the cohesiveness of his body and soul, with a tongue following the guidance of a reasoning mind.

Adam's use of the term "obedience" directs us to consider that obedience includes the condition one is in before the decision to obey is necessary. Adam is *being himself* with the full recognition of his created, ordering, reasoning nature. As Stanley Fish reminds us, reasoning is what a human shares with God and what "testifies to the residence within him of the image of God."[52] If we use "obedience" to describe Adam's state of being long before he must face the choice to obey, we render him consistent with Du-Rocher's created earth, which is held together by obedience and is perhaps best exemplified on the sixth day when God orders the earth to "bring forth" the animals out of her womb, and "The earth obeyed" (*PL* 7.453).[53] For Albert Labriola, it is fundamental to the poem that the state of being in paradise is a state of obedience. He argues that obedience is the only factor that provides a sense of hope within the economy of the poem. For the disobedient angels, "what *is not* (or never?) lost *is* the capability to disobey and to exercise disobedience in any one or all ways." For Adam, however, this state of obedience is such a given that Labriola concludes, "all of *Paradise Lost* engages one question in the epic, posed by Adam to Raphael: 'But say, / What meant that caution join'd *if ye be found / Obedient?*' (*PL* 5.512–14)."[54]

If we accept that obedience is the foundational quality of the poem, and that Adam's very state of being is supported by this quality, what becomes more complicated is demonstrating that this quality is teachable. Michael Allen considers God a Socratic teacher and an "ideal schoolmaster" for his techniques of pedagogical restraint. Allen is concerned mostly with God's mode of address to Adam and the similarity of this address to Milton's teacher.[55] My concern, however, is more with how the state of obedience of each student makes this address possible. While the Miltonic teacher exercises a student's state of devotion through drills in language and reasoning, God exercises Adam by providing him opportunities to worship in his use of language and reasoning. Learning can act as a form of worship for Adam because his very desires work with and not against the order of God's universe. Through worship, God exercises Adam to make him further "sufficient to have stood."

In the scene where readers might most likely go looking for a sign of Adam's own independent power—his "dominion"—we see how Adam's sense of obedience is deeply expressed. Adam names the animals as a result of God's bringing them to him: "I bring them to receive / From thee their names, and pay thee fealty / With low subjection" (*PL* 8.343–45). God does not show the same sense of restraint with Adam that Milton's educator would have exercised in years of gradual, imitative exercises. If, however, the reader assumes that invention refers to an individual composing arguments that incorporate the experience gained from imitation, then Adam's discovery process while naming the animals will be essentially a process of invention where he recombines what he has already learned in his short experience with the existing world.[56]

Rather than asserting his absolute dominion, Adam worships God when he names the animals and when he asks God to add something to the universe. From the beginning of his account of the naming, he pays homage to the source of his sense of reasoning: "I named them, as they passed, and understood / Their nature, with such knowledge God endued / My sudden apprehension" (*PL* 8.352–54). Adam understands the nature of the animals —he "apprehends" them—on the basis of "such knowledge God endued." Just as Adam realizes that his tongue obeys his mind, so also he acknowledges that his mind works by means of the intellectual abilities God has offered him. Whether it is through a grammatical or military drill or through activities of worship, by exercising (and here articulating) one's state of being, one expresses that state of being in and toward its higher form. For Adam, that higher form is his developing place within God's universe.

Adam comes to his fullest appreciation of this universe when he expresses his innermost desire for more (which he discovers from the activity of naming). In the lines that follow the passage above, Adam's apprehension of the nature of the animals, a faculty endued by God, leads to his desire that God would create more: "My sudden apprehension: but in these / I found not what methought I wanted still; / And to the heavenly vision thus presumed" (*PL* 8.354–56). If we notice the placement of the colon after "apprehension," our understanding of this God-given faculty becomes much richer.[57] On the one hand, the colon serves to make all that precedes it a single grammatical unit, thus allowing my previous consideration: Adam is realizing that his apprehension of the nature of the animals comes from God. But the colon also creates an appositive concerning what follows. As an appositive, "what methought I wanted still" renames what precedes it, so that even desire itself will be reconsidered as a homage to the created universe. The desire, "what [he] wanted still," renames the "apprehension," which Adam acknowledges God "endued." For Adam to come to this realization about his desire even more fully, God will intervene in his most active role as educator to lead Adam.

So far, my comparison of Adam to the student in *Of Education* has focused mostly on the similarity between the student's state of devotion and Adam's state of obedience. However, I have done little so far to consider how

God might have acted in the role of teacher to make Adam even more "sufficient to have stood." The reader might argue at this point that God has not really taught Adam; rather, he has allowed Adam to express his already obedient nature. Certainly, if we consider *e-ducation* in its etymological sense, as a "leading out or forth," it requires that a person be led beyond where he previously recognized himself to be. Thus, the analysis that follows will demonstrate that God acts in the role of the most responsible (and indeed responsive) educator who guides his student to recognize continuities in lessons already learned and to appreciate on a greater level the unified system of the universe and his place within this system.

Milton emphasizes the ordered nature of God's presentation of the animals when he draws on the Genesis account of Noah meeting the animals ("two and two unto Noah into the ark") for his description of God overseeing the animals that Adam sees: "As thus he spake, each bird and beast behold / Approaching two and two" (*PL* 8.349–50). It might seem at first glance that God presents the animals to Adam in pairs as a simple grouping device to emphasize the contrast between species. However, each of the pairs also shares a quality with one another: their participation in being a couple. Being in a couple is what Adam is coming to recognize as his desire. Sexual community was always already part of the system even as much as it was previously invisible when Adam performed the earlier "tasks at hand" of naming. God will lead Adam to understand in a more complex fashion his desire to be in a couple himself, while this desire for greater complexity is actually a desire for more of the same.

Although God's Socratic teaching of Adam will result in a benefit beyond exercising obedience (Adam does "get the girl"), under the current analysis, the most important outcome of the reasoning process is how it serves to reinforce Adam's identity as a creature in a world held together by obedience. This process of self-discovery helps Adam to remember and articulate the similarities he has with God and with the animals and reinforces both God's gifts and Adam's humble status. When Adam points out his solitude and makes his request for an additional someone with whom to dwell in paradise, God exploits the way we normally think of desire, as a complaint, by leading Adam to consider further the implications of his desire:

> What callst thou solitude, is not the earth
> With various living creatures, and the air
> Replenished, and all these at thy command
> To come and play before thee, knowst thou not
> Their language and their ways, they also know,
> And reason not contemptibly.   (*PL* 8.369–74)

The answer God leads him to make grants Adam yet another opportunity to testify to God's greatness and enables him to understand his own nature, as he had when God led the animals before him in pairs. Whereas tradition sometimes holds out that the animals might have been able to speak, in *Paradise Lost* they do not speak a language Adam knows. We can recall that after Adam was created, none of the "fair creatures" (*PL* 8.276) he asks about the source of his creation can give him a spoken answer in the way that God eventually does: "Whom thou soughtst I am" (*PL* 8.316). In other words, God's leading question about whether Adam knows their language has a simple answer, "No, only you and I have language, which I first recognized when only you could speak to me, answering you were my creator."

In the reasoning process that follows, Adam recalls the scene of the animals in ordered pairs and what pairs allow them to "rejoice" ("the lion and the lioness") and what pairs do not ("bird with beast, or fish with fowl" [*PL* 8.395]). During this recollection, his understanding of the potential of language as a mode of social relation deepens. Whereas he might be able to speak to the animals, he would be speaking to an "inferior" creature (*PL* 8.382) who cannot speak back. With an inferior, therefore, he could have no "society" (*PL* 8.383–84). Further reasoning about what it would mean to have a society of equals, he declares in a moment of recognition, "of fellowship I speak" (*PL* 8.389). Fellowship with a helpmeet would allow Adam to converse in both ways—in reasoned articulation as he does with God and through sexual relations as the animals have. Therefore, desire in this instance is a desire for more of the same as "the same" is understood in a more complex fashion.

Thus, even as much as God created Adam to be obedient from the beginning, we can see that God's questioning has led Adam further in his sense of obedience. Like the teacher that Milton spoke of in *Of Education*, God teaches Adam on more basic levels and then reinforces how previous lessons are part of a connected system. God explains the goal of this fairly exhausting Socratic procedure, self-knowledge:

> Thus far to try thee, Adam, I was pleased,
> And find thee knowing not of beasts alone,
> Which thou has rightly named, but of thyself,
>
> . . . .
>   I, ere thou spak'st,
> Knew it not good for Man to be alone,
> And no such company as then thou sawst
> Intended thee, for trial only brought,
> To see how thou couldst judge of fit and meet.   (*PL* 8.437–48)

John Leonard writes of these lines, "Adam's real trial turns out not to have been the giving of 'fit and meet' names to the lower species, but the judging of what is fit and meet for himself."[58] I think Leonard is right, but I would like to emphasize that this act of judgment is not just a cognitive or epistemological activity. Adam does not just better understand "himself" as a being separate from God. Rather, the act of naming is an ethical exercise in which God leads Adam to discover himself (through his similarity to and difference from God and the animals) and to pay homage to God and his creation. As with the process of early teaching in Milton's curriculum, God "tempers" Adam so as to "lead and draw [him] in willing obedience" (YP 2:384–85).

As a final consideration of the similarity of Milton's treatise on education and *Paradise Lost*, we might consider the educational function of Adam and Eve's labors. The material we have considered about Adam's naming of the animals, of course, comes from Adam's recollection of this activity to Raphael, who was sent by God to warn him of the coming temptation. Over the first "working dinner," Raphael holds out for Adam the possibility of his development:

> Your bodies may at last turn all to spirit,
>
> . . . .
> If ye be found obedient, and retain
> Unalterably firm his love entire
> Whose progeny you are. Meanwhile enjoy
> Your fill what happiness this happy state
> Can comprehend, incapable of more.   (*PL* 5.497–505)

Here we can see most clearly that obedience would not only be Adam and Eve's submission to God's rule, but also an offering of further developed selfhood, in that their "bodies may at last turn all to spirit" (*PL* 5.497).

Furthermore, Adam recognizes the developing relationship between their happy state and their devotional labors even more than Raphael does. He will recall this relationship in what might seem one of the least likely places, in the "morning quarrel" over his and Eve's daily labors. In Book Nine, Eve presents Adam with the possibility that they might accomplish more separately:

> Let us divide our labours
>
> . . . .
> For while so near each other thus all day
>
> . . . .
> Our day's work brought to little, though begun
> Early, and the hour of supper comes unearned.   (*PL* 9.214–25)

Eve, however, has missed the point of the labor itself, as a material exercise in devotion and the growth of reason in them together and in God's image. Adam's answer illustrates more of the principles of devotional exercise:

> not so strictly hath our Lord imposed
> Labour, as to debar us when we need
> Refreshment, whether food, or talk between,
> Food of the mind, or this sweet intercourse
> Of looks and smiles, for smiles from reason flow,
> To brute denied, and are of love the food,
> Love not the lowest end of human life.
> For not to irksome toil, but to delight
> He made us, and delight to reason joined.   (PL 9.235–43)

Adam thoroughly realizes in this passage their "happy state," but unlike Raphael he has begun to grasp the educational potential of their devotional labors in paradise. Adam recognizes that their daily labors reinforce their relationship with each other and with God. Labor (working as a custodian in the garden) and desire ("sweet intercourse") interact as components of a sense of devotion to their developing role in the created order of things. In *How Milton Works*, Fish argues, "[The] task of laboring in the garden . . . is the task of . . . managing the production of themselves."[59] As with Milton's students or with Puritan soldiers, material labor results in a greater relationship between the inner person and the social and natural world.

In *Paradise Lost*, Adam becomes obedient even further as his appreciation for his place in the created world increases. Because his desires work with the created universe, Adam comes to know the world through worship. Such a correlation between one's sense of desire and the order of the universe might seem to be a paradise that is now truly lost. With desire no longer so clearly part of the order of the universe, humans are left with only God's "umpire conscience" (PL 3.195) as a reminder of the possibility of such a correlation. Conscience may indeed have become yet another repressive force generated by social institutions, leading a philosopher like Michel Foucault to state that, under modern social technologies, "the soul is the prison of the body."[60] It is perhaps only the place of God's paradise that allows such a correlation to occur in a happy sense. Likewise, it may very well have been a sense of place in Milton's nationalistic designs that allowed him to envision an England in which such an education in a "spatious house and ground about it for an Academy" (a limited, specific place) could have been a suitable foundation to educate a nation (another limited, specific place). Although one may or may not consider such a vision paradise, the possibility of a unified system of knowledge and character forming the foundation of education might be, indeed, lost. Character-building goals of education are difficult to discuss without some form of consensus of what that "character" might be. However, certain elements that Milton considers in his curriculum, such as experience and the way experience inscribes the foundation of personhood, still remain with us. Who we are and what we do are not separate things now any more than they have ever been, even as much as now we may do enough different things that are not always recognizable as parts of a single system of culture. It may very well be a goal for future educators to consider how the rules that allow for experience and ultimately for our sense of selfhood might bear some sense of correlation with desire.

University of Illinois at Chicago

NOTES

Earlier versions of this paper were presented at the Conference on John Milton in Murfreesboro and at the International Milton Congress in Pittsburgh. I am especially grateful to Stanley Fish and Michael Lieb, without whom this essay would never have come about. I am also grateful to Jason Rosenblatt for his helpful suggestions and to Albert Labriola, whose patience and encouragement should never cease to amaze us.

1. References to Milton's prose are to *The Complete Prose Works of John Milton,* 8 vols., ed. Don M. Wolfe et al. (New Haven, 1953–1982), 2:366–67, hereafter designated YP and cited parenthetically by volume and page number in the text.

2. Roger Ascham, *The Scholemaster,* ed. John E. B. Mayor (New York, 1967), 10; *De Pueris Institutendis,* in *Desiderius Erasmus concerning the Aim and Method of Education,* ed. William Harrison Woodward (Honolulu, 2002), 185. Thomas M. Conley, *Rhetoric in the European Tradition* (Chicago, 1990), states, "The end of education, in Erasmus' view, was the development of persons of character, an ideal he shared with Quintilian" (120).

3. *Institutio Oratoria,* trans. H. E. Butler (Cambridge, Mass., 1953), 12.1.44–2.31; *The Dialogues of Plato,* 2 vols., trans. B. Jowett (New York, 1937), 1:366–68.

4. For recent responses to the post–9/11 poster "Uncle Sam Wants You to Learn a Foreign Language," see Rosemary G. Feal, "Scaring (Up) 'Foreign' Language Speakers: One Hundred Years of Multitude," *MLA Newsletter* (Winter 2004): 4–5, and Mary Louise Pratt, "Building a New Public Idea about Language," *Profession* (2003): 110–19.

5. See T. W. Baldwin, *William Shakspere's small Latine and lesse Greeke* (Urbana, Ill., 1944), Donald Lemen Clark, *John Milton at St. Paul's* (New York, 1948), and Kenneth Charlton, *Education in Renaissance England* (London, 1965); or, for an outline of educators, see William Harrison Woodward, *Studies in Education during the Age of the Renaissance, 1400–1600,* foreword by Lawrence Stone (New York, 1967). However, extended rigorous consideration of how humanist exercise would actually contribute to a student's moral being is missing from their work. A general exception to this rule includes works that address Erasmus substantially, for his pedagogy is most explicitly devoted to moral training through training in language. See Woodward, *Desiderius Erasmus,* Anthony Grafton and Lisa Jardine, *From Humanism to the Humanities: Education and the Liberal Arts in Fifteenth- and Sixteenth-Century Europe* (London, 1986), and Richard Halpern, *The Poetics of Primitive Accumulation: English Renaissance Cul-*

ture and the Genealogy of Capital (Ithaca, N.Y., 1991). See also Michel Foucault, *The Order of Things: An Archaeology of the Human Sciences* (New York, 1994). While Foucault's study of the sixteenth-century episteme does address the ontological concern that Halpern omits, it does not provide the kind of analysis of the curriculum that Halpern does.

Martin Dzelzainis, "Milton's Classical Republicanism," in *Milton and Republicanism*, ed. David Armitage, Armand Himy, and Quentin Skinner (New York, 1995), writes that *Of Education* is "often dismissed as inconsequential if charming" (14). However, helpful studies of Milton and education include Thomas Festa, "Repairing the Ruins: Milton as Reader and Educator," in *Milton Studies* 43, ed. Albert C. Labriola (Pittsburgh, 2004), 35–63; Barbara Lewalski, "Milton and the Hartlib Circle: Educational Projects and Epic Paideia," in *Literary Milton: Text, Pretext, Context*, ed. Diana Treviño Benet and Michael Lieb (Pittsburgh, 1994), 202–19; Angelica Duran, "The Last Stages of Education: *Paradise Regained* and *Samson Agonistes*," *MQ* 34 (2000): 102–16; Michael Lieb, *The Sinews of Ulysses: Form and Convention in Milton's Works* (Pittsburgh, 1989), and other studies cited below. Of the available studies, only Lieb's (originally published in the *Journal of General Education* 36 [1985]: 245–56) draws the kinds of connections that I am suggesting here between rudimentary exercises and Milton's guiding values.

6. William Empson, *Milton's God*, 2nd ed. (Cambridge, 1981), 146.

7. *Paradise Lost*, 3.99, from John Milton, *Paradise Lost*, ed. Alastair Fowler (London, 1998); hereafter cited by book and line number in the text.

8. Gauri Viswanathan, "Milton, Imperialism, and Education," *Modern Language Quarterly* 59, no. 3 (September 1998): 351. Viswanathan's quote in full reads, "[Milton] took from classical humanist educators like Comenius and Juan Luis Vives a belief in the character-strengthening function provided by Greek and Latin and combined it with the restorative purposes of moral agency." While Milton's ideas on education are often considered in terms of "comenianism," Ernest Sirluck argues, "Milton's conception of a good educational system was fundamentally opposed to that of Comenius" (introduction, YP 2:186). Sirluck's detailed analysis cites the extent of Comenius's democratizing initiatives (which Milton did not share), Comenius's disdain for the trivium and literature generally, and the more vocational prerogatives of Comenius and his followers.

9. Erasmus, *On Copia of Words and Ideas*, trans. Donald King and David Rix (Milwaukee, 1963), 18–19.

10. Above the doorway at St. Paul's School, which Milton attended as an adolescent, was reportedly inscribed the phrase "Ingredere Ut Proficias" [Enter in order to succeed] and painted on the inside of the windows was the phrase "Aut Doce, Aut Disce, Aut Discede" [Teach, learn, or get out!]; see Clark, *John Milton at St. Paul's*, 39.

11. Analysis based on the "rule-governed" nature of a system is often performed to deflate mystical presumptions. See Frank Whigham, *Ambition and Privilege: The Social Tropes of Elizabethan Courtesy Theory* (Berkeley and Los Angeles, 1984), and Arthur J. Jacobson, "The Idolatry of Rules: Writing Law According to Moses, with Reference to Other Jurisprudences," *Deconstruction and the Possibility of Justice*, ed. Drucilla Cornell, Michel Rosenfeld, and David Gray Carlson (New York, 1992).

12. Gregor Reisch, *Margarita Philosophica* (Freiburg im Breisgau, 1503); George Plimpton, *The Education of Shakespeare* (New York, 1933), 2–5.

13. See William G. Riggs, "Poetry and Method in Milton's *Of Education*," *SP* 89 (1992): 445–69. Riggs argues that *Of Education* is based upon "a kind of higher trivium in which poetry has replaced grammar" (445).

14. "Forms" is glossed by Donald Dorian as "paradigms" (YP 2:373 n. 31), and it can also refer to "conjugations."

15. Milton is not suggesting to avoid teaching grammar, but instead to teach it by leading

students to find examples of these principles in their reading: "if after some preparatory grounds of speech by their certain forms got into memory, they were led to the praxis thereof in some chosen short book lesson'd thoroughly to them, they might then forthwith proceed to learn the substance of good things, and Arts in due order, which would bring the whole language quickly into their power" (YP 2:373–74). This method is comparable to Erasmus's in *De Ratione Studii*: "Whilst a knowledge of the rules of accidence and syntax is most necessary to every student, still they should be as few, as simple, and as carefully framed as possible. . . . For it is not by learning rules that we acquire the power of speaking a language, but by daily intercourse with those accustomed to express themselves with exactness and refinement, and by the copious reading of the best authors" (Woodward, *Desiderius Erasmus*, 163–64); see also Ascham, *Scholemaster*, 2–3: "After the three Concordances learned . . . let the master read unto hym the Epistles of *Cicero*, gathered together and chosen out by *Sturmius*, for the capacitie of children."

16. Writing *copia*, or variations on a single phrase or sentence, into commonplace books was a standard activity for early modern schoolboys. Along with Lily's grammar, Erasmus's textbook for further refinement of one's grammatical command was a ubiquitous factor in the English Renaissance. *On Copia of Words and Ideas* was originally dedicated in 1512 to John Colet for use in St. Paul's School. During Erasmus's lifetime, there were at least 85 editions, and the number of editions in the sixteenth century was over 150, with a few editions published as late as 1824 (Erasmus, *On Copia of Words*, 2).

17. John Aubrey, "Minutes of the Life of Mr. John Milton" (1681), in *The Early Lives of Milton*, ed. Helen Darbishire (London, 1932), 12.

18. Lawrence Stone, *The Crisis of the Aristocracy: 1558–1641* (London, 1967); Francis Bacon, *The Advancement of Learning* (1605), ed. Michael Kiernan (Oxford, 2000), 164; David Cressy, "Francis Bacon and the Advancement of Schooling," *History of European Ideas* 2 (1981): 72.

19. Woodward, *De Pueris Instituendis*, 180; Ascham, *The Scholemaster*, 31.

20. Walter Ong, "Latin Language Study as a Renaissance Puberty Rite," *SP* 56 (1959): 103–23.

21. In his introduction to *Accedence Commenc't Grammar*, David P. French characterizes this difference derogatorily: "The *Accedence*, therefore, implicitly rejects Comenian pidgin Latin for the precision of stylistic correctness" (YP 8:69).

22. In perhaps the most controversial instance of his challenging statements of rule, Milton writes, "Wherein we may plainly discover how Christ meant not to be tak'n word for word, but like a wise Physician, administring one excesse against another to reduce us to a perfect mean" (*Doctrine and Discipline of Divorce*, YP 2:282–83).

23. Riggs, "Poetry and Method," 463: "Milton bows handsomely to the rules of his art but allows himself a crucial exemption by opining that 'in them that know art and use judgment' a departure from rule to follow 'nature' 'is no transgression but an inriching of art.' " My argument focuses more on the obedient process of coming to "know art" to the extent that its "nature" is somewhat automatic.

24. Throughout *The Reason of Church-Government*, Milton emphasizes the importance of discipline and the law, which would protect us from "the discretion of men" (YP 1:750). This discipline would require "instruction" (755), be it instruction in the Law, or as we see in the well-known autobiographical passages of the second book, in the works of celebrated poets and thinkers.

25. Lewalski, "Milton and the Hartlib Circle," 202–19.

26. Ernest Sirluck, introduction to YP 2, "*Of Education*" (YP 2:184–216).

27. Lewalski, "Milton and the Hartlib Circle," 203, 207, 208.

28. For alternative views to Lewalski's assertions of conformity in Comenius's pedagogy, see

Jean-Claude Margolin, "The Method of 'Words and Things' in Erasmus's *De Pueris Instituendis* (1529) and Comenius's *Orbis Sensualium Pictus* (1658)," in *Essays on the Works of Erasmus*, ed. Richard L. DeMolen (New Haven, 1978), 221–38, and Jean Piaget, *John Amos Comenius on Education* (New York, 1967), 1–31. Piaget writes, "Comenius has sometimes been criticized for neglecting individuality. It would be easy to show that this is not the case; the importance he attributes to spontaneity, to interest, to the pupil's own ability to verify statements, and to 'autopraxy' would be meaningless if there were no respect for each child's individuality and the ways in which it differs from others" (22–23).

29. See Walter Ong, "Logic and the Epic Muse: Reflections on Noetic Structures in Milton's Milieu," in *Achievements of the Left Hand: Essays on the Prose of John Milton*, ed. Michael Lieb and John T. Shawcross (Amherst, Mass., 1974), 239–68.

30. Clark, *Milton at St. Paul's*, 152–84, esp. 168–84, 158. In his introduction to *Accedence Commenc't Grammar*, French argues against the "exaggerated and distorted" charges that Renaissance schoolmasters were "insensitive tyrants" who "forced [students] to memorize, in Latin, the whole grammar of a language they did not yet understand in the least" (YP 8:43). In his restraints, however, Milton was most cautious of another "insensitive tyranny," of having expectations too great for immature students: "These are not matters to be wrung from poor striplings, like blood out of the nose, or the plucking of untimely fruit" (YP 2:372–73).

31. Frances A. Yates, *The Art of Memory* (Chicago, 1966), 5–7.

32. Ibid., 20; Cicero, *De inventione*, translated by H. M. Hubbell (Cambridge, Mass., 1968), 2.53.159–60.

33. My argument here is consistent with the following autobiographical passage from *The Reason of Church-Government*: "I must say therefore that after I had from my first yeeres by the ceaselesse diligence and care of my father, whom God recompence, bin exercis'd to the tongues, and some sciences, as my age would suffer, by sundry masters and teachers both at home and at the schools, it was found that whether ought was impos'd me by them that had the overlooking, or betak'n to of mine own choise in English, or other tongue, prosing or versing, but chiefly this latter, the stile by certain vital signes it had, was likely to live" (YP 1:808–9).

34. Yates, *The Art of Memory*, 7 .

35. Pierre Bourdieu, *The Logic of Practice*, translated by Richard Nice (Stanford, 1990), 68.

36. Viswanathan, "Milton, Imperialism, and Education," 358.

37. Stephen M. Fallon, *Milton Among the Philosophers: Poetry and Materialism in Seventeenth-Century England* (Ithaca, N.Y., 1991), 80.

38. Stanley Fish, preface to *Surprised by Sin*, 2nd ed. (Cambridge, Mass., 1997), xliv.

39. According to Oliver Morley Ainsworth, *Milton on Education: The Tractate of Education with Supplementary Extracts from Other Writings of Milton* (New Haven, 1928), "The mention of agriculture has led some persons to look upon Milton's proposed Academy as an agricultural school" (17). However, to distance Milton's proposed academy from a vocational school, Ainsworth is more reductive about the role of agriculture: "The reference to the improvement of agriculture, therefore, is probably little more than a courteous recognition of Hartlib's interest in that laudable design" (17).

Milton recognizes the humanizing potential of other material activities when he calls for the civic management of sports and festival pastimes that might "inure and harden our bodies by martial exercises to all warlike skil and performance, and may civilize, adorn and make discreet our minds by the learned and affable meeting of frequent Academies, and the procurement of wise and artfull recitations sweetned with eloquent and gracefull inticements to the love and practice of justice, temperance and fortitude" (*Reason of Church-Government*, YP 1:819).

40. Richard J. DuRocher, *Milton Among the Romans: The Pedagogy and Influence of Milton's Latin Curriculum* (Pittsburgh, 2001), 4.

41. When Milton taught his nephews, "Cato, Varro & Columella de Re rusticâ were the very first Authors they learn't" (Aubrey, "Minutes," 12).

42. DuRocher, *Milton Among the Romans*, 57–58.

43. Robert Thomas Fallon, *Captain or Colonel: The Soldier in Milton's Life and Art* (Columbia, Mo., 1984).

44. Michael Lieb, *The Sinews of Ulysses: Form and Convention in Milton's Works* (Pittsburgh, 1989), 2, 3.

45. See Robert Fallon, ed., *The Christian Soldier: Religious Tracts Published for Soldiers on Both Sides during and after the English Civil Wars, 1642–1648* (Tempe, Ariz., 2003).

46. Boyd M. Berry, *Process of Speech: Puritan Religious Writing and "Paradise Lost"* (Baltimore, 1976), 175, 178. As Fallon notes in *Captain or Colonel,* "Berry shows that the Puritan soldier on the drill ground and battlefield was acting out theological doctrine and the New Model Army 'fought like a gathered Church.'" Fallon argues, however, that the sermons grew out of what the ministers saw on the battlefield, and not vice versa (34 n. 10). My concern here is with the overall educational apparatuses that would have made a certain Puritan sensibility possible, either in the pulpit or on the battlefield.

47. Halpern, *The Poetics of Primitive Accumulation,* similarly argues that Erasmus's pedagogy was, in part, so effective because it formalized the familiar and the "colloquial" by emphasizing social manners and home life as bridges to mastering classical Latin and reading Latin authors (32–33).

48. Clark, *Milton at St. Paul's*, 6.

49. Ong, "Latin Language Study," 105.

50. Jameela Lares, *Milton and the Preaching Arts* (Pittsburgh, 2001), 141–68.

51. Ong, "Latin Language Study," 115.

52. Fish, *Surprised by Sin*, 241.

53. DuRocher, *Milton Among the Romans*, 27.

54. Albert C. Labriola, "'All in All' and 'All in One': Obedience and Disobedience in *Paradise Lost,*" in *"All in All": Unity, Diversity, and the Miltonic Perspective,* ed. Charles W. Durham and Kristin A. Pruitt (Selinsgrove, Pa., 1999), 39–47, quotations from 46, 47.

55. Michael Allen, "Divine Instruction: *Of Education* and the Pedagogy of Raphael, Michael, and the Father," *MQ* 26, no. 4 (December 1992): 113–21.

56. Clark, *Milton at St. Paul's,* reminds us, "The invention of arguments, whether logical or rhetorical, meant, not to invent in the modern sense, but to discover, to look for and find, such arguments as would support the probability of a theme or proposition and convince the persons whom the speaker or writer wishes to persuade" (226).

57. This colon was present in the earliest editions of the poem: *Paradise Lost. A Poem in Ten Books* (London, 1669) and *Paradise Lost. A Poem in Twelve Books,* 2nd ed. (London, 1674). In addition to the Fowler edition, it is also present in *The Complete Poetry of John* Milton, ed. John T. Shawcross, 2nd rev. ed. (Garden City, N.Y., 1971), and *Complete Poems and Major Prose,* ed. Merritt Y. Hughes (New York, 1957).

58. John Leonard, *Naming in Paradise: Milton and the Language of Adam and Eve* (Oxford, 1990), 32.

59. Stanley Fish, *How Milton Works* (Cambridge, Mass., 2001), 528.

60. Michel Foucault, *Discipline and Punish: The Birth of the Prison* (New York, 1979), 30.

CHOOSING DEATH: ADAM'S TEMPTATION TO MARTYRDOM IN *PARADISE LOST*

Margaret Justice Dean

W HILE A D A M ' S M O T I V E S for joining Eve in eating the forbidden fruit have been closely scrutinized, some important issues of his
fall have been overlooked. Generally, Adam's choice to join Eve in disobedience, while fully cognizant that he is choosing to violate the sole command,
is ascribed to chivalrous motives: Eve's fall presents him with the opportunity
to suffer and die for her sake. This attribution may have occluded a more
compelling motivation that dovetails with the religious and political contro-
versies in which Milton participated. I suggest that one of Adam's most
significant motives for disobeying God is idolatry of martyrdom. Application
of Reformation-era standards to Adam's choice of death aligns it with those
chosen by the false martyrs Milton critiques in his prose. This alignment
suggests hitherto neglected aspects of antimartyrology within *Paradise Lost*.
When examined from this perspective, temptation to martyrdom becomes a
significant aspect of Adam's fall.

Milton presents martyrdom as a temptation for Adam in three rhetorical
contexts. Historically, Adam's motives for choosing death resemble those
espoused by false martyrs excoriated by antimartyrologists. Contextually
within the epic narrative, Adam's early acquaintance with Abdiel's example
invites unschooled emulation. Theologically, the motives and consequences
of Adam's passionate, disobedient choice provide a foil for those of the Son,
whose patient, obedient choice sets the standard for martyrdom. Evidence
for placing Adam in these contexts includes the prominence of martyrological controversy in Milton's oeuvre; the dramatic pathos evoked during Adam's
temptation; his early and superficial understanding of martyrdom; the contrast between the Son's true and Adam's false examples; and the effect of
Adam's final words, which suggest a repudiation of his idolatry of martyrdom.
During his temptation in Book Nine, Adam's "heroic" choice engages the
rhetoric and dramatic pathos of martyrdom familiar to Milton and other
readers of John Foxe's *Actes and Monuments*, but examination of the causes
for which Adam dies identifies him as a false martyr, a spiritual suicide who
chooses death rather than "suffering for Truths sake" (*PL* 12.569).[1] Reading

30

Adam's choice of death as a critique of seventeenth-century notions of Foxean martyrdom offers a new perspective on the nature of heroism in *Paradise Lost* by situating it within the martyrological controversy of Milton's day. This essay uses the approach pioneered by Stanley Fish to apply the Reformation-era research of Brad S. Gregory, and that of Laura Lunger Knoppers on *Eikonoklastes,* to Milton's epic. Additionally, it further clarifies the significance of discourses of martyrdom in Milton's oeuvre as delineated by John R. Knott.[2]

I

Milton engages martyrdom as a form of Christian heroism in his prose earlier and more frequently than is generally recognized among scholars. They note his attack on Charles I in *Eikonoklastes,* which attempts to shatter the king's image in order to release the English from their idolatry of his martyrdom. Milton's antimartyrology exposes a false martyr: a criminal perjurer, a tyrant, and a traitor. Even before contending with the king's image, however, Milton's antiprelatical tracts assail Puritan and Anglican icons of the Foxean tradition as well as traditional Roman Catholic saints. As early as 1642 in *The Reason of Church-Government,* he acknowledges his ambition to celebrate in "Epick form . . . the pattern of a Christian *Heroe,*" and though Milton at first suggests the selection of a king or "Knight before the conquest" for this hero, he concludes with a desire "to sing the victorious agonies of Martyrs and Saints" (YP 1:813–17). *Paradise Lost* reflects this early tension in Milton's choice of subject: though initially attracted to romance epic, he explains in Book Nine that he prefers the "higher Argument" of biblical materials and the "better fortitude / Of Patience and Heroic Martyrdom / Unsung" to the celebrated fiction of chivalric tales and the inferior virtues displayed in them.

The Son of God exemplifies this "better fortitude." In his theological treatise, Milton notes, "The greatest example of fortitude is our Saviour Jesus Christ. He displayed fortitude throughout the whole of his life and in his death" (YP 6:739). Among controversialists Milton is not alone in privileging this example. Calvinists, Catholics, and other Christians of this time regarded the Crucifixion as the ultimate example of martyrdom. Gregory describes the centrality of the Son's example: "Jesus's crucifixion was more than the inspiration for elaborate devotional practices: it was the paradigm for what his closest followers could expect."[3] By the time Milton deploys this conventional paradigm in *Eikonoklastes,* he can assume his audience's familiarity with and reverence for biblical martyrdom. He compares Charles I with the biblical standards: Jesus, John the Baptist, and Stephen (YP 3:502). Later alluding to John 5:31, Milton compares Charles's with the martyrdom of

Christ and observes that Charles's is "a negative *Martyrdom*. . . . Martyrs bear witness to the truth, not to themselves. If I beare witness of my self, saith *Christ*, my witness is not true" (YP 3:575). As he discusses Charles's "Meditations upon Death," Milton observes that Charles "imitat[es] therin, not our Saviour, but his Grand-mother *Mary* Queen of Scots" (597). In his epic, Milton compares Adam with the biblical standard.

Before Milton can delineate "the pattern of a Christian Heroe," he must dispel false notions of such patterns. In reaction to English veneration of the martyrs of the *Actes and Monuments*, Milton devotes much in his antiprelatical tracts to antimartyrology (the exposure of false martyrs) at the expense of martyrology (the celebration and memorialization of true ones). When two of Milton's antagonists in these tracts cite Foxe's bishop martyrs and enlist their blood in the cause of prelacy,[4] Milton attacks the credibility of Archbishop Cranmer and Bishops Latimer and Ridley, three of the most famous, whom he labels "halting and time-serving *Prelates*" (YP 1:531–33). Reaching back to medieval legend, he derides the miracles reported as issuing from Bishop Polycarp's blood (YP 1:640–44). In contradistinction to these celebrity martyrs, Milton asserts, "every true Christian will be a *Martyr* when he is called to it," but adds an antimartyrological *caveat*, "not presently does it follow that every one suffering for Religion, is without exception. . . . He is not therfore above all possibility of erring, because hee burnes for some Points of Truth" (YP 1:533). Later, Milton accuses some of "the elect Martyrs and witnesses of their Redeemer" (YP 1:925), whom he exalts in his antiprelatical tracts, of "a jolly slander" and "rash and heedles calumny" (YP 2:722–23).[5]

Ultimately, Milton learns to distrust latter-day martyrs in addition to many earlier ones. He agrees with his opponent on basic tenets in *An Apology against a Pamphlet*, noting, "*there may be a Martyr in a wrong cause, and as courageous in suffering as the best.*"[6] He insists that those seeking truth depend upon the words of Scripture, rather than the testimony of martyrs, "We also reverence the Martyrs but relye only upon the Scriptures" (YP 1:912). These tracts predate *Eikonoklastes* and build toward it; they constitute one reason he was solicited to refute the image of Charles the Martyr because Milton's antiprelatical tracts effectively engage the Reformation-era antimartyrological tradition. He takes this position on Adam the martyr as well. Like the prelate-martyrs Milton derides, Adam suffers "for some Points of Truth." He suffers to affirm God's gifts (Eve and marriage), but idolatry of these gifts leads to his violation of God's command (*PL* 10.137–56).[7]

A review of martyrological tradition will contextualize my argument. Christian culture maintains a definition of martyrdom that was reinforced during the controversy of the Reformation era; it is generally defined as choosing to endure death in defense of religious principles.[8] In response to the first state-sponsored public executions of Lutherans in the 1520s and the subsequent publication of martyrologies about them, controversial tracts arose denouncing the status of some as "false martyrs" while extolling others as "true martyrs." These tracts are termed "antimartyrologies" by historian Brad Gregory because unlike martyrologies, which memorialize and praise these dying witnesses without much discrimination, antimartyrologies discriminate. Antimartyrologies define the "true martyrdom" of their own camp by denouncing the "false martyrdom" of those of the opposing one. This inclusion of antimartyrology within martyrologies served to polarize confessional camps throughout Europe, but it also helped to forge a doctrinal consensus concerning what constituted Christian martyrdom and what did not.[9]

Five guidelines emerged to form this consensus, which generally reached across confessional lines.[10] Disagreement did not concern which guidelines to apply, but how to interpret them (Gregory, 344–47). First, Christ's example determines the pattern of true martyrdom (109–10, 119, 337). While all Christians generally recognize the martyrs of the New Testament and the early church during this period (124, 329–30), the example of Christ at his Crucifixion is the preferred model. He is the innocent yet powerful individual who chooses to allow himself to be publicly executed by civil authorities (whose motives are political under the guise of religion) after an examination that emphasizes his exercise of prerogative, his obedience, his innocence, and the guilt of his persecutors. Motivated by obedience to God and the salvation of humankind, he suffers a painful and humiliating death. Second, a true martyr suffers as a witness to God's truth as described in orthodox Christian doctrine. Adherence to God's truth requires obedience even to death (Matt. 5:10; Gregory, 157, 323, 326, 340). Obedience to and defense of doctrine founded upon Scripture are the primary motives for the martyr's death. As a faithful witness, he or she is an innocent but able defender of doctrine, which the cruel persecutors of faith oppose (318). Third, a true martyr is not a civil criminal. He or she submits to the authorities and suffers under them as a testimony to God. Though he or she may die as a "religious criminal," he or she is obedient to civil laws unless they mandate disobedience to God's law (1 Peter 4:15–16; Gregory, 74, 330, 332). Fourth, a true martyr is not insane. Informed by a careful reading of Scripture, the individual makes a conscious and rational decision to die (100–102). Fifth, a true martyr is not a suicide. He or she is ready to die for his or her testimony, but does not love death or seek it as revenge or escape (102–5).

As John Knott demonstrates, Milton's poetry and prose are deeply involved with issues of martyrdom. The *Actes and Monuments*, which Milton cites specifically three times and may allude to some forty times, assumes the five-point consensus (listed above).[11] In *De Doctrina Christiana* Milton

builds upon this commonly accepted consensus in formulating his own definition of martyrdom: "our firm and, when necessary, open profession of the
true religion, and of our worship of him. . . . when it leads to death or
imprisonment or torture or disgrace. . . . It is generally by martyrdom that the
gospel is propagated. . . . So it is that God's name is sanctified by our words. It
is sanctified by our deeds when they do not fall short of our verbal profession"
(YP 6:701–2).[12] Milton's definition of martyrdom in *De Doctrina Christiana*
emphasizes unjust suffering, but noticeably absent from his version of the
popular consensus is the requirement that the martyr suffer death. Thus,
Milton's definition allows Abdiel to be considered a martyr. Equally noteworthy is Milton's inclusion of opposites of martyrdom. In *De Doctrina Christiana,* he includes a delineation of opposing extremes: "Opposed to this
[martyrdom] is concealment of our religion . . . apostasy . . . profession of
one's faith at the wrong time . . . [and] failure to act in a way which corresponds to our verbal profession" (YP 6:702).[13]

Milton carefully distinguishes between what martyrdom is and is not in
his theological treatise; similarly, he draws this distinction in his controversial
tracts and his narrative poetry. However, discussions of martyrdom in *Paradise Lost,* such as Knott's, do not mention Milton's predilection for antimartyrology with its distinction between false and true martyrs. Though *Eikonoklastes* in 1649 is the most sustained and widely recognized example of his
antimartyrological skill, it is not the only one. Early in his career Milton
commits himself to celebrating heroic martyrdom, but he produces more
attacks on supposed martyrs than monuments to true ones. In this he is the
product of his age. Gregory deplores scholarly neglect of the high incidence
of antimartyrology in European polemical prose of this period and notes the
interdependence of martyrology and antimartyrology.[14] He further explains
the deployment of antimartyrology in order to separate true from false martyrs: "Writers often distinguished true from false martyrs as they exalted their
own witnesses, exhorted fellow believers to perseverance, or prepared for
death from prison. Not merely aware of competing martyr claims, they evidently found it hard to forget about them" (316). Antimartyrology enabled
the faithful to discern, praise, and emulate what is admirable in the true
martyr and to excoriate the idolatry, heresy, crimes, or delusions of the false
one (329). Just as Foxe's book includes the false martyrdoms of Thomas à
Becket and Thomas More in contrast with the Marian martyrs, Milton presents Adam the First as his false martyr to emphasize the truth of Adam the
Second (a title both the New Testament and Milton afford to Jesus or the Son
of God).[15]

Given that most of his contemporaries, as well as Milton himself, acknowledge martyrs in addition to the Son of God, how were the "false" to be

discerned from the "true"? Gregory cites numerous examples of exemplary demeanor of supposed "false" martyrs at their executions as detailed by antimartyrologists who assert that these same individuals are now suffering in hell. The behavior, words, and pathos of these "false" martyrs at the stake or on the block as reported by their detractors are often indistinguishable from those of the "true" martyrs as described by their own advocates. Gregory explains this phenomenon by citing the pervasive *ars moriendi* tradition, which valued steadfastness in suffering and death; most of the martyrs of whatever doctrinal perspective suffered patiently and steadfastly in order to buttress their doctrinal perspective with their demeanor (Gregory, 313–41). Because of their inability to distinguish false martyr from true on the external bases of appearances and behavior, even final words, controversialists resolved this polemical problem by examining doctrine. Gregory notes that this doctrine also constituted "the same criterion by which they identified their martyrological communities" (320). The relevant doctrine is most clearly delineated by Augustine of Hippo. According to Gregory (320) and Knott (155), Christian controversialists of all major confessions relied on Augustine's criteria to distinguish true from false martyrs: "[N]ot the punishment, but the cause, makes a martyr"[16] came to serve as the most reliable and universally accepted method of discrimination. Additionally, sometimes "allegation[s] that false martyrs were condemned for non-religious crimes" were used to discredit their martyrdoms (Gregory, 327).

By the seventeenth century, Augustine's touchstone is so well known that Milton need not cite it; it is implicit in such statements as, "if to die for *the testimony of his own conscience,* be anough to make him Martyr, what Heretic dying for direct blasphemie, as som have don constantly, may not boast a Martyrdom?" (YP 3:576).[17] According to Milton, courageous death for the cause of one's conscience is insufficient if that cause does not square with Scripture: "Heretic[s]" and "Romish Priests" have also been executed for consciences that oppose Scripture (YP 3:575–76). In his controversialist denunciations of false martyrs, Milton joins a host of Reformation-era writers who, by application of Augustine's touchstone, extol the martyrs of their own side while damning those of the opposite.

When Adam's temptation in Book Nine of *Paradise Lost* is examined with an eye to Protestant antimartyrology, readers can discern aspects of Adam's death that expose him as a false martyr. His language and theatricality buttress his romantic heroism. However, the narrative context reveals that Adam's motives involve idolatry, egotism, ambition, heresy, felony, insanity, even suicide. These demonstrate that such heroism is at odds with true martyrdom.

II

Keeping Augustine's touchstone in mind, let us reexamine the impact of the scene of Adam's temptation. Since doctrinally informed readers of martyrological accounts should focus on the causes and motives of the martyr's choice, not the pathos of his or her punishment and suffering, let us examine what in the text constrains us to focus on the pathos of this scene in spite of doctrine. Unfallen Adam is caught off-guard by Eve's fall, but he reacts sympathetically. His seemingly heroic actions and demeanor augment the pathos of his situation. His first response is dramatically physical as he meets Eve, evidence in hand, under the tree of knowledge. Stunned, he is rendered immobile by her choice of death. He drops the garland with which he had intended to crown Eve, his heart's queen (9.890–95). The normally loquacious Adam can speak at first only to himself. His language, attitude, and actions lend him an ethos of martyrdom in this scene. But his soliloquy betrays his motives for violating God's sole command: dread of returning to his previous single state (906–10) and losing his long-sought and dearly beloved human companion (911–13). He will be subject to loneliness again and never recover from his grief for Eve (912–13). Captivated by her beauty, he responds to her as though she were the pathetically beautiful sacrificial victim of Death (896–905). His piling up of rhetorical questions (five in eleven lines, 900–910) reveals the depth of his loss, the permanence of his devotion, his desperation to keep Eve, and the extent to which passion has clouded his thinking. He believes marriage has linked the two inseparably—they can never be severed (915–16). While they seem laden with self-sacrifice, Adam's beliefs place devotion to marriage before devotion to God; in *Tetrachordon* Milton labels this idolatrous affront as "the worshiping of a civil marriage" (YP 2:688).[18]

After the soliloquy, Adam responds to Eve with heroic composure and conviction (9.917–59). Calmly he notes the fact of her choice, comforts her, and assures her of his support. Finally, he announces his immutable decision to die with her because of his identification with and attachment to her. The drama and emotional burden of the scene urge the reader to regard Adam as a heroic martyr—one who, at his first opportunity, volunteers to die for his convictions.[19] However, the narrative context undercuts Adam's words and appearance here (839–999), including his physical and verbal reactions to Eve's disobedience, his voluntary actions, and his attitudes, by presenting them as a snare for the credulous reader, a subtler version of Milton's commentary on William Marshall's frontispiece to *Eikon Basilike*.[20] The drama of this scene is intense, but Adam's language further enhances the pathos of the occasion while revealing his less than Augustinian motives for martyrdom.

Since his decision to die with Eve seems a foregone conclusion (9.907), Adam adopts a fatalistic attitude in his audible response, which further enhances the pathos of his choice (926, 952–54). His words ring with satanic victimization (906, 926); he mingles the language of married love (896–905, 952–59) with that of religious conviction (906–16, 921–51). Were readers, like Adam and Eve, unfamiliar with Augustine's touchstone, such pathos, drama, and language might pass for those of a true martyr because they occlude the cause for which Adam asserts he will die: erotic, married love (915–16).

Adam's final words before his choice of death with Eve take on additional significance in the context of martyrdom. Adam's pathetic "to loose thee were to loose my self" (9.959) certainly urges his attachment to Eve. Many of us read *loose* as a variant of *lose*. Additionally, many read a pun on *loose/lose* indicating Adam's conflation of "loosing" Eve's matrimonial bond and hand with "losing" her as his possession.[21] The phrase emphasizes Adam's possessive and patronizing attitude toward her. His incipient idolatry of Eve and marriage becomes obvious when he asserts he cannot live outside their union. The phrase marks his fatalistic identification with her, which is buttressed by a heretical attempt to make God the author of Adam's sin.[22] His words also echo the paradox of Jesus' words in Luke 9:24, a verse often cited as a proof-text for and exhortation to martyrdom:[23] "For whosoever will save his life shall lose it: but whosoever will lose his life for my sake, the same shall save it" (AV). The scriptural context for these words is Jesus' prophecy of his own martyrdom— his sacrificial obedience as the Son of God. By contrast, Adam's assertions of love for Eve (as for himself) at this juncture resemble both of Milton's descriptions of the causes of suicide as distortions of charity toward oneself: "extravagant self-love, which makes a man love himself more than God" and "perverse hatred of oneself" (YP 6:719).[24] Like the motivations Milton mentions for the suicide, Adam's motivations and actions are those of one "who sin[s] willfully and deliberately."[25] The narrative context of Adam's words, within which this biblical allusion is encapsulated, is their use as a justification for erotic idolatry, extravagant self-love, heretical defamation of God's character, violation of God's sole command, and delusional devotion to death. The allusion thus becomes highly ironic, undercutting Adam's credibility to the scripturally literate reader and suggesting that Adam is, among other things, a "Heretic dying for direct blasphemie" who "boast[s] a Martyrdom." Because he is in the process of making martyrdom an idol instead of a study, Adam assumes that any pathetic choice of death counts as martyrdom.

Adam's own inclination to heroism, yoked to Eve's distortions and promotion of martyrdom, urges him on. Eve's person and reassurance are attractive to Adam, but at least as attractive is the persona she proffers him. Though he may not believe all that Eve relates, her serpent-inspired formulation of martyr as Promethean rebel combines with Adam's new formulation of martyr as victim of love to urge Adam to consort with death.[26] His primary motive may be to keep Eve, but the method he fixes upon is martyrdom in the cause of human love.

While Adam may be attracted to heroic means, he receives strong encouragement from his wife, who presents herself as his audience and admirer. Eve seems impressed with his heroic choice (9.991–93). She encourages her husband's defiance of death as an element in martyrdom for love.[27] Hers is a perversion of martyrdom that urges the form without the substance because she has substituted the cause of human love for divine obedience. The combined effect of Eve's words, of her worship, and of her husband's preferred self-image has disastrous effects on Adam.

The pathos and language of this scene seem to enhance Adam's persona as martyr by tugging at the reader's heartstrings. Doctrinally alert readers, however, know that neither the pathos of severe punishment, nor the apparent courage and steadfastness of the victim facing death, nor the sound of his or her words make the martyr: only the cause for which the martyr dies validates the act. Adam's motives for violation of God's sole command identify Adam as a false martyr and spiritual suicide.[28]

Furthermore, Adam "fails to act in a way that corresponds to [his] verbal profession," the last of several counterindications Milton incorporates into his definition of martyrdom in *De Doctrina Christiana*. In his first speech in the epic, Adam professes obedience to the sole command to abstain from the forbidden fruit, calling it "This one, this easie charge," "The only sign of our obedience left," and "One easie prohibition" (see *PL* 4.421–35). Yet, at the brink of disobedience in Book Nine, Adam denies both his obligation to obey the command and God's faithfulness to his own word in it (9.934–47). Rather than suffering for the sake of obedience to God's truth—offering to die *for* Eve as the Son does, when as the Second Adam he offers to die *for* humankind—Adam chooses paradoxically, heterodoxically, and dramatically to die *with* Eve in a desperate act to keep their marriage alive.

Other readers delineate the contradictions of Adam's inconstancy and idolatry. Most notably, Stanley Fish contrasts Adam's choice of disobedience with the Son's obedience and notes, "the wrongness of disobedience is not a relative wrongness to be balanced against the relative rightness of the form an act of disobedience might take." Fish further develops Adam's inconstancy by quoting his previous convictions "that he owes everything to 'some great Maker.'" Citing Augustine's notion of enjoyment of a thing for its own sake as being "shackled by an inferior love," Fish describes Adam's preference for "the created thing [Eve] to the creator" as idolatry.[29]

Fish does not discuss a specific temptation to martyrdom for either Adam or the reader. However, he asserts that both the reader's and the character's desire for dramatic action in Milton's works—and for "everything of [traditional literary] interest"—comes from "error" (37–38). Fish determines that "it is a creative error"—"always the same error, the failure to identify and cling to the true object of devotion and fear" (36). He calls this "the great error" in reading Milton's works (12), one that also presents itself as a temptation to the characters within it. As Fish observes that readers and characters are attracted to the temptations of plot, history, politics, and knowledge, I assert that they are also attracted to the temptation of martyrdom.[30]

III

Granted, the seventeenth-century English fascination with martyrdom is reflected in Milton's controversial prose, but how can the inexperienced Adam of *Paradise Lost* aspire to martyrdom if he has never heard of the concept, much less seen it enacted? Though Miltonists generally attribute Adam's choice to die with Eve as allegiance to chivalric and Petrarchan values, they ignore the fact that, in Raphael's account of the war in heaven and the events immediately preceding it, Adam is early offered a clearer example of martyrdom than that of chivalry, courtly love, or even Petrarchan love.[31] Raphael's narrative offers Adam his first account of heroism of any kind. The archangel twice refers to "Steeds" (6.17, 391), which pull chariots rather than transport mounted knights. The armored warriors who participate in the war in heaven hail from classical epic rather than romance. Single combat is undertaken without the aid of horses. The chivalric code is neither mentioned nor employed here. No ladies of any sort appear during Raphael's narrative, a situation that denies Adam an introduction to courtly or Petrarchan love. Though an enthusiastic learner, Adam is given no introduction to these traditions of European Christian heroism. However, Abdiel's fortitude and cause as described by Raphael present the angel as a clear example of Milton's definition of martyrdom.[32]

Raphael's heroic narrative emphasizes the quality of Abdiel's martyrdom by opposing it to Satan's false heroism.[33] More subtly than the proem to Book Nine, which contrasts the matter and heroism of romantic epic with those of biblical epic, Raphael's account privileges Abdiel's cause and fortitude by presenting them in immediate opposition to Satan's self-glorification and warmongering. Abdiel's extrabiblical episode comprises nearly a quarter (roughly 300 of 1,200 lines) of Raphael's account of the events immediately preceding the war in heaven in Book Five and the war itself in Book Six.[34] During his speeches from first to last in Books Five (809–48, 877–95) and Six

(131–48, 172–88), Abdiel courageously professes the "true religion and . . . worship" of God. This leads to his disgrace and risk of violence from Satan and his legions in Books Five and Six. Not only do his reported words and behavior suit Milton's definition of martyrdom, these and the cause for which Abdiel suffers are emphasized by the comments of the narrator and by God the Father. Both extol the example of "the dreadless Angel," but the Father's praise spoken from the golden cloud to the heavenly host sets Abdiel's example above that of any angel in the epic:[35]

> who single hast maintaind
> Against revolted multitudes the Cause
> Of Truth, in word mightier then they in Armes;
> And for the testimonie of Truth hast born
> Universal reproach, far worse to beare
> Then violence: for this was all thy care
> To stand approv'd in sight of God.   (6.30–36)

As does Milton in his theological treatise and antimartyrological writing, the Father delineates "the Cause" for which Abdiel suffers, which marks him as a true martyr, rather than the pathos of his suffering or the dramatic prospect of his armed response to Satan. At the onset of the war, Raphael describes the impact of Abdiel's weapon upon Satan's crest, but the preceding depiction of Abdiel's cause and fortitude, as those of a martyr, more effectively enraged and "foil'd" Satan (6.189–200). Adam's introduction to heroism in the events preceding the war in heaven is in the form of martyrdom rather than "Knighterrantry."[36]

"[A]ttentive" (7.51) Adam is entranced by Raphael's narrative. However, the archangel may neglect the attraction of the conventional heroism included within his own account when he warns Adam to "profit . . . [from the] terrible Example . . . Of [Satan's] disobedience" (6.909–11). By warning Adam to avoid Satan's rebellion, but failing to reiterate the necessary connection between Abdiel's cause and his actions, Raphael may allow unfallen Adam to maintain a partial understanding of Abdiel's example. Adam's choice of death in Book Nine demonstrates that he fails to extract and retain appropriate principles of martyrdom from Raphael's account. Instead, guided by his idolatry of Eve, his developing attraction to the notion of the martyr of love serves to eradicate the doctrine embedded in Raphael's narrative. Adam's words and actions in the separation scene, where he presents himself as Eve's courageous defender, demonstrate that he is at least as impressed with Abdiel's heroic actions as he is awed by Satan's punishment.[37] In the midst of his temptation in Book Nine, when Adam should reconsider Abdiel's testimony and the Father's commendation, which emphasize the cause for which the angel suffers, Adam instead reenacts his own dramatic image of Abdiel's courage and constancy. Adam's version of heroism misses martyrdom, devolving into a chivalrous defense of his lady and his marriage rather than bearing "Universal reproach" for "the testimonie of Truth."[38]

Despite Raphael's best intentions, Adam attempts to emulate Abdiel's external example while neglecting his internal motives.[39] In his first attempt to display Abdiel's apparent "Loyaltie, Love," and especially his "Zeale" (5.900), Adam misapplies them. Martyrdom is one legitimate expression of "Zeale," as Milton defines it in his treatise (YP 6:697–703). If "Abdiel is the embodiment of zeal,"[40] Adam is the embodiment of its distortions. Aping Abdiel's zeal, Adam hopes to replicate the angel's heroism. Adam risks reprobation; he even exceeds the angel by risking death out of loyalty, love, and zeal for his relationship with Eve. He proclaims his constancy: his love for Eve and his loyalty to their marriage during his temptation in Book Nine (952–59). Milton labels Adam's evident zeal in defending his marriage as "Ignorant and imprudent" (YP 6:698) because it opposes true zeal, like Abdiel's, which is righteous and expresses "[a]n eager desire to sanctify the divine name, together with a feeling of indignation against things which tend to violation or contempt of religion" (YP 6:697).[41] Instead of indignation against such violation, Adam's blind zeal endorses it.

Before the Fall Adam and Eve have no familiarity with death; neither do they understand martyrdom. Readers might assume they have no need of such knowledge, but when Satan perceives their naivete in these areas, his rhetoric exploits it. He inserts into the serpent's final speech a perversion of martyrdom, which renders it defiance of God rather than obedience to him (10.693–95); correspondingly, Eve promotes this notion in her temptation of Adam (830–33, 969–71). As his temptation progresses, Adam increasingly mistakes blind zeal in human love for martyrdom. One result of these misconstructions is that Adam becomes a false martyr, suffering for his conscientious, but idolatrous, devotion to wrong causes (Eve, marriage, martyrdom itself).

Readers may argue that martyrdom is always invoked as suffering for religious truth;[42] Adam suffers for love of Eve (eros) rather than love of God (agape). Since his suffering does not seem to have what twenty-first-century readers regard as religious motivations, how can Adam qualify for any sort of martyrdom, either true or false? My response is threefold. First, the history of Christian martyrdom, beginning with that of Jesus himself and proceeding through that of the regicides in the Restoration, reveals a blend of religion and politics as a motive for most persecutors and martyrs. Second, Knoppers's research demonstrates that Milton "politicizes" and reconstitutes martyrdom. She illustrates the political implications of martyrological controversy by describing the cult of "the royal martyr" in the late seventeenth century. Furthermore, in the wake of Foxe's book, English views of martyrdom were heavily politicized well before 1649. As Knoppers notes, Milton's prose tracts do not recognize a dichotomy between religious and political truth as a basis for martyrdom.[43] In one example from *Eikonoklastes*, Milton asserts, "he who fights against [political tyranny], and dyes fighting, if his other sins overweigh not, dyes a *Martyr* undoubtedly both of the Faith and of the Common-wealth" (YP 3:530). Finally, Adam, like Charles I, is not a private person, but a monarch and "Patriarch" (*PL* 4.290, 5.506, 9.376). According to Milton's theological treatise, because Adam is the representative head of the entire human race, his affections and actions have universal religious implications (YP 6:384–85).[44]

Because of Adam's status as patriarch of humankind, domestic harmony at the price of religious truth becomes a threat to posterity. In *Eikonoklastes*, Milton castigates Charles I for his zealous devotion to his wife; he accuses Charles of ascribing "*all vertue* to his Wife, in straines that come almost to Sonnetting," at the expense of Parliament "and aspersing the great Counsel of his Kingdom, in comparison of one Woman." Milton also derides Charles's constancy in marriage: "His constancy in what? Not in Religion, for it is op'nly known that her Religion wrought more upon him, then his Religion upon her, and his op'n favouring of Papists, and his hatred of them call'd Puritans [*sic*] . . . made most men suspect she had quite perverted him" (YP 3:420–22). In *Tetrachordon*, Milton discusses the religious implications of the marriage of two persons of different faiths. He notes that the issue for Christians is not "ceremonious defilement, but . . . an irreligious seducement" and "the forc't and servile temptation of loosing our selves" (YP 2:681). Here Milton's concern for "loosing" self indicates "enticement from the true faith" (YP 2:687). Like "the infirme Christian" "unequally yokt" to an infidel, whom Milton discusses in *Tetrachordon*,[45] Charles's religious leadership is sacrificed to domestic and Petrarchan love, which in turn becomes both a religious and political threat to the nation.[46] Adam's assertion that he has "fixt [his] Lot" with Eve (*PL* 9.952) suggests that her (serpent-inspired) religion has wrought more upon him than vice versa. In the case of Reformation-era monarchs and patriarchs, domestic love and religious choice are closely related. Adam's stated motives for eating the forbidden fruit center on love for Eve and devotion to their union (9.953–59), but domestic love becomes religious choice for monarchs beginning with Adam.[47]

Adam's choice is further undermined by its immediate impact in Books Nine and Ten. Since the causes for which Adam suffers cannot measure up to true martyrdom, neither do the effects of his suffering. True martyrs should provide the church with certifiable examples of patience, fortitude, and constancy in the midst of persecution and suffering and thus encourage the faithful to doctrinal and emotional solidarity with the martyrs as well as perseverance in their own quotidian troubles.[48] Ideally, these examples would also convict and convert nonbelievers. Thus, Milton's definition adds, "It is generally by martyrdom that the gospel is propagated." Adam's example has the opposite effects. During the couple's immediate postlapsarian suffering, they bring forth discord and sin in many forms: mutual idolatry (9.1013–33), heresy (9.1009–11), repeated offense—eating the fruit multiple times (9.1004–7), delusion (9.1008–11), and contemplation of suicide (10.999–1028).[49] Mutual recrimination (9.1134–89), self-exculpation (10.125–43), abusive language (10.867–95), even hate (10.834–41) can be added to this long list of less than exemplary actions and attitudes. Adam himself admits that instead of propagating the Gospel, he has "propagated curse" on all he begets (10.728–29). Only in the light of the true martyrdom of the Son, clarified by Michael's teaching, does Adam finally learn to repudiate his distortions.

IV

If Milton's works display more involvement with antimartyrology than martyrology, what is the pattern of true martyrdom implicit within them? Though several of his characters, such as Abdiel (above), fit Milton's definition of martyrdom, the Son of God is the only incarnate pattern of martyrdom in Milton's works.[50] Thus, he asserts in *Of Reformation* that martyrs "are to bee judg'd what they were by the *Gospel,* and not the *Gospel* to be tried by them" (YP 1:603). For Milton the Gospels, especially their accounts of the obedient choice of death by the Son of God, are the gold standard for martyrdom. Furthermore, I build on Dennis Danielson and the antimartyrological tradition in general in asserting that unfallen Adam the First should have set the pattern by voluntarily offering himself as an obedient replacement for fallen Eve.[51] Because Adam the First chooses a disobedient death, Adam the Second chooses an obedient one, which sets the pattern of martyrdom for those following him.[52]

The ironic contrast between the martyrdom of Adam the First and that of Adam the Second bears some illustration. These illustrations demonstrate that, while contemporary martyrs were often presented to the reading public during the sixteenth and seventeenth centuries, the sacrifice of the Son of God was regarded as the ultimate paradigm of martyrdom. Present-day readers easily forget that the Son represents not only the "Saviour of Men" (*PL* 3.412) and "Redeemer" (12.573), but also the preeminent martyr. Thus, Miltonists generally agree with Knott's assertion that in *Paradise Lost* Milton "never developed this ideal [of martyrdom] as fully as one might expect given the pressure he put on it to counterbalance the dramatically powerful example of Satan."[53] I maintain that he employs the ideal of the Son's martyrdom throughout his works but especially in *Paradise Lost*, where Books Three, Ten, and Twelve privilege the example of the Son, and Book Nine presents Adam's example as its foil.

In light of the priority of the Son's example, Milton's first attempt at martyrology might be his early poem, *The Passion*, where he tries to describe the event and paradigm of Jesus's martyrdom. Milton sings Jesus as the ultimate hero, "Most perfect *Heroe*, try'd in heaviest plíght / Of labours huge and hard, too hard for human wight" (13–14). The poet will describe not only Jesus' life of "Dangers, and snares, and wrongs . . . / Which he for us did freely undergo" (11–12) but also focus on "These latter scenes" (22), the scenes of his suffering and death on the cross, which will be described as a martyrdom: "Yet more; the stroke of death he must abide, / Then lies him meekly down fast by his Brethrens side" (20–21). Milton admits failure in this probable ode, but he twice published it with the comment: "This subject the Author finding to be above the yeers he had, when he wrote it, and nothing satisfi'd with what was begun, left it unfinisht" (52). Roy Flannagan comments that " 'The Passion' is generally rated as Milton's worst English poem," but it is noteworthy that he attempted it, that he honors "[t]his subject," that he published it, and that surviving lines can be read as anticipating a martyrology.[54] The Trinity Manuscript records Milton's continuing interest in dramatizing the passion; "Christus patiens" is included among prospective "Outlines for Tragedies" on New Testament themes.[55] When read in liturgical sequence with its companion pieces, the Nativity ode and *Upon the Circumcision*, *The Passion* displays an increasing emphasis on the Son's suffering, but lacks the militancy and ironic contrast of the Nativity ode. *The Passion* also lacks the foil of false martyrdom.[56] Responding to the prelates and *Eikon Basilike* in the 1640s may have provided "the yeers" of experience Milton wanted in 1630.

Paradise Lost contains Milton's most sustained martyrological efforts, yet even these efforts are reinforced by greater emphasis on antimartyrology. The failure of *The Passion* to present such a contrast becomes part of the success of the epic. After presenting the angelic martyrdom of Abdiel in Books Five and Six, the epic sets the tone for the Fall by invoking "Heroic Martyrdom" in contrast with the "tedious havoc [of] fabl'd Knights" in Book Nine.[57] Such a contrast suggests an encounter between true and false heroism on a human level, especially in the arena of martyrdom, embodied in Adam the First and Adam the Second.

In *Paradise Lost*, Books Three, Ten, and Twelve, Milton details the causes for which the Son chooses a martyr's death. However, as early as 1642 in *Apology against a Pamphlet,* Milton outlines his conventional criteria for martyrdom and acknowledges the possibility of courage in a false martyr who serves a wrong cause. He even agrees with his opponent, warning his audience to beware of supposed martyrs who have suffered for the wrong motives, "sometimes in a good cause with a forward ambition displeasing to God. Otherwhiles they that story of them out of blind zeale, or malice may write many things of them untruly."[58] In this tract Milton asserts that a martyr must suffer for the right cause of the Gospel, and must do so only in obedience to God rather than be "vainly ambitious of that honour"; furthermore, the account of the martyrdom must abide by the facts rather than be "misreported, or misunderstood" (YP 1:912).

These standards are reflected in Milton's epic. Book Three presents the Father's sentence in anticipation of Adam's crime, "Dye hee or Justice must; unless for him / Som other able, and as willing, pay / The rigid satisfaction, death for death" (210–12). At first no one volunteers for this task until the Son freely offers himself as satisfaction for Adam's "Treason" (207). The Son puts on mortality so that he can suffer for humankind and thus become an incarnate martyr as well as the savior. Noting his own loss as a parent, God the Father praises the Son for his motives (obedience to God's justice and the salvation of humankind), "for [humankind] I spare / Thee from my bosom and right hand, to save, / By loosing thee a while, the whole Race lost" (278–80). He notes the necessity of the Son's becoming the divine/human replacement of Adam, "Be thou in *Adams* room / The Head of all mankind, though *Adams* Son" (285–86). After the Father's fulsome praise, the heavenly host extol both Father and Son. Their hymn concludes with a celebration of the Son's love, which is expressed in his ultimate sacrifice and example:

> [He] offerd himself to die
> For mans offence. O unexampl'd love,
> Love no where to be found less then Divine!
> Hail Son of God, Saviour of Men, thy Name
> Shall be the copious matter of my Song
> Henceforth, and never shall my Harp thy praise
> Forget, nor from thy Fathers praise disjoine.   (*PL* 3.409–15)

This hymn is accurate martyrological praise, not "misreported, or misunderstood." In a narrative choice, which suggests endorsement of the angels' martyrology, the epic voice joins the heavenly host in celebrating the Son's sacrifice.[59] Their praise contrasts with Eve's "blind zeale or malice," which sings "many things [of them] untruly," as Milton had noted of some martyr idolaters.[60]

In Book Ten, as he receives the Father's command to judge the humans, the Son reminds him of his promise (73–77). The Son emphasizes his obedient resolve and his desire to please his Father. The reader remembers that this martyrdom will serve the highest possible cause, patient obedience to the Father's will; the Son lacks "a forward ambition displeasing to God."

In Book Twelve of *Paradise Lost*, Milton succeeds where *The Passion* had failed "to sing the victorious agonies of Martyrs and Saints." But the epic narrator does not succeed by detailing the agonies of Lawrence, Cyprian, or even John the Baptist or Stephen (though Milton praises all these martyrs in his previous writings—see YP 1:611, 534–35, 546, 561, and 3:502). Rather, he celebrates and explains the Crucifixion of the Son of God. Here, the martyrologist is Michael the Archangel, who delivers a careful exegesis of the Son's motives and actions in order to correct Adam's false notions. Unlike Raphael's narration of Abdiel's heroic resistance,[61] Michael's sermon is repetitive and packed with commentary in order to explicate the causes for which the Second Adam will suffer and die.[62] Obedience is the first, "Obedience to the Law for God, impos'd / On penaltie of death, and suffering death, / The penaltie to thy transgression due" (12.397–99). Fulfillment of God's law by love for God and humans is the second, "Both by obedience and by love, though love / Alone fulfill the Law" (403–4). Life for Adam and his seed, Michael explains, is the third cause. The Son chooses death, so Adam and his chosen seed may live, "Proclaiming Life to all who shall believe" (407). Redemption is the final cause, "his obedience / Imputed becomes theirs by Faith, his merits" (408–9). The Son is innocent of idolatry, heresy, crime, delusion, or suicide; his persecutors are the guilty ones. He is "slaine for bringing Life" (414). Just to make certain Adam gets the point, the archangel notes the Son's choice of death for the life of humankind yet again:

> Thy ransom paid, which Man from death redeems,
> His death for Man, as many as offerd Life
> Neglect not . . .
>   this God-like act
> Annuls thy doom, the death thou shouldst have dy'd,
> In sin for ever lost from life.   (*PL* 12.424–29)

Michael corrects Adam's errors by explicating the ultimate sacrifice of the Son: Adam's false martyrdom results in death for himself and his seed, but the Son's sacrifice offers them life.

In response to Adam's question about the faithful remnants left in the church following the passing of the Apostles, Michael describes their preparation for and perseverance in suffering which "shall amaze / Thir proudest persecuters" (496–97). Though he notes the readiness of the Disciples to endure a death like their master's (444–45), Michael does not describe their executions. In what can be read both as a corrective to idolatry of Foxean martyrs and a coda to Foxe's volumes, the epic omits descriptions of other martyrs' deaths.[63] Milton's views predominate, that "every true Christian will be a Martyr when he is called to it" (YP 1:533) and that such suffering need not include death. Those following the Apostles' teachings should expect persecution and even execution, but they must not exalt heroic death above obedience.[64] By emphasizing the gold standard of the Son's martyrdom, Michael discourages Adam's "forraging after straw." Like his seventeenth-century descendants, Adam must remain in his "firme station . . . under the standard of the Gospell" (YP 1:627). Michael teaches him to eschew false martyrdom and martyr idolatry. As Milton hopes for those idolatrous of Charles the Martyr and misled by his martyrology, Adam "find[s] the grace and good guidance to bethink [himself], and recover" (YP 3:601).

V

Though much attention has been given to Eve's final words in *Paradise Lost*,[65] this does not argue neglect of Adam's parting summary of his lesson learned. Coming as they do in Book Twelve after Michael's sermons explicating the Crucifixion and the history of the persecuted church, as well as the vindication of the just, Adam's final twenty-one lines are marked as such by "last reply'd" (552). They are further emphasized by narrative brackets: "Seer blest" (553) and "Redeemer ever blest" (573). Adam's painful education on the Mount of Speculation in the final books of the epic teaches him to discern, prefer, and emulate the true example of the Son of God as described by the Gospels rather than misleading human notions of martyrdom. Like Milton's assertion in *Of Education,* "The end then of learning is to repair the ruins of our first parents by regaining to know God aright" (YP 2:366–67), Adam summarizes in *Paradise Lost* how he may repair the ruins of his false martyrdom. His words reveal his repentance and doctrinal clear-sightedness. Adam expresses regret for the folly of his aspiration to knowledge too wonderful for him (558–60), but disobedience, not seeking knowledge, was Adam's sin. What he claims to acquire in this process is obedience (561), fear of the Lord (562), acknowledgment of God's presence and providence (562–64), and dependence upon God's mercy rather than human strength (564–69).[66] The last lesson Adam cites is to keep the example of the Son of God ever before him. Adam's final lines can be read as a repudiation of his distortions of martyrdom:[67]

>   that suffering for Truths sake
>   Is fortitude to highest victorie,
>   And to the faithful Death the Gate of Life;
>   Taught this by his example whom I now
>   Acknowledge my Redeemer ever blest.   (*PL* 12.569–73)

Adam acknowledges dependence upon the Son's redemption and the preeminence of his example, which incorporates all of the lessons Adam must learn and culminates in true martyrdom. Finally dispelling the serpent's notions of martyrdom as Promethean rebellion and his own as chivalrous victim, Adam discerns what the Son's example teaches and recites his lesson for readers. Heroic martyrdom is obedience ("to obey is best" [561]). It is a living witness to and maintenance of God's truth in the midst of suffering ("suffering for Truths sake / Is fortitude to highest victorie"), not just any pathetic suffering, not idolatrous defiance of God's command or fatalistic submission to evil. It is neither delusional nor suicidal ("to the faithful Death the Gate of Life"). Rather, it is motivated out of love for God, not forward ambition nor petulant insistence upon what one personally desires ("love with fear the onely God, to walk / As in his presence" [562–63]). Like that of the Disciples, whose life of obedience prepares them for death, Adam's obedience may lead to execution, but it need not include death; it is primarily a choice of life for daily living, like Adam's other lessons (12.581–82). Michael's memorable response validates Adam's entire program of learning, but immediately following Adam's discussion of martyrdom and the significance of the Son's example especially in this arena, the archangel seems to emphasize the lesson of martyrdom: "This having learnt, thou hast attaind the summe / Of wisdome" (575–76).[68] Adam learns "to overcom / By suffering" (11.374–75) the lessons of life: living obedience is better than disobedient, but heroic, sacrifice.

The portrayal of Adam's choice of death in *Paradise Lost*, Book Nine, demonstrates that he does not measure up either to conventional standards for martyrdom or Milton's. In choosing to die for the cause of married love, Adam makes idols of both martyrdom and marriage. Instead of suffering for Truth, Adam sacrifices it, breaking fealty with God in disobedience and self-deceit.[69] After the Fall, in order to correct his misconceived notions, he must study the example of the Son. Adam's choice in Book Nine, line 999, is the culmination of his misconstruction and idolatry of martyrdom. It is a type of spiritual suicide, a delusional heroism of the sort Milton derides in his anti-martyrological prose. By succumbing to this temptation, "the Patriarch of Mankinde"[70] becomes the progenitor and type of those false martyrs and patriarchs Charles I and Archbishop Laud, as well as those Foxean "Prelate-martyrs," Bishops Latimer, Ridley, and Cranmer, so admired by Milton's opponents.

Adam's language in Book Nine also undercuts his delusion of martyrdom. Like the allusion to Jesus' words in Adam's "to loose thee were to loose myself" discussed earlier, Adam's response to Eve, "I, / Who might have liv'd and joyd immortal bliss, / Yet willingly chose rather Death with thee" (1165–67), also ironically echoes Scripture. Moses' challenge to the Israelites encamped on the plains of Moab before they enter the Promised Land presents a similar choice between a life of obedience and the spiritual suicide of disobedience: "I call heaven and earth to record this day against you, that I have set before you life and death, blessing and cursing: therefore choose life, that both thou and thy seed may live" (Deut. 30:19, AV). Adam's words to Eve emphasize his choice of a disobedient death.

In Book Twelve, Michael must re-educate Adam by exegeting the example of the Son: his obedient, unconstrained choice to purchase the lives of Adam and his seed. Adam's temptation in Book Nine confronts him for the first time with the choice of death. His stage presence, heroic persona, pathos, and rhetoric suggest martyrdom to the undiscerning reader, but the domestic, erotic cause for which he dies reveals him as no martyr, but a spiritual suicide. Adam's dramatic choice portrays his fall to the temptation of martyrdom in *Paradise Lost*.

Eastern Kentucky University

NOTES

I first considered the issues raised in this essay during the summer of 1999 in John N. King's NEH seminar at Ohio State University, "The English Reformation," and gratefully acknowledge the role of the National Endowment for the Humanities in providing the initial forum for my study of martyrdom. The longer form of my title suggests my approach owes much to Stanley Fish's *How Milton Works* (Cambridge, Mass., 2001). While I had not read Fish's most recent book before drafting this essay, later perusal of it reveals my internalization of his approach to Milton. Thus, I have added a few appropriate citations from *How Milton Works*.

I am especially grateful to the early readers of this essay: Robert Eldridge, K. Fawn Knight, John R. Knott, Paula D. Kopacz, Albert C. Labriola, Catherine Gimelli Martin, David Lee Miller, and Jesse Swan. Their generosity and patience encouraged me to continue the project. Finally, to John T. Shawcross, my mentor in Milton and early modern studies, I owe the greatest debt of thanks.

Milton texts used throughout are, for poetry, *The Riverside Milton*, ed. Roy Flannagan (Boston, 1998); for prose, *Complete Prose Works of John Milton*, 8 vols., ed. Don M. Wolfe et al. (New Haven, 1953–1982), hereafter designated YP and cited parenthetically by volume and page number. References to the King James or Authorized Version of the English Bible are abbreviated AV.

1. Milton specifically cites the seventh (London, 1631–1632) or eighth edition (London, 1641) of Foxe's *Acts and Monuments* three times. For these citations, see YP 2:424, 425, 426.

Since the seventh and eighth editions were the first complete three-volume editions (the only such editions before or during Milton's lifetime), and he cites volume 3 in 1644, Milton must have used one of these editions. I use the copy of the seventh edition housed in the Special Collections of the University of Kentucky. I abbreviate Foxe's martyrology "*A & M.*"

2. Stanley Fish, *How Milton Works* (Cambridge, Mass., 2001); Brad S. Gregory, *Salvation at Stake* (Cambridge, Mass., 1999); Laura Lunger Knoppers, *Historicizing Milton* (Athens, Ga., 1994), esp. 1–25; John R. Knott, *Discourses of Martyrdom in English Literature, 1563–1694* (Cambridge, 1993). While my essay refers to a handful of Milton's earlier works, it does not attempt a full-scale study of the evolution of his thinking on martyrdom, as does Knott's book. Because of the centrality of martyrology and martyrdom in Milton's oeuvre, such a study requires book-length discussion.

3. Gregory, *Salvation at Stake,* 110. Gregory notes the primacy of God's Word, "the touchstone of the Reformation" (157), and Calvin's discussion of exemplary biblical martyrs headed by Christ (157, 159). Citing Hebrews 12:2, "looking to Jesus the pioneer and perfecter of our faith," Gregory notes scriptural foundation for this paradigm. Also emphasizing the Son's example, Gregory summarizes the near-universal standard of the sacrifice of the Son of God during this period: "Martyrdom was . . . epitomized in the crucifixion of Christ himself" (119).

4. These are antagonists Archbishop James Ussher and Bishop Joseph Hall.

5. Frederick Taft identifies these witnesses as "[William] Prynne, Bastwick, Burton, Leighton, and Lilburne" (YP 1:925 n. 43). The slanderer is William Prynne, according to Lowell Coolidge (YP 2:722–24 nn. 3–10).

6. These are the words of Milton's opponent, the anonymous Modest Confuter. Milton indicates here that they are in agreement (YP 1:912).

7. Compare *PL* 9.952–59 with *PL* 9.990–1004 and 10.198–200.

8. Milton's definition does not include the requirement that all martyrs suffer death. See his definition, cited below in the text, and YP 6:701–3. Interestingly, Milton's definition renders Milton himself a martyr.

9. Gregory, *Salvation at Stake,* 339–41. Generally, the two genres (antimartyrology and martyrology) appear together in the same work.

10. These guidelines are my own extraction from Gregory, *Salvation at Stake*. References to this work are hereafter noted in the text.

11. Knott, *Discourses of Martyrdom,* 151–78. Donald A. Roberts asserts this in *A Milton Encyclopedia,* vol. 3 (Lewisburg, Pa., 1978), 113–14. The three editions of *A & M* in Milton's lifetime were all published in London: 1610 (6th ed.), 1631/32 (7th ed.), 1641 (8th ed.). Seventeenth-century Anglicans and Puritans alike generally revere Foxe's martyrology.

12. As indicated by the three ellipses in this definition, I omit Milton's six proof-texts: Matt. 5:11; Phil. 1:14, 20, 29; Heb. 11:36; and 1 Pet. 3:14.

13. In *De Doctrina Christiana,* Milton typically offers a definition with examples and then presents negatives with their examples. His definition of martyrdom follows this pattern. This presentation of what martyrdom is and is not does not by itself constitute evidence that Milton is more involved with antimartyrology than martyrology. Knott, *Discourses of Martyrdom,* 167, cites Milton's definition but does not detail Milton's concern for its opposites. As with the previous citation, my ellipses here omit Milton's sixteen proof-texts.

14. Gregory, *Salvation at Stake,* comments, "[the denunciations of false martyrs have not been seriously analyzed in relationship to the martyrological sources, without which both are less than well understood. Consequently, it is not entirely surprising that recent scholarship has sometimes missed the meaning of false martyrs. Parallel to martyrology was antimartyrology, in which controversialists attacked those whom fellow believers celebrated. The phenomenon was persistent, widespread, and, in a context of religious controversy, inseparable from martyrdom"

(316). Gregory mentions the Catholic antimartyrologies responding to the *A & M*, such as those of Nicholas Harpsfield, Robert Parsons, Thomas Harding, and Robert Southwell (320–29). The anonymous *Eikon Alethine*, published August 26, 1649, could be cited as one example of contemporary antimartyrology with which Milton was familiar (YP 3:147–49), but Foxe's denunciations of the false martyrdoms of Thomas à Becket and Thomas More demonstrate that by the mid-sixteenth century, antimartyrology was an intrinsic aspect of martyrology.

15. The Son is "The Second Adam." See Rom. 5:12–19, 1 Cor. 15:21–22, and *PL* 3.227–65.

16. See "Letter LXXXIX," *The Confessions and Letters of St. Augustin*, translated by J. G. Cunningham (Grand Rapids, 1978–1979), 1:374. The Latin quotation "Martyrem non facit poena, sed causa" is cited by Knott, *Discourses of Martyrdom*, 155. I cite Gregory's translation of Augustine's sentence in my text (87).

17. This widespread acceptance of Augustine's touchstone is the reason *Eikonoklastes* includes frequent references to the insufficiency of "the cause" for which Charles I dies. For a few examples, see YP 3:349, 413, 421, 530, 532, 533, 599.

18. For Milton's discussion of the temptations to disobedience in the context of marriage to one of a different faith, part of the fourth major point of *Tetrachordon*, see YP 2:680–92.

19. Adam's language urges his religious convictions on the nature of marriage, first in his soliloquy, then in his speech to Eve: "Certain my resolution is to Die / . . . I feel / The Link of Nature draw me . . . / . . . from thy State / Mine never shall be parted, bliss or woe" (*PL* 9.907, 913–16). "Our State cannot be severd, we are one, / One Flesh; to loose thee were to loose my self" (*PL* 9.958–59). While these seem laudatory assertions of Adam's constancy in marriage, from a martyrological perspective, these convictions are insufficient causes for which to die.

20. Adam's image seems to prefigure King Charles at his execution. Milton's comment deriding the image of Charles also fits this scene, "[it] would Martyr him and Saint him to befool the people" (YP 3:343). For his comment on the frontispiece, see YP 3:601. See Knott, *Discourses of Martyrdom*, 161, for this quotation from Charles I, where he claims he dies "the Martyr of the People."

21. Roy Flannagan and John Shawcross, in the preface to *The Riverside Milton*, suggest that Milton's preferred spelling can be read as a pun. They observe, "loose (that is, both *loose* and *lose*)" (xxxii). *The Compact Oxford English Dictionary* corroborates this reading as obsolete; it notes another meaning of "loose" is "to unjoin" or "to unclasp hands." See *King Lear* 5.1.19, *The Riverside Shakespeare* (Boston, 1997), for an earlier example of this usage.

22. Calvin's commentary on Genesis 3:12, in *Commentary on Genesis*, translated by John King (1847; reprint, Carlisle, Pa., 1992), 164, indicates that Adam makes God the author of Adam's sin. In *The Doctrine and Discipline of Divorce*, Milton defends this Calvinist perspective against Arminians who accuse them "of making God the author of sinne" (YP 2:293).

23. Jesus' phrase occurs six times in the Gospels: Matthew 10:39, 16:25; Mark 8:35; Luke 9:24, 17:33; and John 12:25. See Gregory, *Salvation at Stake*, 105–11, 156–57, on proof-texts for martyrdom. He calls Luke 9:24 one of "two classic New Testament passages" urging martyrdom (263).

24. Demonstrating that the cause for which one gives up one's life is the central issue in distinguishing martyrdom from suicide, Milton cites the Gospel parallels to Luke 9:24. He uses John 12:25 to discuss suicide in *De Doctrina Christiana* and extravagant self-love, opposites of the virtue of charity toward oneself, which he illustrates with Matthew 10:39, Mark 8:35 (YP 6:719). Jesus' concern with loving and losing life has multivalent significance for Milton.

25. See Calvin's *Commentary on Genesis* (151–57) and the narrator's comments in *PL* 9.997–1001.

26. See John Donne, "The Funeral," line 19; Shakespeare, *Romeo and Juliet*, 1.2.89–93, 4.5.34–40, 55–58; and Shakespeare's contemporary, Robert Chester, who published *Love's*

Martyr (London, 1601), an anthology that includes "The Phoenix and the Turtle," for a few examples of the popular notion of "love's martyr" during the early modern period. The Counter-Reformation associated this notion with depictions of the martyrdom of Jesus and the ecstatic experiences of Francis of Assisi and Teresa of Avila.

27. Eve's words of encouragement seem an ironic echo of the song of the angels in Book Three, lines 383–415, which adores the Son, honoring his love and future martyrdom. Exulting in their "Union," Eve extols Adam's "glorious trial of exceeding Love, / Illustrious evidence, example high!" (9.961–62, 966). The cause she presses is domestic, erotic love (she repeats "Love" four times, "Death" five times in twenty-nine lines). John Shawcross notes in a personal e-mail (February 11, 2005) that the young Milton uses the phrase "exceeding love" twice to anticipate the agape love that will be demonstrated in the martyrdom of Jesus in *Upon the Circumcision* (lines 15–16). This implicit comparison urges the contrast between the obedient, agape love of the Son versus the idolatrous, erotic love of Adam. The latter can never be the cause of true martyrdom, according to Augustine's touchstone.

28. Other than the obvious motive of eros, Adam's motives include idolatrous desire to keep Eve at his side, extravagant self-love, heretical defamation of God's character, felonious disregard for God's Law, delusional ambitions to martyrdom, and romantic escape from consequences. Calvin's commentary on Genesis adds ambition to Adam's motivations: "[I]t was not only for the sake of complying with the wishes of his wife, that he transgressed the law laid down for him; but being drawn by her into fatal ambition, he became a partaker of the same defection with her. . . . [U]nbelief was the root of the defection [from God's command]. . . . Hence flowed ambition and pride, so that the woman first, and then her husband, desired to exalt themselves against God . . . . unbelief has opened the door to ambition, but ambition has proved the parent of rebellion" (152–53). See also *The Geneva Bible* (Geneva, 1560) gloss on Genesis 3:6 and 3:22.

29. Fish, *How Milton Works,* 34–35, 51–54.

30. Ibid., 37–38, 36, 12, 561–73. Fish's book presents the temptation of plot in Milton's works in general, but especially in *Paradise Regained* and *Comus*. He notes of *Paradise Regained,* "Satan wants (what many readers also want) something to happen; what the Son says (by saying very little) is that everything has already happened, and that all one need do is continue to 'Quaff immortality' (*PL*, V, 638) and praise its bestower" (38). Fish further develops this notion as being "secret—undisclosed, hidden—to those (characters and readers) looking for the evidence of things seen" (67).

31. For a few examples of this widely held belief, see Flannagan, *The Riverside Milton,* 301, 613 n. 261, 614 n. 278, and 615 n. 281. Flannagan discusses Adam as a type of romance knight, volunteering to die for his lady love. For further evidence from the epic, see especially *PL* 5.864–871 (Satan's speech—see Flannagan, 503 n. 245); *PL* 6.15–18 (see Flannagan, 507 n. 9); and *PL* 6.19–43 (Abdiel's words and views). Also see 6.80–98 (Satan's armored forces and heraldry—and Flannagan, 510 n. 34). See *PL* 6.111–30 (Abdiel's response to Satan's rebellion), 6.131–48 (Abdiel's defiant words to Satan before striking him), and Abdiel's further words, "This greeting on thy impious Crest receive" (6.188). See Flannagan, 513 n. 63.

32. Knott, *Discourses of Martyrdom,* 167–68, suggests that Abdiel is one example of martyrdom in the epic. I am indebted to Catherine Gimelli Martin, who early encouraged my pursuit of this approach to *PL* and suggested this discussion of Abdiel.

33. Fish, *How Milton Works,* contrasts "God's writing of the world in book VII of *Paradise Lost* and Satan's efforts in book VI to rewrite it in his own image" (88). However, I note the more immediate contrast between Satan's and Abdiel's means (defiant rebellion versus obedient martyrdom) and causes (glorification of self versus glorification of God).

34. I calculated this percentage as follows: I begin Raphael's account of the war in heaven at *PL* 5.577, with the events immediately preceding the war, and continue counting until line 892 in

Book Six, where the victorious Son returns to the Father's side. The sum of the 892 lines in Book Six and the remaining 330 lines in Book Five is 1,222 lines. To arrive at the percentage of the Abdiel narrative, I begin at 5.803, where Raphael first mentions Abdiel, and count continuously until 6.198, where Satan reels from Abdiel's blow. The total of these lines is 302 lines; 302 divided by 1,222 equals .247, or 24.7 percent.

35. For the narrator's praise, see 5.805–8, 875–76, 896–907; 6.21–28. For the Father's speech, see 6.29–54. Fish, *How Milton Works,* 61–62, also notes the anomaly of this moment and the quality of Abdiel's witness.

36. "Knighterrantry" is a term of abuse Milton employs in *Eikonoklastes* (YP 3:367) to satirize King Charles's use of a prayer from *Arcadia.* This coinage suggests Milton's rejection of the trappings of romance epic as early as 1649.

37. Even before her fall, Adam attempts to portray himself as defender to would-be wandering Eve in the separation scene (9.267–69). During this scene, Adam utters a prophecy, which can be applied to his own, as well as Eve's, fall. They must both beware, "least by some faire appeering good surpris'd / [Reason] dictate false, and misinforme the Will / To do what God expressly hath forbid" (9.354–56). Eve is misled by the "appeering good" presented by the serpent, but Adam is misled by his devotion to Eve, their union, and his misconstruction of martyrdom.

38. While he does not specifically aspire to *false* martyrdom, Adam's linkage of martyrdom, romance, and heroism results in a debasement of all three. Because his motives do not match those of true martyrdom, Adam's version of religious heroism becomes a diminished version of chivalry, of the sort Milton derides in the proem to Book Nine. I am indebted to Jesse Swan for this observation.

39. Adam, like the young scholars Milton describes in *Of Education,* should be taught with "lectures and explanations" which "may lead and draw them in willing obedience, enflam'd with . . . the admiration of virtue; stirr'd up with high hopes of living to be brave men, and worthy patriots, dear to God, and famous to all ages." Also, like them, Adam needs "a speciall reinforcement of constant and sound endoctrinating to set them right and firm, instructing them more amply in the knowledge of vertue and the hatred of vice" (YP 2:384–85, 396). In other words, Adam is naturally inclined to heroic action, but he needs knowledge of principles and recourse to them in order to follow appropriate examples of heroism.

One of Fish's major premises in *How Milton Works* is that "The priority of the inside over the outside is thematized obsessively in Milton's prose and poetry" (23). Adam's penchant for regarding the outside of a situation, rather than seeking to know the internal causes, is one example of his need for further instruction, once he has repented of his disobedience.

40. Flannagan, *The Riverside Milton,* 501 n. 232.

41. Instead of "sanctify [ing] the divine name," Adam speaks evil of it by asserting that God will break his own word rather than punish the humans (9.938–51).

42. The definition of martyrdom I invoke here is the traditional Christian one, rather than the contemporary one, which would include soldiers who support the speaker's cause and who die fighting against overwhelming odds.

43. Knoppers, *Historicizing Milton,* 1–41, esp. 19 and 27.

44. See *De Doctrina Christiana* for a discussion of Adam as representative head of the human race (YP 6:384–85). See also Romans 5:12–19 and 1 Corinthians 15:22 (cited by Milton as proof-texts for the above). See also *PL* 8.637–38.

45. See Milton's discussion of 2 Corinthians 6:14a, "Be ye not unequally yoked together with Infidels," in *Tetrachordon* (YP 2:682–83).

46. The concept of "Love's Martyr" moved from the erotic to religious and political realms in the art of the Counter-Reformation. Catherine Gimelli Martin adds in a private communica-

tion of July 23, 2004, "Like most Protestants, Milton associated the Petrarchan cult of love with Roman Mariolatry and hence false religion."

47. I omit here a discussion of the Reformation-era understanding that the religion of the monarch determines that of the subject. This idea gained prominence with the compromise of the Peace of Augsburg in 1555.

48. For an example of this from Foxe, see "The Utility of This Storie" (*A & M,* 7th ed., 1:PPP2v–PPP3v). See also Gregory, *Salvation at Stake,* 187–96, where he asserts that martyrologies define and reinforce doctrinal boundaries.

49. Martin observes (private communication, July 23, 2004) that Eve's offer of mutual suicide would only repeat their original mistake in reverse, making her a false martyr for Adam after the fact.

50. Such characters in *PL* include the "one just" individual who resists the crowd such as Abdiel, Enoch, and Noah. See Knott, *Discourses of Martyrdom,* 167–68.

51. See Danielson, "Through the Telescope of Typology: What Adam Should Have Done," *MQ* 23, no. 3 (1989): 124. See also Fish, *How Milton Works,* 35.

52. Such an obedient, living sacrifice, like Moses' offer of himself as a replacement for the sinning Israelites in Exodus (32:30–33), might not entail death, but instead enduring and suffering in obedience (as Moses himself does). However, Adam's offer, like Moses', would have to be genuine.

53. Knott, *Discourses of Martyrdom,* 168.

54. Flannagan, *The Riverside Milton,* 50. Knoppers, *Historicizing Milton,* concludes from the conspicuous absence of the Crucifixion in *Paradise Regained:* "In rejecting the passion narratives as models for telling how Christ regains paradise, Milton represses the main emphases of the gospels. . . . The witness of Milton's Son of God counters and challenges the pathos and dramatic appeal not only of the theatrical martyr-kings, but of the Christ whom they imitate" (37). However, such an omission in *Paradise Regained* does not mandate similar omissions in *Paradise Lost* and Milton's other works, or suggest that he does not honor the subject itself.

55. See *The Works of John Milton,* 18 vols. in 21, ed. Frank Allen Patterson et al. (New York, 1931–1938), 18:240–41. I am indebted to Albert C. Labriola for this observation.

56. Worth noting, however, is that both the Nativity ode and *Upon the Circumcision* anticipate the martyrdom of Jesus. The Nativity ode briefly mentions it, since, "The Babe lies yet in smiling Infancy," but he will ultimately "on the bitter cross / . . . redeem our loss; / So both himself and us to glorifie" (151–54). *Upon the Circumcision,* later in the chronology of Jesus' life, is more explicit, urging that the babe, "now bleeds to give us ease" and laments, "Alas, how soon our sin / Sore doth begin / His infancy to sease!" (11–14). This poem concludes with an emphasis on the Second Adam's obedient choice of death in order to satisfy "that great Cov'-nant"; he "seals obedience first with wounding smart / This day, but O ere long / . . . Huge pangs and strong / Will pierce more neer his heart" (21–22, 25–28). Flannagan, *The Riverside Milton,* comments that these three poems (the Nativity ode, *Upon the Circumcision,* and *The Passion*) can be "counted as a part of a trio of poems examining the birth, initiation, and death of Jesus" (50). I add that all three point to Jesus' martyrdom, each with chronologically increasing intensity. I am indebted to Albert C. Labriola for this suggestion.

57. See Knott, *Discourses of Martyrdom,* 151–52, for a brief discussion of this passage.

58. These are again the words of the Modest Confuter. See note 6 above.

59. Flannagan, *The Riverside Milton,* notes of this passage that it is "[a]n apostrophe put in the form of an authorial aside. The author joins the chorus of angels in praising the Son" (428 n. 115). This blending of the epic voice with the angels' song suggests Milton's endorsement of accurate martyrological praise.

60. During Adam's temptation in Book Nine, Eve honors his sacrifice to erotic and domestic "Love" and "Union." She encourages his continuing desire "to have [her] by [his] side," which he first states in 4.484–86. In another contrast between agape and eros, the heavenly host in Book Three praises the Father for "sparing," "loosing," the Son from his "bosom and right hand" in order to save humankind (278–81). Eve's praise emphasizes Adam's jealous possessiveness, which contrasts with the Father's sacrificial love.

61. During their dialogue in Books Five, Seven, and Eight, Raphael corrects unfallen Adam's notions about free will, angelic digestion, angelic union, appropriate knowledge, and domestic relationships, but he does not clarify or correct Adam's notion of heroism. This remains for Michael to accomplish in Book Twelve, lines 386–465, when Adam assumes Satan and the Son will engage in a "Duel."

62. While Michael's sermon may seem belabored and unnecessarily dry to modern readers (see C. S. Lewis's famous comment, in "A Preface to *Paradise Lost*" (New York, 1961), on Books Eleven and Twelve as "an untransmuted lump of futurity" (129) as one such complaint, his careful explication stands in marked contrast to the "false theatricality" Knoppers, *Historicizing Milton,* notes of *Eikon Basilike* and other seventeenth-century works emulating Foxe's book (26–27).

63. Here Milton's epic may build upon the treatise added as one of the final sections of volume 3 in the seventh and eighth editions of *A & M;* Milton explicitly refers to volume 3 from one of these editions in 1644 (see note 1 above). "A Treatise of Afflictions and Persecutions of the Faithfull, Preparing Them with Patience to Suffer Martyrdome" attempts to encourage "all of such as have been persecuted for Truths sake" [A4v]. Though the treatise indicates Christians should expect persecution and prepare for possible execution, it does not recommend martyrdom as the ultimate good.

64. Knoppers, *Historicizing Milton,* suggests Milton may purposely expand the common consensus of martyrdom to include "suffering for Truths sake," which does not include death. This passage does seem to appeal to the Nonconformists of Restoration England. Knoppers's discussion of Milton's expansion of "traditional martyrdom" by the Son's suffering in *Paradise Regained* also fits *Paradise Lost:* "Martyrdom thus delineated can encompass all the faithful in Restoration England (including those who do not suffer the ultimate witness of death). In Milton's hands, the martyrdom of the Son of God becomes an inclusive condition, no longer unique and no longer linked with his kingship—or that of the Stuart monarchs. . . . Milton's model of martyrdom provides crucial hope and encouragement to his fellow dissenters" (38). I am grateful to John R. Knott for suggesting this correction.

65. See, for example, Barbara Lewalski, *"Paradise Lost" and the Rhetoric of Literary Forms* (Princeton, 1985), 277–79.

66. "I learne" (12.561) is present tense, not past. Adam claims his learning begins here and that he will continue to learn "Henceforth" (561).

67. Knott, *Discourses of Martyrdom,* 152, comments on this passage, claiming it helps Adam to "grasp . . . the principle underlying Michael's theology of suffering." Knott continues, "Milton reminds us through Adam's lesson that the example of Christ's suffering is the foundation of Christian martyrdom, the embodiment of the truth to which Christians bear witness" (152). However, Knott's omission of a discussion of antimartyrology or false martyrdom in *Paradise Lost* deprives this description of its full context.

68. There is a semicolon after "wisdome;" (indicating a stop), which stresses martyrdom in the Son's example.

69. For Milton's description of Truth's martyrdom, see YP 2:549–51. See also Truth's

retirement (*PL* 12.535–36). Fish, *How Milton Works*, calls Adam's substitution of idolatry of Eve for obedience to God, "mistak[ing] a base gesture for a noble one" (6).

70. While Flannagan, *The Riverside Milton*, 595 n. 115, notes irony in the use of this epithet for Adam, citing Adam's "possible dereliction of duty," I see an opposite irony in Adam's command to Eve to "Go": it renders him a type of king or bishop patriarch, who forces the conscience of his charge.

"THE WANDRING HEADS OF GALILEANS": MORAL AND KINEMATIC RELATIVITY IN *PARADISE LOST*

J. Christopher Warner

A MONG SEVERAL STUDIES published by Grant McColley in the 1930s on the cosmology of *Paradise Lost* and the development of the astronomical sciences in Milton's century, two of them examine a print controversy between John Wilkins and Alexander Ross over the theory of a heliocentric universe, and they argue Milton's debt to this controversy for the substance of Raphael and Adam's dialogue on the apparent motions of the heavens.[1] Wilkins, publishing anonymously, had championed the Copernican organization of the universe in *The Discovery of a World in the Moone* (two editions in 1638) and *A Discourse Concerning a New Planet* (printed as the second book of *The Discovery's* third edition in 1640). The latter work contains an attack on Alexander Ross's *Commentum de Terrae Motu Circulari: Duobus Libris Refutatum* (1634), a treatise denouncing Philips van Lansbergen and Nathanael Carpenter for their writings in support of the theory of the Earth's diurnal rotation. Ross published his reply to Wilkins in 1646: *The New Planet No Planet; or, The Earth no wandring Star, Except in the wandring heads of Galileans. Here out of the Principles of Divinity, Philosophy, Astronomy, Reason, and Sense, the Earth's immobility is asserted; the true sense of Scripture, in this point, cleared; the Fathers and Philosophers vindicated; divers Theologicall and Philosophicall points handled, and Copernicus his Opinion, as erroneous, ridiculous, and impious, fully refuted.*[2]

McColley acknowledges that the material comprising these several tracts "was extremely commonplace during the early seventeenth century"—such that "Milton could have obtained it from a multiplicity of sources"—but he puts forth that Milton "did not elect to do so."[3] Through side-by-side comparisons of numerous corresponding passages from Wilkins's and Ross's debate and *Paradise Lost*, Book Eight, McColley shows that "virtually all the arguments and ideas, as well as many of the phrases and words employed in [Raphael and Adam's] astronomical dialogue . . . are present in the *Discourse* and *Discovery* of Bishop Wilkins, and in *The New Planet* of Alexander Ross."[4]

Although it may be fair to fault McColley for "somewhat too ambitiously" concluding that Raphael and Adam's dialogue represents a verse composite of passages from these tracts,[5] nevertheless his analysis represented a significant advance in the modern understanding of Milton's range of available sources and his attitudes toward the scientific writings of his contemporaries. Alongside the work of such others as Allan H. Gilbert and Marjorie Nicolson,[6] McColley's analysis of the Ross-Wilkins controversy formed part of that early twentieth-century body of research upon which scholars have since so rewardingly built, not only sharpening our understanding of the structure of *Paradise Lost*'s universe and of Milton's views on the newly emerging theories of the cosmos, but vastly expanding our critical appreciation of the ways in which Milton's engagement with astronomical discoveries, ideas, polemics, even its mechanical models and instruments, profoundly affected "the nature of his poetic art."[7]

In this essay I revisit Alexander Ross's *The New Planet No Planet*, though not with the intention of reviewing his arguments against Copernicanism or, for that matter, attending to anything in the tract as it directly relates to his debate with John Wilkins. Rather, *The New Planet No Planet* has a claim on the interest of literary scholars for the way it appeals to epic poetry and poets in its defense of Ptolemaic and scriptural truth, a practice that has special implications for understanding Milton's own epic project. McColley neglects to mention this feature of Ross's tract when he states, "In their totality, the arguments of Ross against heliocentric astronomy consisted primarily of a mixture of invective, so-called Aristotelian physics, the testimony of the Fathers and literal statements of Scripture."[8] In fact, Ross also routinely cites Virgil to enliven his invective, supply illustrative analogies, and to invoke the authority of ancient wisdom for his claims. But these references to "the Prince of Poets," as Ross calls him, go beyond the mere application of a conventional argumentative technique. I argue in the first part of this essay that Ross enlists Virgil in his battle against the errant Copernicans and Galileans in order to wrest him from Copernicus and Galileo—to retrieve Virgil, that is, from the roles he is made to serve in the former's *De Revolutionibus Orbium Coelestium* and the latter's *Dialogo dei Massimi Sistemi*.[9] Ross understood what was at stake in this dispute. As the author of the most ambitious and best-selling biblical epic to be published in England before *Paradise Lost,* he was invested heavily in the dual basis of biblical epic's authority—the gospel truth in Virgilian dress—which had been seriously challenged by Copernicus and then devastatingly ridiculed by Galileo. When Milton looked back on this dispute, I shall argue in part 2, he likewise saw what was at stake, and he saw how feeble was *The New Planet No Planet*'s attempt at rebuttal. *Paradise Lost* was Milton's occasion to assert, by example, biblical epic's value—its truth and its efficacy—against the very assault that had defeated the energetic but inflexible Alexander Ross.

Milton ventures this assertion by means of a figural relation in *Paradise Lost* between the phenomena of moral and kinematic relativity. He invites us, that is, to apprehend as parallel experiences our unreliable judgments of good and ill, in ourselves and in others, due to our universally fallen condition and partial moral perspectives, on the one hand, and, on the other hand, our unreliable perceptions of movement in the planets and stars due to the circumstance that "apparent motion of any given body may contain a component that could be attributed to motion of the observer rather than the observed object."[10] Hence, my reinvestigation of a minor episode in the seventeenth-century debate over how the universe works will return us, in the end, to our own continuing debate over how Milton works. By considering afresh what form Milton's response to Ross takes in *Paradise Lost,* we will encounter the poem's central interpretive puzzle over which criticism has most agonized. In part 3, I suggest a fresh means to a resolution of the conundrum by viewing Milton's composition of *Paradise Regained,* and his decision to expand *Paradise Lost* from ten books to twelve, also in the light of Alexander Ross's example.[11]

                                        I

Among those besides McColley who have read Alexander Ross's polemical writings, including his *DNB* biographers and students of the seventeenth-century reception of Thomas Hobbes's *Leviathan,*[12] the seemingly inexhaustible energy of Ross's vitriolic wit has made the most lasting impression. That quality, in combination with his primary reliance on painstakingly literal readings of scripture (for example, *"The Sunne is in his glory like a Bridegroome; and in his motion like a Gyant* [citing Ps. 19]; I answer, if the Sunne be in his motion like a Gyant, then sure the Sunne hath motion"),[13] has earned Ross his reputation as a mere blustering defender of philosophical and scientific concepts that he understood no better than the new ones he attacked. As Harinder Singh Marjara rightly reminds us, however, in Ross's and Milton's day "religious and metaphysical reasons" were routinely marshaled to support geo- and heliocentrism because "[t]here was no possibility of verifying either of the hypotheses by the empirical observations of the stars." Even "[t]he advantage of simplicity that the Copernican hypothesis was claimed to have turned out to be more apparent than real," for it "explained retrograde motions of the planets in terms of the changing position of the revolving earth as a platform of observation," and "[s]ince the position of the earth was constantly changing, the calculations became as difficult as when an astronomer used the Ptolemaic model."[14] Ross's style of argument against the new astronomy would not have struck many of his contemporaries as outmoded or irrelevant, therefore, even if these same readers were embarrassed, repelled, or in the end just bored by the accompanying deluge of his acerbic sarcasm.

To be fair, in its milder moments Ross's wit possesses some charm. He opens his attack on Wilkins, for instance, with the charge, "you wrong our common mother, who so many thousand yeares hath been so quiet and stable, that now she should become a wanderer in her old age" (preface, A3ʳ). Likewise, there is some charm in Ross's commonsense arguments, which only the smugness of hindsight enables us now to find laughable. He asserts, for instance, that "[i]f the earth did move the aire, it would cause a sound" (97), while in another place he declares, "the earth must be firme and stable, because it is the foundation of buildings" (99). And yet there is no getting around the fact that Ross's intellectual powers are overwhelmed by the task he sets for himself. My one real objection to McColley's analyses is that by not making this point explicit he gives the impression that Milton turned to the Ross-Wilkins debate because it supplied convenient and balanced synopses of contemporary arguments for and against Ptolemy's and Copernicus's competing models. I think we may assume that Milton understood well enough that Ross was out of his depth in this debate. Indeed, Milton must surely have come to this conclusion before finishing the preface to *The New Planet No Planet,* as he read the following question (which Ross seems not to realize is answered by itself) posed to Wilkins: "[I]f the Earth be a Planet, and each Planet hath its period of time for finishing its course: *Saturne* 30. yeares, *Jupiter* 12. *Mars* 2, &c. What is the time which you will allot to the Earth for the accomplishing of her annuall motion?" (A3ʳ).

In the context of such painful-to-watch ratiocination, Milton would have encountered, and judged, Ross's appeals to Virgil as an ally against the upstart theory of heliocentrism. Besides a couple references to other poets (Ovid, Du Bartas) and a few to Virgil's *Eclogues* and *Georgics,* there are more than twenty citations from Virgil's *Aeneid* serving a range of different purposes. At times, for example, Ross quotes the *Aeneid* merely to embellish his mockery, as in this taunting challenge in the sixth chapter of his treatise as he prepares to examine one of Wilkins's central arguments: "Let us see," sneers Ross, "if you will be as good as your word, which we have not yet found in you; only, large promises without performance. *Larga quidem semper Drance tibi copia fandi* [Always plentiful indeed are your stores for talking, Drances]" (57, quoting *Aeneid* 11.378).[15] In other places, Virgil testifies to historical events in the Bible that were imperfectly known to the pagan Romans. An example is in Ross's response to Wilkins's "*doubt of the truth of the Sunnes going backe"* in answer to Isaiah's prayer (as reported in 2 Kings 20:11). Since there is *"no mention of it in ancient Writers"* (25), Wilkins is skeptical that such an event actually occurred, to which Ross reasonably replies, "if you will doubt or deny all passages and miracles of Scripture, which are not mentioned by the Heathen writers, our Bible will be reduced to a small handfull." But Ross next asserts that the ancients often do testify to God's miracles—through their fables—such as "Saint *Austin* proves" by citing "that Verse in *Virgil"* in which Dido credits a Massylian priestess with the power *"Sistere aquam fluviis, & vertere sidera retro"* (to stay the water of rivers, and turn back the stars) (ibid., quoting *Aeneid* 4.489 and alluding to Augustine's *De Civitate Dei* 21.8).

Finally, for Ross, Virgil also represents a storehouse of enduring wisdom. In the same way that Aristotle was often cited simply as "the Philosopher," Ross now and then invokes the "the Poet" or "Prince of Poets," alongside other authorities, to vouch for truths that have forever been accepted and ought to remain so. At one point, for example, Ross declares that "all the chiefe learned both in Divinitie, Philosophie, and Poetrie" confirm that "the Sunne is in the midst of Heaven," and his example of the third type of "chiefe learned" is "the Prince of Poets," who "speakes both of the Sunne and Moone in the midst of Heaven." Ross quotes the *Aeneid: "Iam medium Phoebus conscenderat igneus orbem. / Phoebe— / Noctivago curru medium pulsabat Olympum"* (Now had fiery Phoebus mounted the middle orb. Phoebe was trampling the mid-heavens in night-roving chariot) (21).[16]

Ross's earliest appeal to Virgil in *The New Planet No Planet* (though it is not a direct quote) occurs in the opening sentence of his dedicatory epistle to Lord Berkley. At first, the allusion seems merely to set the tone for the rest of the tract's satirical assault on the muddle-headed Copernicans: "They who have been long at sea, when they come on shore, think that the Earth moveth as the Sea did, till their brains be settled; even so these men who have been lately traveling in the new found world of the Moon, which swiftly moveth about the Earth, think when they come down hither, that it is the Earth which moveth" (A2ʳ). The nautical analogy in this insult is working on a couple levels, as we shall discover. It reasserts a hallowed truth grounded in the authority of "the Poet," but it also reaffirms the legitimacy and permanence of that authority. In doing so, it signals Ross's intention to do battle on more than just one front, for part of his task in exposing the errors of John Wilkins is to reclaim Virgil's poetry from the corruption and ridicule that it had suffered at the hands of Wilkins's most famous fellow space travelers, Copernicus and Galileo.

To help us understand Ross's motives, I will examine four short excerpts from these astronomers' works alongside others from poetic texts, starting with Copernicus's prior application of the same nautical analogy to explain the phenomenon of kinematic relativity. Citing *Aeneid* 3.72, Copernicus asks his readers,

[W]hy should we not admit that the daily revolution itself is apparent in the heaven, but real in the Earth; and the case is just as if Virgil's Aeneas were saying "We sail out from the harbour, and the land and cities recede"? For when a ship is floating along in calm weather, everything which is outside her is perceived by those who are sailing as moving by a reflection of that motion, and on the other hand they think that they are at rest along with everything that is with them. Naturally the same can happen in the motion of the Earth, so that the whole universe is thought to go round.[17]

Previous to this passage, Copernicus had given the warning, "I think the first necessity is for us to examine carefully what is the relationship of the Earth to the heavens, so that in scrutinising the loftiest heights we do not fall into ignorance of what is nearest, and by the same mistake attribute to the heavens what belongs to the Earth."[18] But from Ross's point of view, Copernicus has fallen into ignorance. The import of the nautical analogy had already been articulated by Lucretius, as Copernicus surely knew, yet here he applies it contrariwise to that ancient's explanation, thereby perversely attributing to the heliocentric model of the universe the authoritative testimony that ought to support the geocentric model. For in the following well-known passage from Lucretius's great "Epicurean epic," *De natura rerum* (quoted from the Loeb prose translation), there can be no mistaking that the comparison between stargazers and sailors corroborates the teaching of Ptolemy.

A ship in which we sail moves on while it seems to stand still, one which remains in its place is thought to pass by; and the hills and plains, which we row by or sail by, seem to be flying astern. The stars all seem to be fixed and stationary in the vaults of ether, yet all are in constant motion, since they rise and return to their far distant settings when they have traversed the sky with bright body. And the sun and moon in like manner appear to remain in their places, while experience proves that they move along.[19]

Thus *The New Planet No Planet*'s opening mockery of Copernicans and Galileans restores the traditional meaning of a Virgilian epic simile. Moreover, by imagining his adversaries "traveling in the new found world of the Moon," Ross not only gets in a joke at the expense of Wilkins, Kepler, and Francis Godwin, for whom fanciful accounts of an inhabited moonscape had served as vehicles to champion the Copernican model of the cosmos;[20] he also aims to characterize their alien modes of reasoning, which included invocations of the ancients without deference to those of their truths that are confirmed by Scripture. Ross evidently hoped that once these travelers had been brought back to Earth and "their brains be settled," they would no longer do such violence to Virgil and the Bible, but return to the brand of conventional learned discourse with which he was familiar, to which he was committed, and without which he felt estranged and angry.

There is a good deal of irony in such an interpretation of Ross's consternation, given his trademark polemical style of amassing what to us are great mountains of irrelevant material for the settling of a physics problem—but again, that is criticism from a privileged perspective. The real irony will surface shortly, when I take up his biblical epic, following our attention to the other excerpts that will frame that discussion. In these passages, Copernicus and Galileo indulge in some polemical mockery of their own, and both writers base their ridicule upon the classical principle of literary decorum. In his prefatory letter to Pope Paul III, Copernicus describes how the Ptolemaists vainly labor to make the disparate parts of their conceptual model cohere. Some of them, he explains, "use only homocentric circles, others eccentric circles and epicycles," yet for both groups "the required consequences do not completely follow." For all their calculations and elaborate models, Copernicus charges, "they have not been able to discover or deduce from the chief thing, that is the form of the universe, and the clear symmetry of its parts. They are just like someone including in a picture hands, feet, head, and other limbs from different places, well painted indeed, but not modelled from the same body, and not in the least matching each other, so that a monster would be produced from them rather than a man."[21]

We recognize Copernicus's classical allusion readily—the opening lines of Horace's *Epistle to the Pisos,* better known as the *Ars poetica* (which I quote from the Loeb prose translation):

If a painter chose to join a human head to the neck of a horse, and to spread feathers of many a hue over limbs picked up now here now there, so that what at the top is a lovely woman ends below in a black and ugly fish, could you, my friends, if favored with a private view, refrain from laughing? Believe me, dear Pisos, quite like such pictures would be a book, whose idle fancies shall be shaped like a sick man's dreams, so that neither head nor foot can be assigned to a single shape.[22]

In contrast to such a freakish image, Copernicus's picture of the universe purports to abide by all the rules of decorum: every piece of data, every calculation and proof, fits naturally with the others and has its proper place in the construction of the whole.

Nor is this merely the achievement of creative ingenuity. Just as the universal knowledge of the human form prohibits the use of foreign body parts in representing individual human beings, thus supplying the criterion by which artistic decorum is judged in Horace's example, there is for Copernicus a fundamental truth, the motion of the Earth, that enables everything in his theory to fit happily within the whole and that supplies what should be acknowledged as the measure by which decorum is evaluated in the cosmological sciences generally. In the following excerpt from *De Revolutionibus Orbium Coelestium*, Copernicus underscores this point by describing the perfect correlation between the universe's order and that of his book:

Thus assuming the motions which I attribute to the Earth in the following work I eventually found by long and intensive study that if the motions of the wandering stars are referred to the circular motion of the Earth and calculated according to the revolution of each star, not only do the phenomena agree with the result, but also it links together the arrangement of all the stars and spheres, and their sizes, and the very heaven, so that nothing can be moved in any part of it without upsetting the other parts and the whole universe. Similarly in the planning of this work I have adopted the following arrangement. In the first book I shall describe all the positions of the spheres, along with the motions which I attribute to the Earth, so that the book will contain as it were the general structure of the universe. In the remaining books I relate the motions of the remaining stars, and all the spheres, to the mobility of the Earth, so that it can be thence established how far the motions and appearances of the remaining stars and spheres can be saved, if they are referred to the motions of the Earth.[23]

We see, then, that the Copernican attack on Ross's world is doubly brazen and damaging: a manifest falsehood not only is affirmed as a truth but asserted to be the axiomatic principle by which the fitness of every component of any future treatise on the subject will have to be judged. By such a measure, that "mixture of invective, so-called Aristotelian physics, the testimony of the Fathers and literal statements of Scripture"[24]—as well as the citations of classical poetry that Ross similarly depends on to construct his arguments—will be laughed at as the "idle fancies" of "a sick man's dreams," a "monster" whose "hands, feet, head, and other limbs" all come "from different places." Virgil's works, as they have been read traditionally, do not abide by that one principle of the Earth's motion that would qualify them for inclusion in astronomical discourse; consequently, *only* if a line quoted from the *Aeneid* can be given an unaccustomed significance—so that it illustrates the manner by which the Earth's motion is mistaken for that of the sun and stars rather than the other way around—will it then be judged suitable for a book on the cosmos. This is a piece of audacity that could but enrage Ross. But he only was capable of responding with additional assemblages of hands, feet, heads, and limbs from different places.

Galileo's mockery of this method would have cut Ross even more deeply. At one point in the *Dialogo dei Massimi Sistemi*, the simpleton who defends the old Ptolemaic order—Simplicio, famously, is his name—protests to his companions, Sagredo and Salviati, that there is more truth to be discerned in the writings of Aristotle than they have been willing to concede. It is only required, as he explains, that we understand all of the philosopher's works so perfectly that it is possible to assemble, in response to any question whatsoever, the relevant passages from their different original locations.[25] Simplicio explains:

Aristotle had not gained so great authority, but for the force of his Demonstrations and the profoundnesse of his arguments; but it is requisite that we understand him, and not onely understand him but have so great familiarity with his Books that we form a perfect *Idea* thereof in our minds, so as that every saying of his may be alwayes, as it were, present in our memory. For he did not write to the vulgar, nor is he obliged to spin out his Sillogismes with the trivial method of disputes; nay rather, using a freedome, he hath sometimes placed the proof of one Proposition amongst Texts which seem to treat of quite another point; and therefore it is requisite to be master of all that vast *Idea*, and to learn how to connect this passage with that, and to combine this Text with another far remote from it; for it is not to be questioned but that he who hath thus studied him knows how to gather from his Books the demonstrations of every knowable deduction, for that they contein all things. (91–92)[26]

Ross does not, in fact, give evidence of so thorough a knowledge of the Aristotelian corpus, but he would presumably maintain that he makes up for this deficiency with his ability to cull from a wider range of works, including Virgil and the most authoritative text of all, the Bible. In Sagredo's devastating rejoinder, however, it is not Simplicio's choice of authority that is targeted for ridicule but the method that he expounds:

But, good *Simplicius*, like as the things scattered here and there in *Aristotle* give you no trouble in collecting them, but that you perswade your self to be able by comparing and connecting several small sentences to extract thence the juice of some desired conclusion, so this, which you and other egregious Philosophers do with the Text of *Aristotle*, I could do by the verses of *Virgil* or of *Ovid*, composing thereof *Centones*, and therewith explaining all the affairs of men and secrets of Nature. But what talk I of *Virgil*, or any other poet? I have a little Book much shorter than *Aristotle* and *Ovid*, in which are conteined all the Sciences, and with very little study one may gather out of it a most perfect *Idea*, and this is the *Alphabet*; and there is no doubt but that he who knows how to couple and dispose aright this and that vowel with those or those other consonants, may gather thence the infallible answers to all doubts and deduce from them the principles of all Sciences and Arts, just in the same manner as the Painter from divers simple colours, laid severally upon his *Palatte*, proceedeth by mixing a little of this and a little of that, with a little of a third, to represent to the life men, plants, buildings, birds, fishes, and in a word, counterfeiting what ever object is visible, though there be not on the *Palatte* all the while either eyes, or feathers, or fins, or leaves, or stones. (92)[27]

Before the multistage satire of this passage even starts, Sagredo lays the foundation with an acutely damning charge: that the Aristotelians have "no trouble" in compiling their proof-texts in answer to a given question because they already have "some desired conclusion" in mind. If that is how the game is played, then any text will do for the purpose: Aristotle, Virgil, Ovid, the Bible, or, for that matter, the most basic building blocks of all, the letters of the alphabet, just as painters (in a clever accommodation of the Horatian simile) mix "simple colours" on their palettes to produce whatever hues they require to "counterfeit" the visible world.[28] For us, though, the first analogy in Sagredo's reply has particular significance—in his reference to "*Centones*," which are literally "patchwork poems" constructed entirely out of lines and half-lines from classical poetry (most frequently, of course, Virgil's). In a marginal note, Salusbury explains that the word *centones* "signif[ies] works composed of many fragments of verses collected out of Poets," and is a "*cunning way to gather Philosophy out of any book whatsoever.*"[29] The second half of this gloss is somewhat misleading, actually. Centos in antiquity tend to be parodic and comical (and frequently obscene), or to serve as compendia of myths and fables; they hardly attempt to "*gather Philosophy*" out of their source texts or to describe "all the affairs of men" or the "secrets of Nature" as Sagredo jokes. In the Middle Ages and Renaissance, the best-known cento was a Christian one, written in the fourth century by Faltonia Betitia Proba, who narrates the Creation story and a condensed version of the life of Christ in 693 hexameter lines pilfered from Virgil.[30] Proba's cento must have enjoyed some popularity in its day because, in one of Saint Jerome's hortatory epistles, he quotes from it while condemning the genre generally. He objects to its trick of making Homer and Virgil, who had been "without Christ," speak as Christians—and he pronounces in the end: "these things are puerile and like the foolery of a quack."[31] By associating the Aristotelians' philosophical method with the composition of cento verse, therefore, Galileo caricatures it as a like form of contemptible trickery—a method for making men without knowledge of the truth speak as if they had it.

The cento probably best known to John Milton, and by far the most ambitious instance of the genre, is Alexander Ross's *Christiad*. An early, four-book version of the poem, titled *Vergilius Evangelisans*, was popular enough to go through two editions in 1634. Ross then revised and expanded his work to full epic length, publishing it in 1638 as the *Virgilii evangelisantis Christiados libri XIII*. Before *Paradise Lost* made its first appearance in 1667, the *Christiad* was printed twice in 1653 in Rotterdam and Zurich, and again in London in 1659.[32] Below, for the purpose of illustration, I quote the opening fifteen lines of Book One. By way of prologue, Ross first identifies himself as a singer formerly of Old Testament history, alluding to his first published works, the *Rerum Iudaicarum Memorabiliorum* in Virgilian hexameters (printed in two parts, 1617 and 1619). He then gives a synopsis of his epic's theme in imitation of the *Aeneid*'s opening lines, upon which Ross mainly depends.

Ille ego qui quondam gracili modulatus avena	*Aeneid* (a)[33]
Carmen, et *Aegypto* egressus per inhospita saxa	*Aeneid* (b) & 5.627
Perque domos *Arabum* vacuas et inania regna	*Aeneid* 6.269
Deduxi *Abramidas;* at nunc horrentia *Christi*	*Aeneid* 1.634
Acta, Deumque cano, coeli qui primus ab oris	*Aeneid* 1.1
Virginis in laetae gremium descendit et orbem	*Georgics* 2.326
Terrarum invisit profugus, *Chananaeaque* venit	*Aeneid* 1.2
Littora, multum Ille et terra jactatus et alto	*Aeneid* 1.3
Ni superum, saevi memorem *Plutonis* ob iram;	*Aeneid* 1.4
Multa quoque in monte est passus dum conderet urbem.	*Aeneid* 1.5
Nam ligno incubuit, dixitque novissima verba,	*Aeneid* 4.650
Et sacram effudit multo cum sanguine vitam;	*Aeneid* 7.534
Atque ausus penetrare sinus nigrantis Averni,	*Aeneid* 1.243
Sed tandem patrias atque altae victor remeavit ad oras?	*Aeneid* 1.7
Evertitque deos *Latii,* et genus omne *Latinum,*	*Aeneid* 1.6
Albanosque patres atque altae moenia *Romae.*	*Aeneid* 1.7

[I am he who once tuned my song on a slender reed, and sang of him who, leaving Egypt, led the children of Abraham across inhospitable rocks and through empty homes and vacant realms of Arabia; but now of the bristling acts of Christ, and of God I sing, he who first from the regions of heaven descended in the lap of the joyful Virgin and, a fugitive, visited this world, and came to Canaan shores, much tormented on earth and sea on account not from above, but of the unforgetting wrath of Pluto. And he suffered long upon the mountain until the time he would build a City. For he set himself on the cross, and said his last words, and poured out sacred life with much blood; and having dared to invade the hollow of black Avernus, did he not at last return victorious to his native regions? and he then overthrew the gods of the Latins, and the whole Latin race, and the Alban lords and walls of lofty Rome.][34]

And so on, for 311 quarto pages—and all of it Virgil, but for the necessary grammatical adjustments, substitutions of proper names and other vocabulary, and, admittedly, here and there a patch having no source in the poet whatsoever. To devote oneself to such a project requires a special brand of zeal, obviously. Hence, Galileo's mockery of centos by name may go a long way to explaining Ross's outrage at those "wandring heads" who express such disdain for his type of learning, his mode of reasoning, and his presumption that strong Christian faith guarantees right and righteous deductions. Faith in the Word was exactly the "vast *Idea*" that was supposed to qualify Ross to cull words—to excerpt phrases and sentences from any text whatsoever, sacred or profane—and to marshal them in support of true propositions or to assemble them in a *Christiad*.

In fact, Ross's assembly of passages from many different source texts is only one way that he asserts that privilege in *The New Planet No Planet*. He also puts on a display of his cento skills. Or perhaps he pays no regard to quoting Virgil accurately, but the distinction is irrelevant so long as the words have been jumbled according to the "vast *Idea*" that authorizes their new order. In one of the samples of Ross's Virgilian quotations supplied above, he points out that "the Prince of Poets speakes both of the Sunne and Moone in the midst of Heaven," and he then cites a little more than two lines from two different places for illustration (21, this time without Ross's italics): "Iam medium Phoebus conscenderat igneus orbem," which he attributes in the margin to the second book of the *Georgics*, and "Phoebe—/ Noctivago curru medium pulsabat Olympum," from *Aeneid, Book Ten*. Actually, the first line is not from the *Georgics* but is a variation on *Aeneid* 8.97: "Sol medium caeli conscenderat igneus orbem." The second excerpt takes some liberties with 10.215–16: "Iamque dies caelo concesserat almaque curru / noctivago Phoebe medium pulsabat Olympum." Interestingly, Ross not only replaces "caeli" with "Phoebus" in the first line, he also replaces "sol" with the word "iam" from 10.215, perhaps justified by this line's affinity to 8.97 in having the "caelo concesserat" construction in the same position as the latter's "caeli conscenderat" (from the second long syllable of the second foot to the end of the fourth foot). Meanwhile, the name "Phoebe" has been removed from 10.216 and placed just above the line to make room for "curru," which Ross has transferred from its position at the end of 10.215.

Except for the marginal misattribution of *Aeneid* 8.97 to *Georgics, Book Two* (perhaps a printer's error?), Ross is not quoting carelessly. These are changes by design. But then, *what* design? If their purpose is to demonstrate that Virgil attributes motion to the sun and moon, the alterations cannot be justified: the original lines show exactly that. Hence, it seems strange that Ross would not keep the lines intact, lest readers who detect the textual discrepancies have a lower estimate of his authority in this debate. I suggest the opposite. By these "misquotes," Ross means to assert his authority, reminding us, no less, of his supreme authority in this business—his special warrant to wield Virgil in defense of the truth. He is, after all, cento poet extraordinaire, compiler of the *Christiad,* and as we already know of him, his style of countering attacks against his materials and his methods is to fire back more of the same. So—against Sagredo's impious ridicule of cento poetry, Ross retorts with cento poetry, and he gets in the last word(s, rearranged).

II

In turning to consider what Milton could have derived from the spectacle of *The New Planet No Planet*—besides, that is, the "arguments and ideas, as well as many of the phrases and words" that McColley discovers in *Paradise Lost,* Book Eight—we ought first to remark what Milton saw and made sure to avoid. It was the same fatal error that doomed the Vatican's censorship of Galileo. Both Ross and Pope Urban VIII believed that the Bible unambiguously testifies to the truth of a geocentric universe, so for them accepting that truth was a test of one's faith in the literal truth of Scripture and the lifegiving tenets of Christianity. "[Y]ou are very preposterous," Ross scolds John Wilkins as he is coming to the end of his treatise, "for you will have the truth of Scripture confirmed by Astronomie, but you will not have the truth of Astronomie confirmed by Scripture: sure one would thinke that Astronomicall truths had more need of the Scripture confirmation, then the Scripture of them" (117). In *Paradise Lost,* as is well known, Milton simply denies that astronomy and Scripture need confirm one another. The dramatic scene of Adam and Eve's fall is an immobile Earth at the center of the universe, sure[35]—but Raphael poses the possibility of an alternative without anxiety: "What if the Sun / Be Centre to the World[?] . . . what if . . . / The Planet Earth, so steadfast though she seem, / Insensibly three different Motions move?"[36] As the first parent's mentoring angel previously had instructed him—referring then to the calculation of time and the seasons, but the axiom is shown to apply equally to their relationship to God and life in Eden—"whether Heav'n move or Earth, / *Imports not*" (8.70–71; emphasis added).

Of course, adopting this easier perspective requires self-assurance of one's ability to judge what imports and what imports not in matters that "may prove dangerous and pernicious to Divinitie," as Ross fears of heliocentrism (118); and similarly, as the author of exegetical and polemical works himself, Milton would have had to be confident, at least hopeful, that his own practice of citing material out of many different sources would be exempt from the ridicule that Copernicus and Galileo directed at their adversaries. Not just the biblical passages alongside Cicero and Suetonius in the political tracts (concerned as these are with creating a godly republic, after all), but Homer amid the biblical passages of *De Doctrina Christiana*—all must be relevant to the purpose, every citation in conformity with some particular, central truth that is mandatory for all fruitful discourse on the subject (like the motion of the Earth in astronomical treatises, according to Copernicus), a truth that alone warrants the selection and combination of diverse materials in pursuit of related truths.[37] Only if this strict standard of decorum is observed can the method of "connect[ing] this passage with that" and "combin[ing] this Text with another far remote from it," as Simplicio describes, be justified.

The burden of observing this standard in a biblical epic would be daunting indeed, as Sagredo's mockery of cento poetry underscores, for in a sense cento poets only take to an extreme what any composer of biblical epic must do: retell biblical history in language imbued with traces of earlier exemplars of the epic form. The biblical epic poet aspires to sing the good news of Christ (to "justify the ways of God to men" [*PL* 1.26]), yet all the while he invokes the familiar names, events, and imagery of pre-Christian epic tradition—its characteristic figures of speech and familiar turns of phrase—in a bid, on the one hand, to have his song partake of the acknowledged cultural prestige of this ancient genre, and, on the other hand, to bolster that prestige by infusing new matter into the genre and investing it with new authority, notably the Word of God. The result is pastiche, a monster made out of mismatched limbs. Does not *Paradise Lost* fit this description? Satan grutches that God "hath hither thrust me down / Into this gloom of *Tartarus*" (2.857–58); Eden is a "Spot more delicious" than such "Gardens feign'd" as "renown'd / *Alcinoüs*, host of old *Laertes' Son*" (9.439–41). How can a poet use schemes and tropes borrowed from the plains of Troy to represent the angels' war in heaven without arousing laughter? or invite associations between Adam and Aeneas, Eve and Dido, even for the ostensible purpose of contrast, without trivializing the tragedy of the Fall? To justify the ways of God to men is challenge enough, as Empson has gone to lengths to emphasize.[38] So why complicate the assignment further, why risk undermining one's efforts, by attempting the feat with an inappropriate combination of materials when, instead, one could devote one's time to polishing and publishing a theological treatise by the title *De Doctrina Christiana?*

Paradise Lost, though, "pursues / Things unattempted yet in Prose or Rhyme" (1.15–16), says Milton. In some respects this claim is very preposterous, since there were countless prose works given to justifying the ways of God and not just a few biblical epics and other verse versions of stories from Scripture, including, in that Virgilian cento by Proba, Adam and Eve's fall. But then, Milton criticism has long enjoyed the rewarding labor of striving to articulate the many particular means by which *Paradise Lost* does its work—of discovering the myriad "Things" that Milton's epic attempts in all their complexity, subtlety, and interpretive difficulty. One of these "things attempted," I propose, is a justification of biblical epic's seemingly absurd pastichelike nature by way of the poem's thematizing of a different absurdity, one that we saw put into relief by the Ross-Wilkins debate: the error of attributing to another object motion that belongs to oneself. The problem of kinematic relativity, to wit, becomes the model for *Paradise Lost*'s involvement of its readers in the problem of moral relativity, defined not only as the potential to attribute to another being badness that belongs to oneself but, more broadly, the potential to misattribute qualities of any sort to other beings, whether noble or ignoble, based upon the unreliable perspective of one's own fallen nature. On the strength of this figurative correspondence, Milton endeavors to make functional the biblical epic's patchwork of body parts that decorum would seem to dictate should not go together.

Kinematic and moral relativity are explicitly correlated in two passages of *Paradise Lost* whose relationship is signaled, I suggest, by their like location in consecutive books, one near the beginning of Book Eight and the other near the beginning of Book Nine. The first is Adam's opening expression of puzzlement in his dialogue with Raphael "concerning celestial Motions" (as the argument describes their topic). Here Adam expresses precisely the right doubt about the Ptolemaic explanation of the cosmos, the same that Copernicus famously cited as the source of his skepticism—namely, the suspiciously high speed at which the distant sun, planets, and stars in their respective spheres would have to be traveling in order to orbit the Earth in just twenty-four hours. Given, too, Adam's assumption that the heavenly bodies are "nobler" than the Earth, he wonders that they could have been created to provide it such "service," especially when an alternative explanation of their apparent motion is available.[39] As he says to Raphael,

> When I behold this goodly Frame, this World
> Of Heav'n and Earth consisting, and compute
> Thir magnitudes, this Earth a spot, a grain,
> An Atom, with the Firmament compar'd
> And all her number'd Stars, that seem to roll
> Spaces incomprehensible (for such
> Thir distance argues and thir swift return
> Diurnal) merely to officiate light
> Round this opacous Earth, this punctual spot,
> One day and night; in all thir vast survey
> Useless besides; reasoning I oft admire,
> How Nature wise and frugal could commit
> Such disproportions, with superfluous hand
> So many nobler Bodies to create,
> Greater so manifold to this one,
> For aught appears, and on thir Orbs impose
> Such restless revolution day by day
> Repeated, while the sedentary Earth,
> That better might with far less compass move,
> Serv'd by more noble than herself, attains
> Her end without least motion, and receives

As Tribute such a sumless journey brought
Of incorporeal speed, her warmth and light;
Speed, to describe whose swiftness Number fails.   (8.15–38)

Adam receives no firm answer to the part of his query having to do with "celestial Motion," but instead, according to the argument's digest, he is "doubtfully answer'd, and exhorted to search rather things more worthy of knowledge." The "great Architect" has "conceal[ed]" certain "secrets" of the "Fabric of the Heav'ns" from men and even angels, says Raphael (8.72–76), so whereas "to read his wond'rous Works" in "Heav'n / . . . as the Book of God before thee set" (8.66–68) is blameless up to a point, to "Conjecture" overmuch about the organization of the universe, or the movements of its bodies, will achieve little else but "to move / His laughter" (8.76–78). So, Raphael advises Adam, "Think only what concerns thee and thy being" (8.174), and what concerns him is to serve God's will ("him serve and fear" [8.168])—to continue to live in obedience and innocence. Accordingly, Raphael responds less "doubtfully" to that part of Adam's query which expresses moral judgment, insofar as Adam seeks clarification on the relative goodness—as opposed to the relative motion—of the Earth and sun, the stars and planets. Addressing Adam's surprise that the tiny and "sedentary Earth" could be "Serv'd" by "Bodies" that are "more noble than herself" (8.28–34), Raphael asks Adam to "consider first, that Great / Or Bright infers not Excellence: the Earth / Though, in comparison of Heav'n, so small, / Nor glistering, may of solid good contain / More plenty than the Sun that barren shines" (8.90–94). So far this seems waffling; but then, Raphael suddenly expands the scope of this discourse on the relative goodness of created things so as to eliminate the ambiguity: "Yet," he tells Adam, "not to Earth are those bright Luminaries / Officious, but to thee Earth's habitant" (8.98–99). Among the heavenly bodies there *is* a way to measure relative goodness, then, but it is not by any sort of comparison between the bodies themselves (their relative bigness or brightness, for instance), but rather, it is by assessing their relative good service to Adam and his kind. Hence, Raphael's request of Adam to consider that the earth "may of solid good contain / More plenty than the Sun that barren shines" appears now to recommend that judgment unequivocally, since the Earth is "solid" and the Earth is where God's "plenty" has been put for Adam and Eve's benefit. In sum, as Adam in the future gazes up into the night sky, the problem of kinematic relativity will continue to make it impossible for him to decide between earthly versus heavenly motion; but with the understanding now that the goodness of heavenly objects is measured by their goodness *to him,* he has the firm foundation that he needs to "search" the sky for "things more worthy of knowledge"—that is, to evaluate the nature and comparative excellence of each celestial body's service to his being, whether it be to light up his days and give him warmth, nourish his garden and fill his stomach, aid him in his navigations, establish his calendar and set his clock, or simply excite his admiration.

This particular combination of dispelled and "doubtfully answer'd" doubts positions us in a most deliberate way for the description of Satan's orbital flight around the Earth at the beginning of Book Nine:

> The Sun was sunk, and after him the Star
> Of *Hesperus,* whose Office is to bring
> Twilight upon the Earth, short Arbiter
> Twixt Day and Night, and now from end to end
> Night's Hemisphere had veil'd the Horizon round:
> When *Satan* who late fled before the threats
> Of *Gabriel* out of *Eden,* now improv'd
> In meditated fraud and malice, bent
> On Man's destruction, maugre what might hap
> Of heavier on himself, fearless return'd.
> By Night he fled, and at Midnight return'd
> From compassing the Earth, cautious of day,
> Since *Uriel* Regent of the Sun descri'd
> His entrance, and forewarn'd the Cherubim
> That kept thir watch; thence full of anguish driv'n,
> The space of seven continu'd Nights he rode
> With darkness, thrice the Equinoctial Line
> He circl'd, four times cross'd the Car of Night
> From Pole to Pole, traversing each Colure;
>   On th'eighth return'd, and on the Coast averse
> From entrance or Cherubic Watch, by stealth
> Found unsuspected way.   (9.48–69)

The passage begins with a reminder of the moral principle articulated above in the excerpt quoted from Book Eight: behind the sinking sun follows Hesperus, the evening star, which has a good "Office" to perform—"to bring / Twilight upon the Earth" (9.49–50). But then our attention is turned to Satan. Though varying in his course, he attends the night as it goes round the globe, orbiting the earth eight times in as many days.[40] He maintains the same rate of speed, in other words, as the other celestial objects slowly wheeling their way across the sky, and presumably, to any hypothetical observer on Earth, he would appear to be one of them.

There are only two potential human observers at this time, and so soon after Raphael and Adam's dialogue on the heavens in Book Eight, Satan's journey undoubtedly invites us to ponder—*what if* Adam and Eve had happened to see his luster (diminished, but not extinguished) as they set their gazes above them one evening? We can state exactly what is the uncertainty and also the error that would accompany their mistaking him as a star or planet. First, they would not with certainty know this object to be a satellite moving around the Earth. It might be that its apparent motion is but kinematic illusion, like the apparent motion of all the other bodies in the cosmos. Second, they would certainly not suspect that the object could be "bent / On Man's destruction" and motivated, in this ill office, by "meditated fraud and malice" (9.55–56). They would naturally attribute to Satan what belongs to all the stars and planets, each to its own degree but without exception: good service to themselves.

Such a hypothetical misjudgment anticipates Satan's temptation of Eve, coming right up in Book Nine, when she will attribute to the strangely speaking serpent an ability that does not properly belong to beasts; when she will attribute to the serpent goodwill toward her that is not genuine; and when she will attribute to the forbidden fruit a power that it does not possess. It also looks immediately back to the episode that now seems to bridge Raphael and Adam's dialogue on the cosmos and Satan's orbital journey—when Adam describes his overwhelming emotion at the sight of Eve, attributing to her more wisdom and virtue she possesses (8.546–59), and when Raphael, admonishing Adam for his overestimate, attributes to him (so Adam protests) more impairing "passion" than he had experienced (8.588). But really, this is an omnipresent theme of *Paradise Lost*, extending beyond the actors in its drama to involve too its observers, the readers of the poem and the judges of its decorum, in the same difficulties of relative perspective and moral judgment. Complementarily, the plethora of classical references, echoes, and allusions, the epic similes and Virgilian imitations that are omnipresent in *Paradise Lost*, do more than just supply the necessary epic atmosphere or palimpsest that allows the poem to claim its ancient patrimony. They function as they cannot help but function, given the biblical basis and Christian purpose of this "advent'rous Song" (1.13)—as pieces out of place, threatening to provoke unseemly reactions. To be sure, laughter potentially is one of them: we have all heard of Milton's epic poem, *The Rape of the Apple*. But laughter has not been the typical response, and we can be confident that it was not Milton's design. Instead, the epic elements in *Paradise Lost* cooperate with other features of the poem to engage readers in experiences similar to those of its principal characters: experiences of perspectival and moral uncertainty, of seeing with a "maladaptive eye"[41] and feeling the lure of attributing to heavenly things what is earthly and to earthly things what is heavenly, of feeling the temptation, that is, to attribute one's own fallen character to the unfallen while attributing nobility to the ignoble.

So we are back on familiar, though contested, ground: Milton's charac-teristic manner of challenging readers to sort out points of likeness and unlikeness in classical allusions that seem devised to generate the maximum ambiguity and incertitude. One of the best-known instances is the poet's commentary on the "naked beauty" of Eve—that she was "more adorn'd, / More lovely than *Pandora,* whom the Gods / Endow'd with all thir gifts, and O too like / In sad event" (4.713–16). The question is whether it is too easy merely to draw a line that absolutely differentiates the timing of this state-ment's two comparisons: that is, we are invited right now to compare the beauty of mythical Pandora and of Eve. Eve's is greater, but the harm that she brings into the world will not be comparable to Pandora's—it will not even exist—until later, at her fall. Thus, one must be careful at this point in the Genesis story not to attribute to unfallen Eve any guile or other moral failing that was instilled in Pandora from the start (God made Eve beautiful and with the free will to do good or ill; Hermes made Pandora beautiful but he predetermined her to be bad, despite the good qualities bestowed on her by the other gods). Such a distinction may be too facile because the evil that was put into Pandora is not stressed by Milton; he calls our attention instead to the "Gods" who "Endow'd" Pandora "with all thir gifts." By this he may have just intended to reinforce the tragic irony of "the sad event" in each case, the tragic irony that women so blessed with beauty and other virtues should be the cause of so much sorrow. Or perhaps there is a suggestion, in this em-phasis on the gods' gifts, that something in the very nature of gifts from gods, something in God's gifts to Eve, is destructive or destined to backfire—her desire, for one thing, to improve herself, to rise up, to traffic one day with angels amid celestial heights.[42]

An illustration that starts in the opposite direction is Satan's "All is not lost" / let us "wage by force or guile eternal War" speech (1.106–24), which reminds us of any number of epic heroes rallying their troops before battle in Homer and Virgil and other poets, though it is more specifically modeled on Aeneas's post-shipwreck address to his soaking *socii* on the Libyan beach, in which he urges them to "press on" (*durate*) despite their misfortunes (*Aeneid* 1.198–207). Milton even includes the revelation of Satan's stifled anguish at the conclusion of his address, similar to Aeneas's: "So spake th'Apostate Angel, though in pain, / Vaunting aloud, but rackt with deep despair" (1.125–26); compare "Talia uoce refert curisque ingentibus aeger / spem uultu simulat, premit altum corde dolorem" (Such things he said, and sick with heavy cares he simulates hope in his face, suppresses sorrow deep in his heart) (1.208–9). The episode invites us to associate Satan and Aeneas, ob-viously but imprecisely: it spurs us into interpretive activity, sorting out the various ways Satan is like and unlike Aeneas.[43] The basic points have been well enumerated: both have been violently "cast out" (Aeneas from Troy, most recently from the sea; Satan from heaven); both have a responsibility to shore up their followers' morale and reconfirm their commitment to the mission; both are victims of divine displeasure, except in Satan's case his sinful rebellion provoked the wrath of the one true God whereas the vicissitudes of *pius* Aeneas are the consequence of factionalism in the pantheon, with Juno's hatred sometimes spoiling the effects of Jupiter's good favor. And while Satan has an eternity of justly deserved misery ahead of him, Aeneas will fulfill his heaven-appointed fate by reaching Latium and founding the race of Rome. Thus, one should resist the temptation to attribute to Satan heroic nobility or pitiable sorrows such as Aeneas's, since Aeneas is caught in the middle of an Olympian power struggle that is beyond his influence and comprehension, whereas Satan knew God's love and could still be knowing it but for his self-born pride. Again, though, we are aware that many readers of *Paradise Lost* have rejected this too-easy distribution of likenesses and unlikenesses. In their view it willfully ignores the complexity of the passage, insisting as it does upon presumed moral certainties that the Virgilian echo would seem to rattle rather than reinforce (all the more so, if we consider the ambiguities and dark implications of the *Aeneid* itself).[44]

And so, as I hinted at the outset, this essay has managed to traverse from the Ross-Wilkins to the Fish-Rumrich debate, where the words "moral relativity" in the title probably destined it. If we could be confident that Milton requires us, always and without qualification, to cling to that key principle that is the premise of the Fall's tragedy—that doing God's will is the only good— then we would understand the following: although making moral judgments frequently seems as difficult and deceptive a process as correctly distinguishing between one's own motion and that of other bodies, there is a fundamental difference between these two experiences of relativity, for which the Word of God supplies an independent means of verification that is clear enough on the essential points. Hence, *Paradise Lost* exercises our powers of moral discernment: it challenges us to overcome our impaired, fallen perspective and the confusions of moral uncertainty, and it chastens us if we are caught attributing nobility or baseness to things that are really the opposite. The pastichelike qualities of the poem would therefore be justified on the basis of this didactic, faith-bracing function. In contrast, if we believe that the poem's generation of ambiguities and multiple perspectives deliberately exceeds the capacity of any single principle to bring them under bridle, then we would interpret its thematic correlation of kinematic and moral relativity as evidence that Milton recognized the fundamentally illusory nature of human perception and knowledge, that he embraced life's deep uncertainties (not excepting the mysteries of God and of good and evil), and that in *Paradise Lost* he therefore immerses his readers in this experience of an unfathomable universe to show that even the most cherished moral and spiritual tenets have to be held provisionally. The pastichelike qualities of the poem would therefore be justified on the basis of this didactic, faith-complicating function.

Without an independent means of ascertaining which of these interpretations is the correct one, the decision rests inevitably upon which portrait of the poet one finds more plausible: either Milton is Fish's Puritan pedagogue whom Rumrich complains is "a redundant pedant who already knows the truth of things, humiliates and berates his charges for their errors, and with obnoxious superiority requires conformity to traditional beliefs,"[45] or, Milton is Rumrich's "poet of indeterminacy who found ways to incorporate the uncertain and the evolving into his most highly realized works of art," who eschews pat answers because he knows that "[t]he equivocal nature of human knowledge makes interpretive and therefore moral certainty an impossibility."[46] Fish contends that this account describes Richard Rorty, not Milton,[47] and he interprets the energy with which Rumrich and others argue for such a Milton as a yearning for wish-fulfillment: "If," says Fish,

you can link the so-called literary work with revolutionary sentiments, or with the crisis of the nation state, or with the emancipation of the liberal subject from the hegemony of religion and political tyranny, you're doing the Lord's, or rather the proletariat's, work. . . . That's why so many critics have a stake in demonstrating that the Milton they admire professionally has the right political values—their values—and believe that if he were alive today he would be against the war in Iraq and for multiculturalism.[48]

III

Perhaps, in a manner of speaking, Milton anticipated the Fish-Rumrich controversy, and that is why he made *Paradise Regained* "so cold"—as Alan Fisher characterizes the poem in his essay, "Why Is *Paradise Regained* So Cold?"[49] Perhaps Milton realized that the moral uncertainties of *Paradise Lost,* in large part produced by its construction out of materials native to epic but alien to the faith, were befuddling some of the very readers he would have pegged as fit to face its challenges. There may even have been a few budding Blakes among his acquaintances who hinted their suspicion that the old blind poet had gone over to the dark side despite his inclinations otherwise. In *Paradise Regained,* then, we get a poem that leaves no doubt which is the right perspective for readers to measure against their own. "Much of the 'coldness' we find in Jesus" as he resists the successive temptations of Satan in the desert, says Fisher, "is the difference we can sense between what we might say and what Jesus does say. . . . A simple no, however weak, is enough;

though an accurate, eloquent, thorough no is better" (201). Jeffrey Morris, for one, has characterized this effect in the terms of motion and morality that have here concerned us—"Milton," he observes, "portrays [Christ] as the calm, immovable center of chaotic, disorienting movement"[50]—and this "center," this example of perfectly unwavering obedience to God's will, we are charged with keeping fixed in our minds *as* perfection, whatever our own potentially disorienting angles of perspective on his words and deeds. In the final scene of the poem, after angels have rescued Jesus "[f]rom his uneasy station" (4.584) atop the pinnacle where he was placed by Satan, he is taken up to heaven where "Angelic Choirs / Sung Heavenly Anthems of his victory / Over temptation and the Temptor proud" (4.593–95): he is the "True Image of the Father," they rejoice; "whether thron'd / In the bosom of bliss" or "remote from Heaven," in "human form, / Wand'ring the Wilderness" (4.596–600), he is always, forever, "still expressing / The Son of God"— "whatever [his] place," whatever his "Habit, or state, or *motion*" (4.600–602; my emphasis).

If, finally, *Paradise Regained* has this aim of instructing us how to be readers of *Paradise Lost,* then our attention is drawn again to Alexander Ross and a different kind of example that he could have set for Milton. For it seems we have lit upon a new explanation of Milton's decision to convert *Paradise Lost* from an epic in ten books to an epic in twelve, which he did in 1674 following the publication of *Paradise Regained* in 1671. This re-division, I suggest, retrospectively makes *Paradise Regained* a supplement to *Paradise Lost*—not just a separate sequel, but an extension comparable to the thirteenth book of the *Aeneid* by Maffeo Vegio (still printed in most editions of Virgil through the early seventeenth century), and comparable to the thirteenth book of Alexander Ross's *Christiad,* which Ross presumably included on the model of Vegio's *Supplement* (as it was usually titled).[51] After Virgil's famously abrupt ending of *Aeneid,* Book Twelve, Vegio continues the story of the exiled Trojans' victory against the Latins by describing Aeneas's marriage to Lavinia, his initial laying of foundations for a new city, and then, after Venus perceives that the time is ripe and has obtained Jupiter's approval, his translation into a deity among the stars (drawing on Ovid's description in the *Metamorphoses,* but without its irreverence). In this manner, Vegio completes Aeneas's tale as the journey of a good man toward his ultimate destination in heaven, consistent with the Christian Everyman's pilgrimage to eternal life and authorizing, retroactively, the perspective that discerns truth in Virgil's epic of the "false and lying gods."[52] Ross's thirteenth book of the *Christiad* likewise describes the translation of its hero to heaven, and it does much more of a "supplementary" nature, stressing the past, future, and what Ross urges should be the present-day impact of Christ's coming: he sings of the founding of Christ's church, looks ahead to Judgment Day, laments England's current civil strife and the threat of renewed Turkish attacks against Europe, and appeals to Christians everywhere to live harmoniously.

In sum, a ten-book epic is an epic in ten books, but a twelve-book epic is in need of a supplement. *Paradise Regained* would fit that bill—though it is in four books rather than a single "thirteenth," and despite Christ's ascension at the end being only a temporary sojourn to restore physical strength after his long desert fast. By depicting Christ's imperviousness to temptation, *Paradise Regained* looks back to Milton's "epic proper": it stresses the import of Adam and Eve's story by calling on readers to imitate their Savior rather than their oldest ancestors. Whereas *Paradise Lost* supplies opportunities to swerve from that goal and to attribute such swerving to someone or something else, *Paradise Regained* stages the perspective that keeps to the right path, the angle of vision from which readers must acknowledge their departures and by which they must strive to "justify"—in the sense, *to adjust or arrange exactly*—their own. In this respect, Fisher asserts, its "purpose is plain: we are to hear temptation just as Jesus does; we are to register its impact and wrestle with it—and then judge how well our responses to it match those of the 'perfect man'" (201). The purpose of *Paradise Regained*, we might say in other words, is to stabilize the wandering heads of readers of *Paradise Lost*.

Le Moyne College

NOTES

I am indebted to my colleague Maura Brady for her helpful critique of an early draft of this essay, and to Michael Lieb and Albert Labriola for their recommendations for further revisions.

1. Grant McColley, "Milton's Dialogue on Astronomy: The Principal Immediate Sources," *PMLA* 52 (1937): 728–62, and "The Ross-Wilkins Controversy," *Annals of Science* 3 (1938): 153–89 (the latter is reprinted in *John Wilkins and Seventeenth-Century British Linguistics*, ed. Joseph L. Subbiondo [Amsterdam, 1992], 95–131; however, I cite the original pagination of this essay below). For McColley's other articles on Milton and seventeenth-century astronomy, see "The Theory of a Plurality of Worlds as a Factor in Milton's Attitude toward the Copernican Hypothesis," *MLN* 47 (1932): 319–25; "The Theory of the Diurnal Rotation of the Earth," *Isis* 26 (1937): 392–402; and "The Astronomy of *Paradise Lost*," *SP* 34 (1937): 209–47. Though much abridged, material from these essays is incorporated in McColley's monograph study, *"Paradise Lost": An Account of Its Growth and Major Origins, with a Discussion of Milton's Use of Sources and Literary Patterns* (Chicago, 1940).

2. Wilkins published his treatises while serving as private chaplain to William Fiennes, First Viscount Saye and Sele. Ross, by 1546, had lost his living at St. Mary's, Carisbrooke (on the Isle of

Wight); he was possibly residing in London, perhaps in his former occupation as a schoolmaster. For the most detailed and sympathetic account of Ross's career, see John R. Glenn, introduction to *A Critical Edition of Alexander Ross's 1647 "Mystagogus Poeticus," or "The Muses Interpreter"* (New York, 1987), 1–59.

    3. McColley, "Milton's Dialogue," 728 n. 2.

    4. Ibid., 753; compare McColley, "Ross-Wilkins Controversy," 163.

    5. See Kester Svendsen, *Milton and Science* (Cambridge, Mass., 1956), 258 n. 4, for this critique of McColley's judgment in "Milton's Dialogue," 754.

    6. See especially three essays by Allan H. Gilbert—"Milton and Galileo," *SP* 19 (1922): 152–85; "The Outside Shell of Milton's World," *SP* 20 (1923): 444–47; "Milton's Textbook of Astronomy," *PMLA* 38 (1923): 297–307—and Marjorie Nicolson, "Milton and the Telescope," *ELH* 2 (1935): 1–32. To some degree these and other studies published between 1900 and 1940 on the role of astronomy in Milton's poetic imagination reflect the academy's effort to correct information and interpretations in the initial major study of the subject, Thomas N. Orchard's *The Astronomy of Milton's "Paradise Lost"* (London, 1896), but McColley's essays also endeavor to refute some of Gilbert's conclusions, in particular the claim that Milton relied heavily on Galileo's *Dialogo dei Massimi Sistemi*.

    7. Again quoting McColley, "Milton's Dialogue," 754, who affirms that his investigation of Milton's reliance on Wilkins and Ross leads first to the question of what help it offers to understanding Milton's poetic aims and methods. The bibliography of studies on the relation between seventeenth-century astronomy and Milton's poetry, especially the impact of Galileo's telescope on Milton's management of narrative perspective, is immense indeed. The first major postwar treatments of this relation, in Svendsen, *Milton and Science,* 43–113, and Walter Clyde Curry, *Milton's Ontology, Cosmogony and Physics* (Lexington, Ky., 1957), came to play a role for scholars in the latter half of the twentieth century which was comparable to Orchard's for the first (see previous note)—that is, a common point of reference for conclusions in need of qualification or correction. In addition to the studies cited in subsequent notes in connection to specific points of my essay, the following works comprise the essential critical context for any examination of the new astronomy's impact on Milton's composition of *Paradise Lost:* J. H. Adamson, "Kepler and Milton," *MLN* 74 (1959): 683–85; Arthur O. Lovejoy, "Milton's Dialogue on Astronomy," in *Reason and Imagination,* ed. Joseph Anthony Mazzeo (New York, 1962), 129–42; John Arthos, "Milton, Andreini, and Galileo: Some Considerations on the Manner and Form of *Paradise Lost,*" in *Approaches to "Paradise Lost": The York Tercentenary Lectures,* ed. C. A. Patrides (London, 1968), 163–79; Lawrence Babb, *The Moral Cosmos of "Paradise Lost"* (East Lansing, Mich., 1970); Malabika Sarkar, " 'The Visible Diurnal Sphere': Astronomical Images of Space and Time in *Paradise Lost,*" *MQ* 18 (1984): 1–5; Neil Harris, "Galileo as Symbol: The 'Tuscan Artist' in *Paradise Lost,*" *Annali del'Instituto e Museo di Storia della Scienze di Firenze* 10, no. 2 (1985): 3–29; Jürgen Klein, *Astronomie und Anthropozentrik: Die Copernicanische Wende bei John Donne, John Milton und den Cambridge Platonists* (Frankfurt, 1986), 217–77; Anita Lawson, " 'The Golden Sun in Splendor Likest Heaven': Johannes Kepler's *Epitome* and *Paradise Lost,* Book 3," *MQ* 21 (1987): 46–51; Julia M. Walker, "Milton and Galileo: The Art of Intellectual Canonization," in *Milton Studies* 25, ed. James D. Simmonds (Pittsburgh, 1989), 109–23; Donald Friedman, "Galileo and the Art of Seeing," in *Milton in Italy: Contexts, Images, Contradictions,* ed. Mario A. DiCesare (Binghamton, 1991), 159–74; Judith Scherer Herz, " 'For Whom this Glorious Sight?': Dante, Milton, and the Galileo Question," in *Milton in Italy,* 146–57; Harinder Singh Marjara, *Contemplation of Created Things: Science in "Paradise Lost"* (Toronto, 1992), esp. 38–162; Annabel Patterson, "Imagining New Worlds: Milton, Galileo, and the 'Good Old Cause,' " in *The Witness of Times: Manifestations of Ideology in Seventeenth Century England,* ed. Katherine Z. Keller and Gerald J. Schiffhorst (Pittsburgh, 1993), 238–60;

Regina Schwartz, "Through the Optic Glass: Voyeurism and *Paradise Lost*," in *Desire in the Renaissance: Psychoanalysis and Literature,* ed. Valeria Finucci and Regina Schwartz (Princeton, 1994), 146–66; Denise Albanese, *New Science, New World* (Durham, 1996), 121–47; Amy Boesky, "Milton, Galileo, and Sunspots: Optics and Certainty in *Paradise Lost*," in *Milton Studies* 34, ed. Albert C. Labriola (Pittsburgh, 1996), 23–43; Derek N. C. Wood, "Milton and Galileo," *MQ* 35 (2001): 50–52; Maura Brady, "Galileo in Action: The 'Telescope' in *Paradise Lost*," in *Milton Studies* 44, ed. Albert C. Labriola (Pittsburgh, 2005), 129–52.

8. McColley, "Ross-Wilkins Controversy," 157.

9. Compare what I take to be a complementary analysis of Galileo's references to classical poetry in his letters and in the *Dialogo*, within the context of an account of seventeenth-century tensions between traditional humanistic discursive practices and emergent scientific ones, in Albanese, *New Science, New World,* 148–85. Also compare Erwin Panofsky, *Galileo as a Critic of the Arts* (The Hague, 1954).

10. Julian B. Barbour, *The Discovery of Dynamics: A Study from a Machian Point of View of the Discovery and the Structure of Dynamical Theories* (Oxford, 2001), 243. Originally published as the first of a proposed two-volume study titled *Absolute or Relative Motion? The Discovery of Dynamics* (Cambridge, 1989), Barbour's book provides an excellent overview of the "absolute/relative problem" in dynamical theories from Aristotle through Newton.

11. I will approach the question of Ross's example for Milton (and address the implications of this example to contemporary Milton criticism) from a different angle than I attempt in *The Augustinian Epic, Petrarch to Milton* (Ann Arbor, 2005), where my treatment of both poets occurs within the context of a history of neo-Latin and vernacular epic that emphasizes the extent of their shared aims and methods.

12. For a representative assessment of Ross's attack on Hobbes in *Leviathan Drawn Out with a Hook* (1653), see Samuel I. Mintz, *The Hunting of Leviathan: Seventeenth-Century Reactions to the Materialism and Moral Philosophy of Thomas Hobbes* (Cambridge, 1962), 55.

13. Ross, *The New Planet No Planet,* 18, with his (or his printer's) italics; subsequent citations to this work are supplied parenthetically in the text.

14. Marjara, *Contemplation of Created Things,* 134.

15. This and subsequent references to Virgil's epic are to the text and numbering in *P. Vergili Maronis Opera,* ed. R. A. B. Mynors (Oxford, 1969), with my translations.

16. Here Ross quotes from *Aeneid* 8.97 and 10.215–16. The discrepancies between these lines in Virgil's text and Ross's quotation shall be discussed shortly.

17. [N]eque fateamur ipsius cotidianae reuolutionis in caelo apparentiam esse, et in terra ueritatem? Et haec perinde se habere, ac si diceret Virgilianus Aeneas: Prouehimur portu, terraeque urbesque recedunt. Quoniam fluitante sub tranquillitate nauigio, cuncta quae extrinsecus sunt, ad motus illius imaginem moueri cernuntur a nauigantibus, ac uicissim se quiescere putant cum omnibus quae secum sunt. Ita nimirum in motu terrae potest contingere, ut totus ciruire mundus existimetur. From Nicolaus Copernicus, *De Revolutionibus Orbium Coelestium* (Nuremberg, 1543; rpt. in facsimile, New York, 1965), 6^r, with abbreviations silently expanded; translated by A. M. Duncan, *Copernicus: On the Revolutions of the Heavenly Spheres* (Newton Abbot, Devon, 1976), 44. By 1646, the date of *The New Planet No Planet,* Copernicus's *De Revolutionibus Orbium Coelestium* had been published four times: twice in Basel (1543 and 1566) and twice in Amsterdam (1617 and 1640).

18. [A]nte omnia puto necessarium, ut diligenter animaduertamus, quae sit ad coelum terrae habitudo, ne dum excelsissima scrutari uolumus, quae nobis proxima sunt, ignoremus, ac eodem errore quae telluris sunt attribuamus coelestibus. From Copernicus, *De Revolutionibus,* 3^r; Duncan, *Copernicus,* 39–40.

19.

Qua vehimur navi, fertur, cum stare videtur;
quae manet in statione, ea praeter creditur ire.
et fugere ad puppim colles campique videntur
quos agimus praeter navem velisque volamus.
Sidera cessare aetheriis adfixa cavernis
cuncta videntur, et adsiduo sunt omnia motu,
quandoquidem longos obitus exorta revisunt,
cum permensa suo sunt caelum corpore claro.
solque pari ratione manere et luna videtur
in statione, ea quae ferri res indicat ipsa.   (4.387–96)

Text and translation (with paragraph break deleted) cited from *Lucretius: On the Nature of Things*, ed. and trans. W. H. D. Rouse, Loeb Classical Library; 3rd rev. ed. by Martin F. Smith (Cambridge, Mass., 1992).

20. Kepler's famous *Somnium* (reporting his dream-journey to the moon) was printed in 1634, and Godwin's *Man in the Moone; or, A Discourse of a Voyage Thither* appeared the same year as Wilkins's *Discovery of a New World* (1638). For a discussion of these and like works of the new astronomy, the satires they elicited, and their possible impression on Milton, see John S. Tanner, "'And Every Star Perhaps a World of Destined Habitation': Milton and Moonmen," *Extrapolation: A Journal of Science Fiction and Fantasy* 30 (1989): 267–79.

21. Alii nanque circulis homocentris solum, alii eccentris et epicyclis, quibus tamen quaesita ad plenum non assequuntur. . . . Rem quoque praecipuam, hoc est mundi formam, ac partium eius certam symmetriam non potuerunt inuenire, uel ex illis colligere. Sed accidit eis perinde, ac si quis e diuersis locis, manus, pedes, caput, aliaque membra, optime quidem, sed non unius corporis comparatione, depicta sumeret, nullatenus inuicem sibi respondentibus, ut monstrum potius quam homo ex illis componeretur. From Copernicus, *De Revolutionibus*, iii^v; Duncan, *Copernicus*, 25.

22.

Humano capiti cervicem pictor equinam
iungere si velit, et varias inducere plumas
undique collatis membris, ut turpiter atrum
desinat in piscem mulier formosa superne,
spectatum admissi risum teneatis, amici?
credite, Pisones, isti tabulae fore librum
persimilem, cuius, velut aegri somnia, vanae
fingentur species, ut nec pes nec caput uni
reddatur formae.   (1–9)

Text and translation from *Horace: Satires, Epistles, and Ars Poetica*, ed. and trans. H. Rushton Fairclough, Loeb Classical Library, 2nd rev. ed. (Cambridge, Mass., 1929).

23. Atque ita ego positis motibus, quos terrae infra in opere tribuo, multa et longa obseruatione tandem reperi, quod si reliquorum syderum errantium motus, ad terrae circulationem conferantur, et supputentur pro cuiusque syderis reuolutione, non modo illorum phaenomena inde sequantur, sed et syderum atque orbium omnium ordines, magnitudines, et coelum ipsum ita connectat, ut in nulla sui parte possit transponi aliquid, sine reliquarum partium, ac totius uniuersitatis confusione. Proin de quoque et in progressu operis hunc sequutus sum ordinem ut in primo libro describam omnes positiones orbium, cum terrae, quos ei tribuo, motibus, ut is liber contineat communem quasi constitutionem uniuersi. In reliquis uero libris postea confero

reliquorum syderum atque omnium orbium motus, cum terrae mobilitate, ut inde colligi possit, quatenus reliquorum syderum atque orbium motus et apparentiae saluari possint, si ad terrae motus conferantur. From Copernicus, *De Revolutionibus*, iiii^r; Duncan, *Copernicus*, 26.

24. Quoting McColley, "Ross-Wilkins Controversy," 157.

25. I cite the English translation by Thomas Salusbury (with the corresponding text of the 1632 Italian edition provided in the notes) published in *Mathematical Collections and Translations in Two Tomes* (1661 and 1665). The first volume contains *The Systeme of the World: In Four Dialogues. Wherein the Two Grand Systemes of Ptolomy and Copernicus are largely discoursed of: And the Reasons, both Philosophical and Physical, as well on the one side as the other, impartially and indefinitely propounded: By Galileus Galileus Linceus, A Gentleman of Florence: Extraordinary Professor of the Mathematicks in the University of Pisa; and Chief Mathematician to the Grand Duke of Tuscany*. I have not cited the *Dialogue on the Great World Systems in the Salusbury Translation,* ed. Giorgio de Santillana (Chicago, 1953), because there Salusbury's English has been "corrected" and "edited" beyond recognition in order "to meet the needs of the modern reader" (viii). I have, however, silently supplied and deleted a few marks of punctuation in the following quotes in line with modern expectations but without risk of altering the sense. A modern English translation of Galileo's *Dialogo* is by Stillman Drake in Galileo Galilei, *Dialogue Concerning the Two Chief World Systems—Ptolemaic and Copernican,* 2nd rev. ed. (Berkeley and Los Angeles, 1967).

26. Aristotile non si è acquistata sì grande autorità se non per la forza delle sue dimostrazioni e della profondità de i suoi discorsi: ma bisogna intenderlo, e non solamente intenderlo, ma aver tanta gran pratica ne' suoi libri, che se ne sia formata un'idea perfettissima, in modo che ogni suo detto vi sia sempre innanzi alla mente; perchè e' non ha scritto per il volgo, nè si è obligato a infilzare i suoi silogismi col metodo triviale ordinato, anzi, servendosi del perturbato, ha messo talvolta la prova di una proposizione fra testi che par che trattino di ogni altra cosa: e però bisogna aver tutta quella grande idea, e saper combinar questo passo con quello, accozzar questo testo con un altro remotissimo; ch'e non è dubbio che chi averà questa pratica, saprà cavar da' suoi libri le dimostrazioni di ogni scibile, perchè in essi è ogni cosa. From Galileo Galilei, *Dialogo Sopra i Due Massimi Sistemi del Mondo Tolemaico e Copernicano,* 2 vols., ed. Ottavio Besomi and Mario Helbing (Padua, 1998), 1:117.

27. Ma, Sig. Simplicio mio, come l'esser le cose disseminate in qua e in là non vi dà fastidio, e che voi crediate con l' accozzamento e con la combinazione di varie particelle trarne il sugo, questo che voi e gli altri filosofi bravi farete con i testi d'Aristotile, farò io con i versi di Virgilio o di Ovidio, formandone centoni ed esplicando con quelli tutti gli affari de gli uomini e i segreti della natura. Ma che dico io di Virgilio o di altro poeta? io ho un libretto assai più breve d'Aristotile e d'Ovidio, nel quale si contengono tutte le scienze, e con pochissimo studio altri se ne può formare una perfettissima idea: e questo è l'alfabeto; e non è dubbio che quello che saprà ben accoppiare e ordinare questa e quella vocale con quelle consonanti o con quell'altre, ne caverà le riposte verissime a tutti i dubbi e ne trarrà gli insegnamenti di tutte le scienze e di tutte le arti, in quella maniera appunto che il pittore da i semplici colori diversi, separatamente posti sopra la tavolozza, va, con l'accozzare un poco di questo con un poco di quello e di quell'altro, figurando uomini, piante, fabbriche, uccelli, pesci, ed in somma imitando tutti gli oggetti visibili, senza che su la tavolozza sieno nè occhi nè penne nè squamme nè foglie nè sassi (Galileo, *Dialogo,* 1:117–18).

28. In this passage, Galileo is also echoing Lucretius's analogy between the alphabet that he uses to compose his verses and the basic elements of the universe that in different combinations produce all things; see Rouse, *Lucretius: On the Nature of Things,* 2.688–99.

29. In the context of an otherwise nuanced analysis of how "Galileo's anti-Aristotelian polemic models a contrarian legitimation for scientific inquiry, where the Aeneid and the Odys-

sey . . . have meaning primarily as negative occasions of the practice appropriate to natural philosophy" (155), Albanese also quotes Sagredo's reply to Simplicio (*New Science, New Worlds,* 153); however, she misunderstands Salusbury's gloss on *centones,* stating that "they appear to resemble commonplace books" (219 n. 9; compare lead-in sentence to the quote on 153).

30. A modern edition and translation is in *The Golden Bough, the Oaken Cross: The Virgilian Cento of Faltonia Betitia Proba,* ed. and trans. Elizabeth A. Clark and Diane F. Hatch (Ann Arbor, 1981). For a history of cento poetry, see Octave Delepierre, *Centoniana, ou Encyclopedie du centon,* Miscellanies of the Philobiblon Society, 1866–1868, vols. 10–11; reprinted as *Revue analytique des ouvrages écrits en centons, depuis les temps anciens jusqu'au XIXᵉ siècle* (Geneva, 1968). A recent study of late classical Virgilian centos is Scott McGill's *Virgil Recomposed: The Mythological and Secular Centos in Antiquity* (Oxford, 2005).

31. Quasi non legerimus Homerocentonas et Vergiliocentonas, ac non sic etiam Maronem sine Christo possimus dicere Christianum . . . puerilia sunt haec et circulatorum ludo similia. From Epistle no. 53, *Saint Jérôme lettres,* 8 vols., ed. Jérôme Labourt (Paris, 1949–1963), 3:16.

32. Another cento poem by Ross, the *Psychomachia Virgiliana* depicting the defeat of vices by Christian virtues, was published posthumously in Rotterdam in 1661; it is discussed in Delepierre, *Centoniana* (1968), 324–34 and Glenn, *Ross's "Mystagogus Poeticus,"* 37–38, 59 n. 130.

33. I have supplied book and line references to the evident sources for Ross's lines (he gives only the book numbers, sometimes erroneously). The first line of this excerpt and the first word of the second line—cited as (a) and (b)—are from that opening passage of the *Aeneid* (dismissed now as spurious) in which the poet announces his transition from pastoral themes to martial. Mynors prints it in *P. Vergili Maronis Opera,* xii.

34. Ross, *Christiados,* 1–2; I quote my translation of this passage from *The Augustinian Epic,* 146.

35. For a convenient account of the poem's Ptolemaic setting, see Anthony Low, "The Astronomy of *Paradise Lost,*" *ELN* 8 (1971): 263–67.

36. *PL* 8.122–30. All citations of Milton's works in this essay are from *Complete Poems and Major Prose,* ed. Merritt Y. Hughes (New York, 1957); hereafter cited by book and line number in the text.

37. Compare the now benchmark study of Milton's evolving conception and employment of scriptural "places" by Dayton Haskin, *Milton's Burden of Interpretation* (Philadelphia, 1994).

38. William Empson, *Milton's God* (1961; rev. ed. London, 1965).

39. Marjara, *Contemplation of Created Things,* 136–37, briefly reviews the range of opinions on the question of the "inherent dignity" of the Earth from Copernicus to Milton (with reference to Ross's rejection of such dignity in *The New Planet No Planet,* 60), and notes that the anthropocentric assumption that heavenly bodies exist for the service and pleasure of humankind was widely shared in the period. Ross is in agreement with this idea (58).

40. For an account of Satan's course on his journey and the number of his orbits around the Earth (including a ninth and tenth within the Earth's atmosphere, as described in 9.69–86), see Sherry Lutz Zivley, "Satan in Orbit: *Paradise Lost,* IX: 48–86," *MQ* 31 (1997): 130–36. See also Malabika Sarkar, "Satan's Astronomical Journey, 'Paradise Lost,' IX. 63–66," *N&Q,* n.s. 26 (1979): 417–22, an analysis of Satan's relation to the sun and Earth's shadow at different stages of his travels.

41. This phrase is Stevie Davies's; see *Milton* (New York, 1991), 95–152. Other studies that stress particularly the problems and challenges of perspective in *Paradise Lost,* and which provide much of the critical context for the discussion that follows, include Jackson I. Cope, *The Metaphoric Structure of "Paradise Lost"* (Baltimore, 1962), 50–148; Stanley Fish, *Surprised by Sin: The Reader in "Paradise Lost"* (London, 1967); Philip Brockbank, "'Within the Visible

Diurnal Spheare': The Moving World of *Paradise Lost*," in Patrides, *Approaches to "Paradise Lost*," 199–221; Dustin Griffin, "Milton's Hell: Perspectives on the Fallen," in *Milton Studies* 13, ed. James D. Simmonds (Pittsburgh, 1979), 237–54; Linda Gregerson, "The Limbs of Truth: Milton's Use of Simile in *Paradise Lost*," in *Milton Studies* 14, ed. James D. Simmonds (Pittsburgh, 1980), 135–52; John R. Mulder, "The Lyric Dimension of *Paradise Lost*," in *Milton Studies* 23, ed. James D. Simmonds (Pittsburgh, 1987), 145–63; John Rumrich, *Milton Unbound: Controversy and Reinterpretation* (Cambridge, 1996), esp. 94–117; Luisa Calè, *Visione e cosmo: La prospettiva nel "Paradise Lost"* (Rome, 1997), esp. 35–93, and on the interrelation of motion and perspective, 176–87; Peter C. Herman, "*Paradise Lost*, the Miltonic 'Or,' and the Poetics of Incertitude," *SEL* 43 (2003): 181–211; David Gay, *The Endless Kingdom: Milton's Scriptural Society* (Newark, Del., 2002), 63–98; Neil Forsyth, *The Satanic Epic* (Princeton, 2003), esp. 77–113.

42. George F. Butler, "Milton's Pandora: Eve, Sin, and the Mythographic Tradition," in *Milton Studies* 44, edited by Albert C. Labriola (Pittsburgh, 2005), 153–78, aims to discover just the right sets of distinctions that this passage calls for. "Sin, not Eve," Butler concludes, "is Pandora's true archetype, a role that Milton reinforces through his complex web of mythological subtexts. He thus follows the mythographic and exegetical tradition in making Pandora, or Sin, the source of suffering, while he simultaneously departs from that tradition by making Eve, the false Pandora, a symbol of regeneration" (173).

43. For analyses that sift points of likeness from points of unlikeness between Adam and Aeneas, Eve and Dido, see Wolfgang H. Rudat, "Milton's Dido and Aeneas: The Fall in *Paradise Lost* and the Vergilian Tradition," *Classical and Modern Literature* 2 (1981): 33–46; André Verbart, "Milton on Vergil: Dido and Aeneas in *Paradise Lost*," *English Studies* 78 (1997): 111–26; and compare Warner, *The Augustinian Epic*, 156–82.

44. For example, Forsyth, *The Satanic Epic*, 84–85. See also David Quint, "The Virgilian Coordinates of *Paradise Lost*," *Materiali e discussioni per l'annalisi dei testi classici* 52 (2004): 177–97.

45. Rumrich, *Milton Unbound*, 21.

46. Ibid., 24, 12.

47. Stanley Fish, *Surprised by Sin*, 2nd ed. (Cambridge, Mass., 1997), xli.

48. Stanley Fish, "Why Milton Matters: Or Against Historicism," in *Milton Studies* 44, ed. Albert C. Labriola (Pittsburgh, 2005), 10.

49. Alan Fisher, "Why Is *Paradise Regained* So Cold?" in *Milton Studies* 14, ed. James D. Simmonds (Pittsburgh, 1980), 195–217; hereafter cited in the text by page number.

50. Jeffrey B. Morris, "Disorientation and Disruption in *Paradise Regained*," in *Milton Studies* 26, ed. James D. Simmonds (Pittsburgh, 1990), 234.

51. This parallel between Vegio's and Ross's thirteenth books has previously been remarked upon by Anna Cox Brinton, *Maphaeus Vegius and His Thirteenth Book of the "Aeneid": A Chapter on Virgil in the Renaissance* (Stanford, 1930), 38; and by John R. Glenn, *Ross's "Mystagogus Poeticus*," 11.

52. Translation of Virgil's words in Dante's *Inferno* (1.72). Michael C. J. Putnam, in the introduction to *Maffeo Vegio: Short Epics*, The I Tatti Renaissance Library (Cambridge, Mass., 2004), denies that Vegio encourages any allegorical or anagogical interpretation of Aeneas's journey, let alone intends that Aeneas's "stellification" should be interpreted as Christian translation (xviii). In *The Augustinian Epic* (62–63), however, I note one passage in which Vegio explicitly invokes the "ages of man" or "stages of maturation" allegory.

SINUOUS RHYTHMS AND SERPENTINE LINES: MILTON, THE BAROQUE, AND THE ENGLISH LANDSCAPE GARDEN REVISITED

Dirk den Hartog

I

THIS ESSAY DRAWS together and supplements three recurring discussions of aspects of *Paradise Lost* that have hitherto proceeded for the most part separately: the rhythms of its blank verse, the relevance to the poem of the concept of the baroque, and the role of the poem in the history of English garden design. Something still needs to be said about the expressiveness of the poem's rhythms, especially in the pastoral sections of the poem, and it seems to me that this significantly enhances the well-developed understanding we already have of *Paradise Lost* as baroque.[1] The same also goes for the complex relations between Milton's Eden and the development of the English landscape garden, well examined though these have been.[2] The connection is one side of the poem's life within that symbiosis of the literary and the visual arts that rose to its peak in England in the eighteenth century.[3] This essay deals with a yet unexplored aspect of this interchange between *Paradise Lost* and gardening, which the dual literary-visual literacy of many of the poem's eighteenth-century admirers may have enabled: the possible relations between the imagery and, more importantly, the blank-verse rhythms of the pastoral sections of Milton's poem, and that essential feature of the new eighteenth-century English style, the serpentine line. In doing this it moves beyond Milton to some eighteenth-century gardenist writings that he influenced, writings that themselves linked the pastoral sections of *Paradise Lost* to their accounts of contemporary gardens: Stephen Switzer's *Ichnographia rustica* (1718), and those two markedly Miltonic blank-verse poems, James Thomson's *The Seasons* (1726–1730) and William Mason's *The English Garden* (1772–1781).

Persuasive detailed analysis of the rhythms of *Paradise Lost* has been surprisingly rare. Milton's prefatory assertion of the virtue of blank verse, equating it with freedom and variety, made consideration of the poem's "numbers" an essential item of critical commentary. This, of course, became a rallying cry in the reaction to neoclassicism that ensued in the following century, with John Dryden's disapproval and attempted 1671 rewriting of the poem into a drama in heroic couplets (as *The State of Innocence, and Fall of Man*) soon becoming a minority position.[4] Yet while ensuing commentary on the poem has included its rhythms as an important ground for admiration, the claim has remained a rather general one. Joseph Addison's precise identification of stylistic traits in his groundbreaking discussion of the poem as epic noted how the insertion or omission of syllables gave "a greater variety to [the poem's] numbers." And Thomas Gray, the critically changeable Oliver Goldsmith, and later William Hazlitt all commented on the expressive relation of such variety to the feeling and meaning conveyed. But none of these commentaries provided properly explained examples. Even in our own times such an assiduous and skillful close reader of Milton as Christopher Ricks has despaired of the possibility of sufficiently objective detailed analysis of rhythm and music in the poem, supporting this by convincing demonstration of the failed attempts in commentaries he otherwise admires.[5]

I hope to show that Ricks has given up too soon on this score. This being no easy task, I will begin by advancing two principles on the interpretation of rhythm in poetry in general, which inform my reading of the rhythms of *Paradise Lost* here. The first is that whenever a poem establishes any kind of metric regularity, it cannot but set up in the reader an expectation of its continuance: in this it draws on the roughly isochronic nature of spoken English in general. So when such expectation is thwarted, an instinctive response is to compress and elongate sounds to regularize the deviating element at least partially. It may take a fraction longer to say "the catapult on the floor" than "the cat on the floor," but one naturally quickens the pace on "catapult" to avoid what seems an unnatural deferment of the second stress. I suggest that it is this reaction that is largely responsible for the dramatic power of, for instance, Satan's spectacular ejection from heaven:

> Him the Almighty Power
> Hurld headlong flaming from th'Ethereal Skie
> With hideous ruine and combustion down
> To bottomless perdition, there to dwell
> In Adamantine Chains and penal Fire,
> Who durst defie th'Omnipotent to Arms.   (1.44–49)

"Ethereal," "bottomless perdition," "Adamantine," "th'Omnipotent"— by vocally reading this passage, one quickens the pace at each point that such highly polysyllabic words occur, in an attempt to make the surplus of syllables fit into the emphatic duplet rhythm that we begin to expect from the end of the first line (carrying over from the end of the previous sentence) and that persists amid these complications—reasserting itself most powerfully at the end of the sentence. The expressive effect of the quickening is a sense of dramatic compression that is released in the ensuing moments where monosyllabic word and stress concur—coming to a climax on that final "Arms." Addison rightly saw that Milton's taste for Latinisms made his diction contribute to the poem's sublimity; he might also have added how the concomitant insertion of extra syllables is one way in which that sublimity is achieved.[6]

However, another important principle in considering rhythm in poetry, as I. A. Richards insists, is that it cannot be considered in isolation from meaning.[7] Thus, a hypothetical variant passage that ends with the line "And wants to invite the Omnipotent to tea" would be no more sublime than the (to us) endearingly homely "No fear lest dinner cool" (5.396), which Addison singles out as a stylistic lapse.[8] Rather, it is in the simultaneous apprehension of meaning and rhythm as one reads of Satan's ejection, and the mutual influence of these elements on each other in our minds, that the impression of grandeur is created. This grandeur was well defined some decades ago by Murray Roston. For Roston the poem's central baroque theme, which he sees as "infinite strength overcoming powerful resistance in order to demonstrate its might," is expressed both in narrative and style. Moments equivalent to those quickenings and compressions in the passage just discussed (Roston's analysis deals mainly with the rhythmic effects of enjambed phrases) are thus for him a literary equivalent to what Heinrich Wölfflin defines as the style of the baroque in the visual arts, "when a scene refuses to be contained within the limits of the canvas and seems to burst out of its frame." So at "Ethereal," "Adamantine," "Omnipotent," and so on, our quickenings both compress the noniambic polysyllables into the iambic frame of the line and fail to quite do so, thus registering a fleeting impression of bursting out as we read past them.[9]

The verse of Satan's ejection reflects the heroic side of *Paradise Lost* as baroque: the baroque of splendor and magnificence, of powerfully opposing forces and dynamic movement toward infinite vistas—the sense of space made imaginable by Copernicus and Bruno.[10] In his Italian travels in 1638–1639 Milton would have experienced this side of the baroque in Rome, especially at St. Peter's, including Bernini's recently completed Baldachino, or in the Palazzo Barberini, where Milton attended a concert in February 1639, and where he would almost certainly have seen Pietro da Cortona's nearly completed ceiling fresco, "The Triumph of Divine Providence" (1633–1638).[11]

Yet as Roston recognizes in his concluding chapter, the baroque has also its pastoral side, marked by a sense of the cornucopian abundance of the natural world. This is certainly the style of Milton's Eden, in which "Nature boon / Powrd forth profuse on Hill and Dale and Plaine" (4.242–43) and where Eve, asked by Adam to "bring forth and poure / Abundance" (5.314–15) from her stores to honor Raphael's visit, "Heaps with unsparing hand" (5.343–44), an action that prefigures her destiny, announced by Raphael, as:

> Mother of Mankind, whose fruitful Womb
> Shall fill the World more numerous with thy Sons
> Than with these various fruits the Trees of God
> Have heaped this Table.   (5.388–91)

It is also the style of much of the account of the Creation in Book Seven. As has been variously argued, it expresses a feeling for life that reflects Milton's experience of painters such as Rubens, Jan Brueghel, Bassano, and Tintoretto, along with the lavish profusion of forms, both human and natural, on the Cortona ceiling fresco and in baroque architectural moldings.[12] Such sensuous profusion typifies the mixture of metaphysics and naturalism that Roy Daniells, drawing on J. R. Martin, has seen as characteristic of the baroque and Milton as baroque, in which, as Roston has convincingly argued, the impulse is "to celebrate divine creation." (Diane McColley has more recently given an eloquent and highly convincing account of the poem in these terms, though relating its philosophical optimism mainly to prebaroque works of art.)[13]

Perhaps because of the very profuse availability of cornucopian imagery in the poem for ready citation, neither Roston nor anyone else has commented on the rhythms in which the sense of abundance is expressed. But consider the following:

> Or the flourie lap
> Of some irriguous Valley spread her store,
> Flours of all hue, and without Thorne the Rose:
> Another side, umbrageous Grots and Caves
> Of coole recess, o'er which the mantling Vine
> Layes forth her purple Grape, and gently creeps
> Luxuriant.   (4.254–60)

"Irriguous" and "umbrageous" are as pointedly Latinate here as "adamantine" and "omnipotent" in the passage cited from Book One above (Milton's use of "irriguous" here is the second recorded in the *OED*, the first being Jeremy Taylor in 1651).[14] The deviation from the underlying iambic rhythm that they potentially impose is equally profound. The same goes for the more common but equally polysyllabic "luxuriant" that completes the enjambment at the passage's end. But because rhythm and meaning work interactively on each other, the effect here is not dramatically reverberative, as in the heroic style of Satan's ejection and other like instances, but one that might be characterized, by a visual analogy, as sinuosity. Here we have both extra syllables and thus a potential quickening of pace, *and* a constraint on realizing this potential due to our awareness of the Edenic landscape, the serene amplitude of which makes any such straightforward quickening incongruous. Rather, it seems more appropriate here to let one's voice (overt or silent) move more slowly along the arhythmic syllables that the polysyllabic words introduce. This entails an elongated enunciation of the polysyllabic Latinisms, which in these instances emphasize variations in pitch that a more rapid articulation would obscure. (With all three instances here, "irriguous," "umbrageous," and "luxuriant," there is a rise in pitch on the second syllable that then falls for the third and fourth.) These variations in pitch complement the rhythmic variations, deferring the expected iambic stresses to create an effect of what we might call undulance—to use a synonym of "sinuous" that covers matters of both sight and sound.

Sometimes, as in the passage discussed, sinuosity is concentrated over a number of lines. At others only a single line is involved, as with the momentary ripple—a graceful rather than a reverberative quickening—introduced by the three-syllabled adjective describing angelic taste in drink: "And not disrelish thirst / Of nectarous draughts between" (5.305–6). Or the similar "amorous" in: "Yielded with coy submission, modest pride / And sweet reluctant amorous delay" (4.310–11), and: "All but the wakeful Nightingale; / She all night long her amorous descant sung" (4.602–3), and the "spirit of love and amorous delight" (8.477) that Eve inspires in Adam. Only in the last of these examples does a need for lexical variation dictate the use of the three-syllabled "amorous" rather than the two-syllabled synonym, "loving." The same applies to that other typically Miltonic choice of "odorous" as an alternative to "fragrant," as in the "odorous bushie shrub" that "fenc'd up the verdant wall" of the Edenic bower (4.696–97) or the better known "odorous gums and balm" of Eden's "rich trees" (4.248).

This expressiveness is sometimes specifically mimetic and sometimes not. Eve's gracefulness in general is suggested by the rhythmic sinuosity of the above-quoted line (4.311), not her coyness in particular, and it is more an evocation of the serpentine meander of the valley than its moisture that is brought to mind with "irriguous," the rhythm affecting one more than the unsurprising meaning of the word. Yet these two latter qualities are cognate and both are subsumed in an overall sense of cornucopian bounty that the sinuosity finally signifies. Where the mimesis is locally specific it is so in a way that is in keeping with the overall style, as with Adam's "Hyacinthin Locks," which "Round from his parted forelock manly hung / Clustring" (4.302–3), or with "Yet higher than thir tops / The verdurous wall of Paradise up sprung"

(4.142–43), where the obscure Latinism limns the wall to the imagination as undulant in shape. (The only recorded English poet before Milton to use "verdurous" was Michael Drayton.[15]) Or, quite differently, there is the framing pictorial detail of the Edenic marriage bed, where, over Adam and Eve's "naked limbs the flourie roof / Showrd roses" (4.772–73). Here, as we move from the phrase preceding the line break to the one after it, the lessening of syllables amid the balance of varied sound and alliterative and assonantal repetition suggests sudden voluptuous release.

With the "sense" so "variously drawn out," each rhythmic nuance functions doubly, as both expressive in its own right and as an element within an overall variousness in the metric composition. Most obviously, there is the pleasing variety derived from the juxtaposition of undulance with other sensuous qualities expressed by rhythm and sound, as in "The verdurous wall of Paradise up sprung" (4.143) where the initial undulance is balanced by the clustered accents and assonance of the final phrase, which gives us the wall's thrusting solidity. But undulance can also be present as something hinted at amid a surge of thrusting energy, as in "Forth flourish't thick the clustring vine" (7.320) (where one cannot but hover between assigning two and three syllables to "clustring"). Or there can be a fuller melding of different qualities, such as a steadying thrust amid undulance, as when Eve goes "forth among her Fruits and Flours" (8.44), and they "at her coming sprung / And toucht by her fair tendance gladlier grew" (8.46–47). Or a soft transition from one quality to another, as where undulance subsides to calm in the "liquid lapse of murmuring streams" (8.263) that Adam is aware of at his first awakening, where both the sibilance and the soft-consonant assonance sway from ongoing movement in the second and fourth words, respectively, to come together in a concluding rest on the fifth. Or the similar effect with the "circumfluous waters calm" (7.270) of the oceans at Creation.

Throughout, in fact, effects of rhythm need to be considered in the context of patterns of assonance and alliteration. In the opening lines of the "flourie lap" example, for instance (4.254–60), "irriguous valley" flows so smoothly out of its rhythmic frame because it continues the alternation of *l* and *r* begun in "flourie lap." Something of the same kind is at work in the soft consonant and short *u* vowel assonance of the famous injunction to "feed on thoughts, that voluntarie move / Harmonious numbers" (3.37–38), except that here we have, as it were, a two-stage swelling from the rhythmic frame, with "harmonious numbers" echoing "voluntarie move" in sound while amplifying its impression of syllabic excess, not so much by a greater number of syllables as by the extension of the assonance further toward the conclusion of the phrase. Conversely, polysyllabic insertions are least attractive when such euphony is lacking, as in: "Now gentle gales Fanning thir odoriferous wings dispense / Native perfumes" (4.156–58), where "odoriferous" simply chokes up the line, to no point.[16] The same applies to the "marriageable arms" that the Vine "spous'd . . . twines" about the Elm in Eden's orchard (5.215–17): these vegetal nuptials lack charm because they *sound* awkward. With sinuosity, too, we again have the style of the baroque, as characterized by Wölfflin's idea of the "atectonic," whereby, "the mass of . . . the wall . . . lost its inner structure. . . . *All hard and pointed shapes were blunted and softened, and everything angular became rounded.*"[17]

There is also perhaps a more specific analogy between the relationship in baroque architecture of framing members (columns, pilasters, strips, and niches) and enclosed materials, and the interplay of regularity and irregularity in Milton's rhythmic sinuosity, in which the regular iambic stresses are the equivalent of the framing members of architecture. Thus, the effect in Milton of an opulent rhythmic swelling out of the duplet metric frame is akin to the baroque architectural effect Wölfflin observes by which "the decorative filling [is made] too large, so that it overflows its allotted space." The verse of Satan's ejection is like "the perpetual state of friction between recess and frame" in baroque ceilings, which "make us fear that the filling will burst out of the frames."[18] Somewhat differently, the frame-obscuring sinuosity of the rhythm in the "flourie lap" passage recalls Cortona's "Triumph of Divine Providence" in the Palazzo Barberini, in which the *quadratura* ceiling frame that divides the central from surrounding frescoes is both obscured by superimposed painted bodies which reach up or travel from one frescoed scene to another, and itself merges partially with the frescoes through the continuity of the painted sculptural figures of the frame and the figures of the frescoes. It would be drawing far too long a bow to speculate that Milton's experience of works like Cortona's might have been an inspirational source for his Edenic rhythms, but the simple parallel does illuminate their nature.

The fully baroque sensuous form of this rhythm is enforced by a comparison with a passage in which Spenser might seem to be doing something similar:

> Low his lascivious arms adown did creepe,
> That themselves dipping in the silver dew,
> Their fleecy showers they tenderly did steepe,
> Which drops of Christall seemed for wantonness to weepe.
> Infinite streames continually did well
> Out of this fountain, sweet and faire to see,
> The which unto an ample laver fell.   (*Faerie Queene* 2.11.61–67)

Here also are two moments of rhythmic sinuosity—"low his lascivious arms" and "infinite streams continually did well / Out." But they are briefly flourished steps aside from the generally weary plod of the verse's regularity: as a whole one is much more conscious of the frame than of the interruptions to it. With Milton, by contrast, rhythmic variousness is pervasive: framing regularity is not only set aside more often by moments of sinuosity, but also, to keep to the passage under discussion, by phrases where clustered accents express the actions denoted, as in "spread her store" and "layes forth her purple Grape" (4.255, 259). As with Cortona's ceiling, order exists at the limits of variety.

To talk of the *movement* of Milton's verse as having such sensuous qualities both supports and is supported by Jean Hagstrum's comment, almost fifty years ago, that Milton's verse was neither pictorial, nor just musical, but rather kinesthetic.

Milton is more intent on having us feel in a kind of kinesthetic sensation the full opulence of nature itself than on having us see its particulars. . . . The fresh water, the orient pearl, the sands of gold, the purple grapes, . . . the "flowr's of all hue"—all create an idea streaked with sensuous recollections, in a sense the antithesis of a visual scene that implies an idea.[19]

Our response to poetic rhythm is central to kinesthetic sensation, as it is in our subphysical movement in response to the movement of the verse in which the kinesthesis occurs. This is why reading Milton brings to mind not just stylistic parallels between the verse and baroque art, as just discussed, but also, in the indirectly subliminal way Hagstrum's formulation suggests, memories of classical, Renaissance, or baroque artworks themselves. Hazlitt put this well when he said that in Milton "the persons of Adam and Eve, of Satan, etc. are always accompanied, in our imagination, with the grandeur of the naked figure; they convey to us *the ideas* of sculpture" (my italics).[20] This imaginative interaction between the literary and the visual will be the focus of the second part of this essay.

II

It is with the baroque sinuosity of Milton's Edenic rhythms in mind that I now want to revisit that amply discussed question of the relation between *Paradise Lost* and the history of garden design. Existing studies have approached this from two directions: the influence of existing gardens, Italian or English, upon the poem, and the influence of the poem upon the later "natural," "English"-style gardens that began to come into fashion some decades after the poem was published. Of course, in his landmark commentary on the relationship, *History of the Modern Taste in Gardening* (1782), Horace Walpole ruled out the first line of influence altogether, arguing that Milton alone, in the "vigour

of [his] boundless imagination," and without having "seen a glimpse of anything like what he [had] imagined," freed English garden design from the
European formalism imposed by "education [and] custom."[21] Even before
this, however, Addison had discreetly murmured in a footnote that Milton
"would never have been able . . . to have laid out his Paradise, had he not seen
the . . . gardens of Italy" in his 1638–1639 tour. In recent decades, scholars
such as Roland Frye, Stanley Koehler, and John Dixon Hunt have confirmed
Addison's claim in ample and convincing detail, Frye and Koehler elaborating
stylistic analogies between Milton's Eden and Italian baroque gardens and
Hunt using similar material to expose the chauvinism of Walpole's truncated
history. Charlotte Otten has written similarly of the influence of existing
English gardens on Milton's picture of Eden.[22] Pursuing the other direction,
both Koehler and Hunt have also stressed that Milton was still *one* of the
important influences upon the development of the English garden. That this is
so is very clear from both the writing of eighteenth-century gardenists such as
Stephen Switzer and in eighteenth-century poetry about gardens, such as the
poet-gardenist William Mason's *The English Garden* (1782–1791)—the first
attempt to write a long poem, modeled on Virgil's *Georgics*, about the "English garden"—and which quotes verbatim at some length (1.453–58) from
Milton's Eden.[23]

Nevertheless, the nature of this Miltonic influence still warrants further
attention. Hunt has written in some detail on Milton's influence in giving
"inspiration and justification," "advice and retrospective sanction" to the
eighteenth-century landscape movement in matters such as naturalness, variety, and the management of water. He cites various instances where such
features occur in gardens or are referred to in garden writings in ways that
suggest the influence of Milton's depiction: often the relationship is explicitly
acknowledged.[24] One question he leaves unexplored, however, is a possible
correspondence between the style of gardens and the *style* of the poetry. In
general terms, at least, Stephen Switzer, was aware of such an analogy, believing that "the Designer should make use of the Poets in forming his Imagination," and holding that Addison's classification of classical epics into the great
(Homer), the beautiful (Virgil), and the strange (Ovid) should also be applied
to styles of garden design. Hence, while Pope's description of Windsor Forest
was "sweet," Milton's "inimitable description of Paradise" was "Noble and
Majestic."[25] What relevance might this stylistic analogizing have to one important aspect of the English garden that Hunt mentions in an unelaborated
note as bearing Miltonic authorization: the serpentine line? What relation is
there, that is, between the sinuous and the serpentine? Is there conscious
awareness of the analogy at this specific level, and in relation to what ele-

ments of style? Is the nature of this relationship simply—or even mainly—a matter of causality or legitimation, or both?

To begin with the last of these questions, one must acknowledge that an abundance of sources has already been documented to explain the rise of the serpentine line as a landscape feature, from the general stylistic journey of the form from mannerism to the rococo and thence, specifically, to the garden, to the new feeling for the undulant line in seventeenth-century landscape painters, to the more recent influence of the Chinese ideal of *sharawadgi*, to the effect of practical decisions such as Switzer's innovative retention at Castle Howard of an existing curved laneway, and to the influence of Hogarth's celebration of the form as "the line of beauty."[26] Milton's sinuous rhythms could only have played a very supplementary causal role in this profusion of determination. It is intriguing to wonder whether such an influence was perhaps one of the things Jonathan Richardson had in mind when declaring that, "after having read Milton, one sees nature with better eyes than before, beauties appear, which else had been unregarded." But the comment is frustratingly unillustrated, and while Richardson quotes Milton extensively, especially in his chapter on the sublime, where he refers to "the Musick of the Words" and "the Pleasure . . . in the Sound," none of *these* quotations are in fact from the Eden or the related Creation sections of the poem.[27]

More likely than causality, therefore, is the alternative mentioned in Hunt's passing comment that *Paradise Lost* "gave authority" for the serpentine line. Hogarth, for whom Milton was a favorite author, gives us a striking example of this in *The Analysis of Beauty* (1733), where he illustrates the "interlacing . . . of serpentine lines" in "one of the most pleasing movements in country dancing," by the image of Milton's angels dancing about the sacred hill in "Mazes intricate / Eccentric, intervolved, yet regular / Then most, when most irregular they seem" (5.621–24). Here, too, Milton's role is to confer legitimacy rather than transmit memories of Italian gardens. Indeed, the serpentine line was not a pronounced feature of these gardens, unlike those elements, such as variety, surprise and the sloping site, which anti-Walpolean revisionists like Hunt discern as passing from Italian baroque origins into icons of Englishness at Milton's hands.[28]

A further understanding of the analogy of the sinuous and the serpentine, however, is given to us by that highly literary gardenist, Stephen Switzer, in the Miltonic echoes that at times invest his description of natural forms in *Ichnographia rustica* (1718). Switzer expresses his general stylistic preference by conflating Miltonic allusions and endorsing "Places that are set off not by nice Art, but by luxury of Nature." In a way impossible to Milton but typical of eighteenth-century Miltonists and Milton-loving gardenists like

Switzer, however, the metaphor of the serpentine is now used, free of morally ambiguous connotations, to figure what is now held to be the quintessentially natural form. So, for Switzer, in "natural Gardening" it is "the loose Serpentine Line" that "[seems] to be the most entertaining," since: "the Owner does not see all his business at once, but is insensibly led from one Place to another, and from a Lawn to a Hill, or a Dale."[29] Thus, when Switzer asserts that, in a garden design "the whole should correspond together by the *mazie error* of its natural avenues and meanders" (my italics), he similarly lends Miltonic authority to the form that for him typifies naturalness. But is something more going on elsewhere when, noting this "loose Serpentine line" in foliage, Switzer tropes it charmingly with Eve's hair, referring to "the *loose Tresses* of a tree or Plant, that is easily fann'd by every gentle Breeze of Air" (my italics). Or, when he later declares, arguing against topiary, that, "The careless and *loose tresses* of Nature, that are easily moved by the least Breath of Wind, offer more to the Imagination than the most delicate Pyramid" (my italics).[30]

Switzer's allusion to "loose tresses" surely plays on that lovely Miltonic image of Eve leaning "half-embracing" on Adam, so that, "Half her swelling breast / Naked met his under the flowing gold / Of her loose tresses hid" (4.495–97), with its sensuous masterstroke by which the hair as veil is used both to half-cover and to erotically enhance Eve's breasts. This troping thus sets up in our imagination a symbiotic interplay of the literary and the visual, by which our imaging of the naturalistic detail is infused anthropomorphically by the literary echo. Milton himself could rely on this interactiveness, as *Paradise Lost* was written at a time when Stuart patronage of the visual arts had established a dual literary and visual literacy as a mark of the educated person.[31] For such a person, too, reading Switzer and recalling Milton, a further cross-media interaction was also available in the way that the imaging of Eve here also recalls the 1531–1535 nude version of Titian's paintings of the penitent Mary Magdalen, which Milton probably saw in the Medici collections on one of his two stays in Florence on his 1638–1639 travels in Italy. The Grand Duke Ferdinand de Medici's history of championing Galileo would have made his collections, which then held the picture, an especially appropriate place for Milton, the anti-Catholic aesthete, to visit.[32] (Titian's Magdalens would also seem to be evoked by the later image of Eve at Adam's feet, "with tears that ceased not flowing / and tresses all disordered" [10.910–11].)

A further echo, too, is the Caroline fashion for "disordine" hairstyle and dress promoted by cavalier poets like Richard Lovelace and Robert Herrick (poetic advocate of "a sweet disorder in the dress") and court painters like Lely and Anthony Van Dyck, the latter painter being, in the words of a mid-seventeenth-century commentator, William Sanderson, the "first painter that e'er put Ladies dresse into a careless Romance."[33] Switzer's troping on Eve's hair can thus be seen as part of a process by which the sexual insolence typified by Lovelace's demand that Amarantha let her hair "fly as unconfined / As its calm ravisher, the wind" ("To Amarantha") is transmuted, via Milton, into a diffused eroticism in which the depiction of real-life gardens and landscapes is invested with echoes of the precariously innocent voluptuousness of Milton's idyll. This is perhaps why William Mason was to see the English garden that his poem celebrated as conducive to leading a life that was "free, yet not licentious" (*The English Garden*, 3.567). Interestingly, at a moment in garden history when the objective presence in gardens of actual mythological statuary was about to be challenged,[34] such a symbiosis of Milton's text and landscaped form in a gardenist like Switzer reveals a persisting, subjectively imagined mythological presence, which looks forward to Keatsian tropes such as the "light-winged dryad of the trees" ("Ode to a Nightingale," 1819) and the personified Autumn's "hair / soft-lifted by the winnowing wind" ("To Autumn," 1819).

The symbiotic relationship between literary and visual art, by which a conjoint literary-visual awareness became a significant form of multimedia aesthetic experience, had come in eighteenth-century England to involve gardening as much as painting—a relationship to which *Paradise Lost* was ideally suited. The Renaissance had revived the classical practice by which the evocation of literary references in gardens had been an important element of the garden experience itself. Traditionally this had involved classical literature, largely Ovidian mythology.[35] The distinctive fusion of the Christian and the classical in *Paradise Lost* played a large part in extending this practice into the cultivation of what Diane McColley has called "paradisal consciousness,"[36] so that a hundred years later, William Mason, clergyman as well as poet, literary scholar, and gardenist, could still speak of his enthusiasm for classical ornament in gardens (perhaps with a glance at emerging evangelical disapproval) as a "harmless idolatry."[37] Thus, we have, representatively, the title of John Lawrence's 1728 work, *Paradise Regained; or, The Art of Gardening*.[38] In a similar spirit, the Milton-loving Switzer declared that in "a Country Seat . . . every person makes to himself a kind of a new Creation."[39] Beyond this, contemporary belief in Milton's Eden as a source of the "English" garden, however chauvinistically deluded, automatically implied, by the stylistic analogy, that some present-day gardens recreated the setting for Milton's retelling of the biblical narrative. Horace Walpole's reference to Milton's "prophetic eye of taste" also suggests, in fact, that Milton is not just a progenitor but also the inspired revealer of a divinely preferred gardening style, which replaced styles "unworthy of the almighty hand that had planted the delights of Paradise." So, when Walpole saw the movement of water in rivers and fountains at Hagley and Stourhead as the realization of Milton's Edenic prototype, he implied a conjoint multimedia experience of the literary and visual, in terms of poem and garden, by which to experience the one was imaginatively to recall the other.[40]

Switzer's allusions to Eve's hair are to be understood within this broad symbiosis. Specifically, they indicate the role played by eighteenth-century Miltonizing and Miltonic allusion in linking Edenic sinuosity in *Paradise Lost* with the serpentine line as a feature of the newly emerged English landscape garden. This is not a conjunction of literary allusion and a direct experience of a garden—as in the setting of a literary program of statuary in a garden (Virgil at Stourhead or Ovid at the Villa d'Este)—and only sometimes is it the linking of a literary work with a specified actual place, as Walpole does with Milton and Hagley.[41] However, the drawing together of literary reference with natural details that are not specifically located, as with Switzer here, can be seen as modeling for the reader a habit of association to be put into practice in real life locations: with Switzer's trope in mind the Milton-lover can associate any free-flowing foliage anywhere with Eve's "loose tresses."

Somewhat surprisingly, though, the serpentine line is not stylistically prominent in Milton's poem as an image, even within the pastoral sections. There are some memorable instances, such as the country-dancing angels that pleased Hogarth and the elephant who "wreathed / His lithe proboscis" (4.346–47). And there is the serpent itself, whom we first see simply *as* serpent, weaving "with Gordian twine / His braided train" (4.348–49), and then, possessed by Satan, putting on a virtuoso display of being "erect / Amidst his circling spires" (10.501–2) to catch Eve's notice. Later, leading her off to see the tree of life, he "swiftly rowl[s] in tangles, and make[s] intricate seem strait" (10.631–32). But neither here, nor when Adam and Eve "haste" to "their morning's rural work" (5.211), or when Eve goes "forth among her Fruits and Flowers" (8.44) or "bet[akes] her to the groves" (9.398), are we told whether the paths themselves are undulant or straight. "Walks" and "Allies" are mentioned (see, for example, 4.626–27, 9.1107, 11.270), but not their form. The "serpentine meanders" that eighteenth-century gardenists such as Switzer and Langley so often recommended as the proper path of flowing water[42] are hinted at in the "four main streams" into which the waters from the garden divide, to go "wandering many a famous realm" (4.233, 234), in the "crisped brooks / Rolling . . . with mazie error" (4.237–39) and in "the watry throng . . . with Serpent errour wandring" (7.297–303) in the description of the creation of the oceans. And there is Eve's hair, of course, as discussed above, and in that other, even more famous image of it, where "She as a veil down to the slender waist / Her unadorned golden tresses wore / Dishevelled, but in wanton ringlets waved" (4.304–6) (which also recalls

Botticelli's "Birth of Venus," 1482, a painting Milton would have seen in the Medici collection at Florence, and in which the undulant sweep of Venus's golden hair flows down her side to curve in to cover her pudenda.[43]) Quantitatively, however, imagery of the sinuous is not important: even the Milton-loving Stephen Switzer sees Virgil as the chief literary inspiration here ("How sweetly is Virgil's Muse delighted, with a winding Valley, and a lofty Hill").[44]

So it is at the level of the "numbers," finally, that the relationship of the sinuous and the serpentine can best be explored. Can the kind of aesthetic symbiosis just discussed be entertained for the relationship of the serpentine line and Milton's sinuous *rhythms?* A Miltonizing poet like James Thomson is interesting here in his bringing together Milton's rhythms and an eighteenth-century sense of nature and the landscape, where the serpentine line is now frequently introduced and celebrated as a sensuous form alone, either as the metaphor itself, now free of moral ambiguities, as in the Switzer quote above, or as "winding" (perhaps the most frequently used adjective in eighteenth-century garden writing):

> See, where the winding Vale her lavish Stores,
> Irriguous, spreads. See how the Lilly drinks
> The latent Rill, scarce oozing thro' the Grass,
> Of Growth luxuriant; or the humid Bank,
> In fair Profusion, decks!   ("Spring," 496–500)

Milton's style is strongly present here, as is his baroque celebration of the created material world, that sense of life pouring forth, "inexhaustive . . . in fair Profusion." Thomson modulates the cornucopian vision onto a more naturalistic plane, interfusing it into a contemporary landscape, so that Milton's Edenic "mantling Vine . . . [that] gently creeps / Luxuriant" (4.258–60) here becomes the more prosaic and unclassical "Grass, of Growth luxuriant." One aspect of this is the embedding, in "where the winding vale her lavish stores, / Irriguous, spreads," of the serpentine image in a Miltonically sinuous rhythm: Thomson reworks Milton's "or the flourie lap / Of som irriguous Valley spread her store" (4.254–55), using Milton's arcanely Latinate "irriguous" while transposing it into the Miltonic habit of placing the polysyllabic adjective after the noun, often with enjambment, and substituting "winding" for the Persephone allusion of "flourie." (Reference to "irriguous" plains or vales becomes, in fact, quite a commonplace in eighteenth-century landscape poetry and not uncommon in prose descriptions of gardens and land-scapes.[45]) This is in one sense a loss, a thinning of associative texture. But in compensation its new collocation of serpentine form and sinuous rhythm arguably enacts a new symbiosis of the visual and the literary, so where Milton's idealized Eden is enriched by echoes of classical mythology, Thomson's nature is enriched by the evocative presence of Milton's style. In the writer this might just be a matter of making the sound congruent with the sense. But for the properly practiced reader the link models, in the literary text, a cross-media awareness by which the kinesthetic experience of sinuous rhythm is enriched by memories of the serpentine form evoked by the visual image the rhythm accompanies. Conversely, might the pleasure of a Milton enthusiast in the undulant forms of an English landscape garden be enhanced by a subliminal association with the sinuosity of the poetry?

Such juxtapositions of rhythm and image may seem coincidental. As we saw earlier with Milton, sinuosity is one of a number of expressive deviations from iambic regularity that together constitute the variousness of his "numbers." So when half a century later the clerical poet and gardenist, William Mason, echoes and adapts Milton's famous preface in asserting an analogy between the "natural" freedom and variety of blank verse and "natural" gardening, he may only have been thinking of a congruence on this general level:

Numbers of the most varied kind were most proper to illustrate a subject whose every charm springs from variety, and which, painting Nature as scorning control, should employ a versification for that end as unlettered as Nature itself. Art at the same time, in rural improvements, pervading the province of Nature, unseen, and unfelt, seemed to bear a striking analogy to that species of verse, the harmony of which results from measured quantity and varied cadence, without the too studied arrangement of final syllables, or regular return of consonant sounds.[46]

The whole thrust of Mason's poem, with its Miltonic style and verbatim quotation from *Paradise Lost* (1.453–59), is to link Milton's Eden with the eighteenth-century gardening style that Mason celebrated: to read Mason's poem is to imaginatively reenact its coalescence of mythological and real gardens. And within this there is also a concern to delineate particular qualities rhythmically, or, as he puts it, "by modulation meet / Of varied cadence . . . to form / [a] magic sympathy of sense with sound."[47] A clear example is the apostrophe to the art of gardening at the beginning of the second book: "Hail to the Art . . . / that bids Magnificence / Abate its meteor glare, and learn to shine / Benevolently mild" (2.1–5).

Where the transition from the reverberative "bids Magnificence / Abate" (to go back to the adjective I used in analyzing Satan's ejection passage) to the undulant "shine / Benevolently mild," is expressively in keeping with the change of reference, as well as being a pleasing variation in the overall pattern created by the modulation. More specifically relevant still, touches of Miltonic sinuosity of rhythm frequently accompany Mason's many celebratory allusions to the visually serpentine, "the curve that Nature loves"

(4.4–5), thus modeling for the reader a cross-media awareness akin to that in the Thomson example above. Hence, we have "Who ever loves to undulate and sport / In many a winding train" (1.311–12) and "careless lines, whose undulating forms / Play thro' the varied canvas" (1.273–74). Likewise, there is the instruction to guide water through a landscape design: "as a river pent / By fringed banks, weave its irriguous way / Thro' lawn and shade alternate" (1.121–23), where again, as in the Thomson example above, the Miltonic "irriguous" creates a rhythmic complement to the relatively non-Miltonic image of undulant form, "weave," supplementing the kinesthesis with visual traces. One might also cite the reworking of Milton's "umbrageous grots and caves / Of cool recess, o'er which the mantling vine / Lays forth her purple grape, and gently creeps / Luxuriant" (4.57–60) into Mason's "solemn grot, / Oe'r which an ancient vine luxuriant flung / Its purple clusters" (2.540–42), though the latter's "solemn grot" substitutes an awkwardly staccato assonance for the delicious assonance of the former's "umbrageous grots and caves." In general, however, moments like these offer one reason why *The English Garden* (1772–1781) does not quite deserve the blanket dismissal that it is usually given as poetry (as in a reference of Hunt's to its "turgid blank verse"), rather than as historical document.[48]

Arcane Miltonic Latinisms such as "umbrageous," "verdurous," or "circumfluous" become almost widely used in eighteenth-century and nineteenth-century poetry, chiefly in pastoral settings and often echoing Milton with an effect similar to the above Thomson and Mason examples. Thus, we have Cowper's "Umbrageous walks and solitary paths" ("Retirement" [1782], 258) and Shenstone's "A group of elms umbrageous rose" ("Elegy XV"). (The *Poetry Full-Text Database* lists ninety-three uses of "umbrageous" in the eighteenth century, with repeated uses by major poets like Thomson and Cowper; this subsides to seventy in the next century, with few usages by major poets.) Then there is Henry Brooke's splendidly onomatopeic "Circumfluous rolls the long disparted tide" ("Universal Beauty" [1735]) (compare Milton's "circumfluous waters calm" [7.270]). Most famously, of course, are the "verdurous glooms and winding mossy ways" of Keats's "Ode to a Nightingale." In all these examples the rhythmically sinuous effect of the Latinisms resonates with the imagery of undulance, either where the collocation is explicit, or where it is implied, as in Cowper's walks and paths, which suggest themselves as not just shady and secluded, but either winding in themselves or inviting of a sauntering casualness in the walker's tread. Likewise, the rhythmic suggestiveness of Keats's "verdurous" (try substituting "leafy") suffuses his "glooms" as well as his "winding ways."

These ruminations perhaps have some bearing on the question of how *Paradise Lost* might be taught in the future, if it will be so at all. Forty-five years ago, Jean Hagstrum argued at the conclusion of *The Sister Arts* that knowledge of the visual context of poets like Milton was as necessary for students as that of "philosophical and purely literary relationships."[49] In a present-day world where the visual is displacing the literary in its more demanding forms, and in which it is thus even harder than when Hagstrum wrote to kindle substantive undergraduate interest in poetry like Milton's, a renewed pedagogic emphasis on the interdependence of the literary and visual arts, a reaffirmation of their lapsed sisterhood, would seem highly desirable. The popularity of Philip Pullman's *Dark Materials* trilogy has re-awakened curiosity in *Paradise Lost* as an idea, but to develop this into an enjoyment of the poetry itself will involve re-creating in newer readers that ability to enjoy verbal rhythm and sonority on which, in the past, taste for the grand style has so fulsomely relied. A good approach to this might be to begin to cultivate that awareness of stylistic analogy of the kind that at least some earlier readers of *Paradise Lost* probably took with them when they went forth into their gardens.

Ormond College, University of Melbourne.

NOTES

1. My chief point of reference here is Murray Roston's *Milton and the Baroque* (London, 1980); earlier contributions are Roy Daniells, *Milton, Mannerism and Baroque* (Toronto, 1963), and Margaret Bottrall, "The Baroque Element in Milton," in *English Miscellany*, ed. M. Praz (Rome, 1950). Stanley Koehler also makes significant use of the idea of the baroque in his "Milton and the Art of Landscape," in *Milton Studies* 8, ed. James D. Simmonds (Pittsburgh, 1975), 3–40, but while he uses this to describe the landscape features in Milton's Eden, he does not consider it in relation to the style of *Paradise Lost*. Roland M. Frye's comprehensive work on Milton and the visual arts, *Milton's Imagery and the Visual Arts* (Princeton, N.J., 1978), contains a number of pertinent observations on specifically baroque parallels to aspects of *Paradise Lost*.

2. See, for instance, Horace Walpole, *The History of the Modern Taste in Gardening* (1782; reprint, New York, 1995); John Dixon Hunt, "Milton and the Making of the English Landscape Garden," in *Milton Studies* 15, ed. James D. Simmonds (Pittsburgh, 1981), 81–105. See also Koehler, "Milton and Landscape," and Charlotte F. Otten, "My Native Element: Milton's Paradise and English Gardens," in *Milton Studies* 5, ed. James D. Simmonds (Pittsburgh, 1973), 249–67.

3. For the rise of this dual literacy in England, see Norman K. Farmer, *Poets and the Visual Arts in Renaissance England* (Austin, Tex., 1984). For its development, see Jean Hagstrum, *The Sister Arts* (Chicago, 1958).

4. See J. W. Good, *Studies in the Milton Tradition* (1915; reprint, New York, 1967), 147, 163; also 160–65, 230–35 for a survey of the continuing late seventeenth- and eighteenth-century debate on the relative merits of rhyme and blank verse, focusing on Milton.

5. Joseph Addison, *The Spectator* 285 (January 26, 1712); Thomas Gray, "Observations on English Metre," in *The Works of Thomas Gray in Prose and Verse*, ed. Edmund Gosse (London,

1884), 1:532–33; Oliver Goldsmith, "The Poetical Scale (1758), cited in Good, *Milton Tradition,* 195 n. 105; William Hazlitt, *Lectures on the English Poets,* 8th ed. (1818; London, 1939), 61–63; see Christopher Ricks, "A Note on Rhythm and Music," *Milton's Grand Style* (Oxford, 1963), 24–26. For several recent analyses of the overlapping issue of the expressiveness of blank-verse lineation in *Paradise Lost,* see Richard Bradford, " 'Verse Only to the Eye': Line Endings in *Paradise Lost,*" *Essays in Criticism,* 33 (1983): 187–204, and Archie Burnett, " 'Sense Variously Drawn Out': The Line in *Paradise Lost,*" *Literary Imagination* 5 (Winter 2003): 69–92.

6. Addison, *The Spectator* 285 (January 26, 1712), cited from *The Spectator* 165, 4 vols. (London, 1945), 4:351.

7. I. A. Richards, *The Principles of Literary Criticism* (London, 1926), chap. 17.

8. Addison, *Spectator* 285 (January 26, 1712).

9. Roston, *Milton and Baroque,* 151, 161. For Wölfflin's discussion of baroque art as reversing the "tectonic" clarity of Renaissance classicism, see his *Renaissance and Baroque,* trans. Peter Murray (London, 1961), part 1, chap. 4, especially the comparison of Michelangelo's Sistine chapel ceiling with Annibale Carracci's ceiling of the Galleria Farnese. See also his *Principles of Art History,* trans. M. D. Hottinger (New York, 1932), chap. 3.

10. For Roston's argument that these figures were important intellectual sources of the baroque, see *Milton and Baroque,* chap. 1, esp. 35–40.

11. For a recent account of what is known about what Milton saw on his Italian journey, see Barbara K. Lewalski, *The Life of John Milton* (Malden, Mass., 2000), chap. 4. For Milton's two stays in Rome, see 94–96 and 99–102. See also Roland Frye, *Milton's Imagery and the Visual Arts* (Princeton, N.J., 1978), 23–31.

12. Roston, *Milton and Baroque,* 47–49, emphasises Milton's experience of baroque architecture and the Cortona ceiling, but others have also argued for a complementary knowledge of the oil paintings of the period, for example, B. Sprague Allen, *Tides in English Taste, 1619–1800,* 2 vols. (1937; reprint, New York, 1958), 2:120; Hannah Demaray, "Milton's 'Perfect' Paradise and the Landscapes of Italy," *MQ* 8, no. 2 (1974): 33–41. With reference to Milton's visit to the Palazzo Barberini, where the Cortona ceiling had recently been completed, see Lewalski, *Life of Milton,* 99–100; Mindele Anne Treip, " 'Celestial Patronage': Allegorical Ceiling Cycles of the 1630s and the Iconography of Milton's Muse," in *Milton in Italy,* ed. Mario A. Di Cesare (New York, 1991), 237–80, esp. 268–73; and Otten, "My Native Element," 258.

13. Daniells, *Milton, Mannerism, Baroque,* 62–63, 166. For the formulation of "the baroque" that Daniells draws on at these points, see J. R. Martin, "The Baroque from the Viewpoint of the Art Historian," *Journal of Aesthetics and Art Criticism* 14, no. 2 (1954): 164–71. Roston, *Milton and the Baroque,* 167–75; Diane McColley, *A Gust for Paradise: Milton's Eden and the Visual Arts* (Urbana, 1993).

14. Jeremy Taylor, *English Poetry: The English Poetry Full-Text Database* (Cambridge, 1992–1995); available at http://collections.chadwyck.co.uk, lists it as the only poetic usage during the seventeenth century.

15. Ibid.

16. See *Poetry Full-Text Database* for the decline in the modest popularity of this word after the seventeenth century.

17. Wölfflin, *Renaissance and Baroque,* 47.

18. Ibid., 55–56.

19. See Hagstrum, *The Sister Arts,* 126; for a summary of views of Milton as musical rather than visual, see Hagstrum, 123–24; see also T. S. Eliot, "Milton" (1947), reprinted in T. S. Eliot, *Selected Essays* (London, 1951).

20. Hazlitt, "On Shakespeare and Milton," *Lectures on the English Poets,* 59–60.

21. Walpole, *The History of Modern Taste,* 29, 31.

22. For Addison's comment, see *The Spectator,* 5 vols., ed. D. F. Bond (Oxford, 1965), 3:564. Frye, *Milton's Imagery,* chap. 13; Hunt, "Milton and the English Garden"; Koehler, "Milton and Landscape"; Otten, "My Native Element." The idea of Milton as source is also qualified by cases made for the influence upon him of landscape painting; see, for example, Allen, *Tides in Taste,* 2: 117–20, and Demaray, "Milton's 'Perfect' Paradise," 133–41.

23. See John Dixon Hunt, "Gard'ning Can Speak Proper English," in *Culture and Cultivation in Early Modern England: Writing and the Land,* ed. M. Leslie and T. Raylow (Leicester, 1992), 195–222. Stephen Switzer, *Ichnographia rustica,* 3 vols. (1718; reprint, New York, 1982); William Mason, *The English Garden: A Poem* (New York, 1982).

24. John Dixon Hunt and Peter Willis, *The Genius of the Place: The English Landscape Garden, 1620–1820* (1975; reprint, Cambridge, Mass., 1988), 79. See also Hunt, "Milton and the Making of the English Landscape Garden," 85–90.

25. Switzer, *Ichnographia rustica,* 3:6–8.

26. In William Hogarth, *The Analysis of Beauty* (1733) (Oxford, 1955). For an overview of the influences behind the rise of the serpentine line in the eighteenth century, see Allen, *Tides in Taste,* vol. 2, chaps. 16–18. For Switzer's retention of the naturally undulant Henderskelf Lane at Castle Howard, see Tom Turner, *English Garden Design: History and Style since 1650* (Woodbridge, Suffolk, 1986), 86–87. For a detailed case for the influence of "sharawadgi," especially as conveyed to England by an album of engravings of Chinese gardens brought to England by Father Matteo Ripa and coming into the hands of Lord Burlington, see Rudolf Wittkower, "English Neo-Palladianism, the Landscape Garden, China and the Enlightenment," *Palladio and English Palladianism* (London, 1974), chap. 12, esp. 184–87. A critique of this argument and an alternative proposal for the greater influence of Italian theatrical designs, in particular those of Filippo Juvarra on William Kent, has been made out in S. Lang, "The Genesis of the English Landscape Garden," in *The Picturesque Garden and Its Influence Outside the British Isles,* ed. Nikolaus Pevsner (Washington, D.C., 1974), 1–30.

27. Jonathan Richardson, *An Essay on the Theory of Painting* (1725; reprint, Menston, England, 1971), 11–12, 244–45.

28. Hunt and Willis, *Genius of the Place,* 79. Hogarth's fondness for Milton is witnessed, for instance, in Hogarth's "Self-Portrait with Pug" of 1745, which includes both a palette on which is inscribed "the Line of Beauty" and a canvas resting on three volumes: of Shakespeare, Swift, and Milton. For a discussion of this work, see Ronald Paulson, *Hogarth,* 3 vols. (New Brunswick, N.J., 1992), 2:260–64. Quotation from Hogarth, *The Analysis of Beauty,* 160.

29. Switzer, *Ichnographia rustica,* 3:47, 106–7. There are early seventeenth-century uses of "serpentine" without moral connotation, though these are in contexts which make such ambiguity irrelevant; see *Oxford English Dictionary.*

30. Switzer, *Ichnographia rustica,* 3:36, 2–3, 46.

31. See Hagstrum, *The Sister Arts,* 108–12; also Farmer, *Poets and the Visual Arts,* 53–65. Hagstrum demonstrates very convincingly how a familiarity with the forms of neoclassical painting, for example, the habit of allegorical personification, can help us to appreciate not just Milton but what he calls "neo-classical poetry" in general.

32. Demaray, "Milton's 'Perfect' Paradise," 34. For the provenance of Titian's 1531–1535 nude Magdalen, see Harold E. Wethey, *The Paintings of Titian,* 3 vols. (New York, 1969), 1:143–44.

33. On the interrelations of these painters and poets (including also Edmund Waller), see Farmer, *Poets and the Visual Arts,* chap. 5. The comment on Van Dyck comes from Sanderson's *Graphice* (1658), cited in Farmer, 65.

34. On this development, see William Whately, *Observations on Modern Gardening* (1770), in John Dixon Hunt, *Gardens and the Picturesque: Studies in the History of Landscape Architecture* (Cambridge, Mass., 1992), chap. 3.

35. For Italy on this point, see John Dixon Hunt, "Ovid in the Garden," *Garden and Grove: The Italian Renaissance Garden in the English Imagination, 1600–1750* (London, 1986), chap. 4; for eighteenth-century England, see Philip Ayres, *Classical Culture: The Idea of Rome in Eighteenth Century England* (Cambridge, 1997), 142–51.

36. McColley, *A Gust for Paradise*, 12–13

37. Mason, *The English Garden*, 3:507. For contemporary evangelical dismissal of classical statuary in gardens, see Wesley's hostile reaction in 1776 to Flitcroft's Pantheon at Stourhead, cited in Ayres, *Classical Culture*, 142.

38. Cited in Good, *Milton Tradition*, 270.

39. Switzer, *Ichnographia rustica*, 3:iii.

40. Walpole, *The History of Modern Taste*, 29–31.

41. On Virgil at Stourhead, see David Watkin, *The English Vision: The Picturesque in Architecture, Landscape and Garden Design* (London, 1982), 28–29; on Ovid at the Villa d'Este, see Hunt, *Garden and Grove*, chap. 4.

42. See, for example, Batty Langley, *New Principles of Gardening*, cited in Hunt and Willis, *Genius of the Place*, 181; Switzer, *Ichnographia Rustica*, 3:47.

43. For a thorough discussion of the extant traditions for pictorial representation of Eve in Milton's time, see Frye, *Milton's Imagery*, 272–80; on Eve's hair in particular, see 272–74. Frye does not consider the question of which of these representations Milton had seen personally, however. He also does not consider the possibility of a Venus as source for this detail, though he does treat the Venus-Eve connection in more general terms (276–77.)

44. Switzer, *Ichnographia rustica*, 3:107.

45. According to the *Poetry Full-Text Database,* Milton's use of "irriguous" in Book Four of *Paradise Lost* was the only time the word was used in seventeenth-century poetry. In the following century, however, it was used fifty-seven times, the number dwindling to seven in the nineteenth century. For prose usage, see, for instance, Walpole's *The History of Modern Taste,* 21, and Arthur Young, *A Six Months' Tour thro' the North of England,* 2nd ed., 4 vols. (London, 1771); see lengthy extracts reprinted from vols. 1–3 in *The English Garden: Literary Sources and Documents,* 3 vols., ed. Michael Charlesworth (East Sussex, 1993), 2:249–85. "Irriguous" occurs on 258, 264, 276, and 284.

46. Mason, preface to *The English Garden,* vii–viii, from 1982 reprint of the poem.

47. Mason, *The English Garden,* 2:252–56.

48. Hunt, "Milton and the Making of the English Landscape Garden," 90; also, Hunt and Willis, *Genius of the Place,* 308, and in Hunt's preface to the 1982 Garland reprint of the poem. See also the offhand reference to "the very indifferent poet William Mason" in F. R. Cowell, *The Garden as a Fine Art* (Boston, 1978), 184. On poems of Mason's other than *The English Garden,* see Richard Terry, "Gray and Poetic Diction," in *Thomas Gray: Contemporary Essays,* ed. W. B. Hutchings and William Ruddick (Liverpool, 1993), 73–111, esp. 96–103.

49. Hagstrum, *The Sister Arts,* 318.

"A NICE AND PHILOSOPHICAL ACCOUNT OF THE ORIGIN OF ALL THINGS": ACCOMMODATION IN BURNET'S *SACRED THEORY* (1681) AND *PARADISE LOST*

Kevin Killeen

MILTON IMPLIES THROUGHOUT *Paradise Lost* that his monist philosophy is merely extrapolated from Scripture and that it arises logically from the biblical text as an explanatory philosophical device, to account for Creation and the Fall. This has widely been treated as an exegetical absurdity, a licentious if not preposterous overreading of the Scriptures. In what sense did Milton, a writer who repeatedly accounts himself a literal reader of Scripture and who cites the biblical injunction not to add to the Word, imagine that his monist philosophy arose from the Bible?[1] One response is to discard Milton's claims to literal interpretation of the Bible in relation to *Paradise Lost*. Such a solution, however, is surely at odds with Milton's stringent attention to biblical hermeneutics. A more plausible response is what Peter Harrison calls late-seventeenth-century "modifications of the literal," chief among which was the use of biblical accommodation.[2] Accommodation became an important means by which extensive scientific-philosophical schemes might be superimposed upon Scripture. The "elasticity" in readings of the Bible that consider themselves literal, but which seem to us nothing of the sort, was by no means confined to Milton. The importance of accommodation (and its increasing complexity) as a tool for harmonizing biblical thought with natural philosophy is evident in a range of thinkers, from John Wilkins to Boyle to Joseph Glanvill, all of whom invoke the theory of biblical accommodation within their natural philosophy.[3] This essay presents a near-contemporaneous parallel to Milton's practice, Thomas Burnet's *Sacred Theory of the Earth* (1681), a "scientific" account of the Creation and deluge that was both influential and contentious, precipitating a flood of replies and extensive correspondence. The responses to Burnet engage *The Sacred Theory* on two levels, debating both its exegetical method and its natural philosophy. William Whiston's *New Theory of the Earth*, for example, opens with a lengthy discussion of biblical hermeneutics before dealing with the "science" of the text, while Burnet's communication with Isaac Newton on the subject (1681) addresses in depth the degree to which Moses "compressed" the truth. These debates share with *Paradise Lost* a concern with the nature of accommodated truth in the Bible. They ask how far the biblical writers simplified and compromised their explanations for an Israelite audience considered unable to comprehend the true complexity of Creation.

While Milton's monism has aroused frequent incredulity, his theory of and use of accommodation (insofar as it relates to the presentation of heaven and God's speech) has been treated as relatively uncontentious. This essay argues that the scope of accommodation theory underwent a major and contentious change in the period, a change that is evident in both *Paradise Lost* and the "sacred earth" controversy. Linking Milton and Burnet, writing fourteen years apart, goes against a long-standing tendency to see Milton enmeshed in old science and unsophisticated philosophy. The scientific-philosophical currency and acumen of his monist argument is not, however, my point. Rather, this essay addresses issues of contemporaneous exegesis in the latter half of the century, and how it created the hermeneutic possibility of incorporating science and philosophy into one's scriptural interpretation. In this respect, Milton's practice accords with natural philosophers and theologians, from Boyle to Burnet, who, uniquely in this late-seventeenth-century era, saw the Scriptures as compatible with their science. Accommodation, whose traditional function was to explain biblical rhetoric, became the exegetical tool that allowed emerging scientific and philosophical ideas to meld with Scripture.[4]

The disquiet over Milton's monist philosophy (in terms of both its role as embellishment for a scriptural epic and its internal coherence) is long-standing. Samuel Johnson comments, in a magisterial manner, that Milton "has unhappily perplexed his poetry with his philosophy." Milton commits, for many commentators, both a theological and poetic impropriety in having Raphael discuss theories of matter (not to mention theories of lunch) during a mission to forewarn Adam and Eve of the impending Fall.[5] *Paradise Lost* presents the Fall not only in its moral valences—of obedience, temptation, and will—but also in terms of the physical mechanisms that constitute the shift from a state of grace to the state of fallenness. This is, for some, a poetic and theological idiosyncrasy too far. The very substance of Adam and Eve thickens as an organic consequence of their actions, leaving them too "gross" for paradise, and they are ejected from Eden in an emetic as much as a judicial sense: "Eject him tainted now, and purge him off / As a distemper."[6] This curiously physical account of the expulsion has been described by Stephen Fallon as Eden's "ontological immune system." Fallon's *Milton Among the Philosophers* is perhaps the most cogent demonstration of the radical consistency of Milton's philosophy of matter. Monism, he shows, underlies a range of action in *Paradise Lost,* from the devils' fallenness to the animate substance out of which Adam and Eve are composed, from the sexuality of angels, to the battle strategies of the war in heaven.[7] Demonstrating how ubiquitous the monism is, however, does not so much solve the problem of Milton's theological decorum as make it more pressing. The monist ideas of *Paradise Lost* are not merely extraneous, nor are they confined to Raphael's credal statement of the philosophy, on the "one first matter" of the universe (*PL* 5.469–505). Raphael's notion of a single-substance cosmos is superimposed upon the story of the Creation and the Fall in rigorous detail. *Paradise Lost* does not propose merely that its scientific-philosophical scheme is "godly" or that it demonstrates God's providential action. Rather, it presents a correlation of scriptural text and the natural world, to discover what latent truths might be contained within the biblical narratives.

Gerald Reedy argues that a fundamental shift occurred in the cultural and religious thought in the latter half of the seventeenth century. Theological scholarship became preoccupied with the scope of the biblical truthdomain, its jurisdiction outside the realms of doctrine and church government. Where the civil war era was concerned with questions of grace and election, or of the sacraments and the liturgy, for example, Reedy suggests that a new set of priorities appeared, attempting to discern in what manner Scripture was true:

By what analogy do we compare the truth of Scripture to the truth of other objects of mind and sense? Is it true as something we can see or feel? As true as the predictable sum of the angles of a triangle or the ratio of the circumference to the diameter of a circle? Is it true because we believe its authors or because something inherent in it compels assent? . . . What about it is true? Its history, its doctrine, its prophecy, its miracles?[8]

The attempts by Milton and Burnet to incorporate complex philosophical and scientific schemes into their understanding of the Bible participate in this endeavor to explain the nature of scriptural truth. Such a scriptural focus is resolutely not characterized by the kind of textual insularity of later or modern-day scriptural literalism. As Georgia Christopher puts it, "Whatever the claims of nineteenth-century fundamentalists, God's word in the first two centuries after the Reformation was *not* equated with the lexical surface of the Bible, nor with the exact wording of any particular passage."[9] Biblical interpretation in the late seventeenth century exhibits a surprising receptivity to seemingly extraneous matter. This receptivity is facilitated, in part at least, by the changing role of accommodation, which becomes the exegetical tool through which ancillary truths discovered elsewhere—in the natural world, in the realms of reason and philosophical thought—could be fused with the stuff of Scripture.

The importance of Milton's hermeneutics has been increasingly recognized in recent years, in particular the link between his hermeneutic strategies and the natural world of the garden. Karen Edwards, for example, notes in *Milton and the Natural World,* the importance of "Bible-reading practices" to the discovery of a "richly indeterminate" natural world, "its openness to constant rereading and reviewing."[10] Diane McColley reads the command to root out Satan from the garden, and resize him—"search through this garden, leave unsearcht no nook" (*PL* 4.789)—as a call for proliferation in interpretation, as an injunction to close reading.[11] Dayton Haskin investigates the landscape of Eden as a site of concealment as much as revelation, of such profusion that it continually resists interpretation.[12] Milton's biblical interpretative practices are relevant not only in assessing the complex, suggestive landscape and the natural world of the epic, but also in any discussion of the science and philosophy of *Paradise Lost*. To this end, a deeper understanding of the changing role of accommodation in the era is an important element.

POURING THE OCEAN INTO A NUTSHELL:
THEOLOGICAL ACCOMMODATION

Accommodation did not traditionally have such a grand facilitating role, to integrate physical, metaphysical, and theological truths. Accommodation at core is the mode by which God communicates aspects of himself, bridging the gap between limited human capacity and the conceptual vastness of the deity—it negotiates the knotty problem that a central attribute of the divine is his unknowability.[13] Alongside this difficulty is a correlate sense of human cognitive deficiency. John Wollebius, for example, in his *Abridgement of Christian Divinity* (1650), explaining how "God's essence is by us incomprehensible," uses the perhaps inaccurate but nevertheless beautiful image, "For there is no proportion between finite and infinite, no more then between a nut-shell and the Ocean."[14] Accommodation is the cognitive leap that bridges the gap, that construes aspects of infinity for our comprehension, that pours the ocean into the nutshell, so to speak. Walter Charleton (1652) similarly invokes the nature and scale of the ocean as an apposite analogy for the inconceivability of God. He compares the immense disproportion to trying to conceive of a "chiliagon," a thousand-sided figure that, though finite, exceeds all efforts at visualization. Likewise, in the impossibility of imagining the entire ocean, we begin to recognize the scale of the conceptual problem, the absurdity, of "thinking" God. He notes, however, that we may justly claim to have seen the sea, though we only see a portion of it.[15] Accommodation theorizes the nature of this portion. It is the measure of the Scriptures' capacity for enabling us to conceive of God.

Central to this debate is the epistemological status of scriptural language. Accommodation works in two directions: first, the Scriptures contain a divine "condescension" of his unknowable form—a writing down to human deficiency—and second, in some accounts at least, including Milton's, there is an attendant human ennobling in the work of "translating" these images.[16] The first of these generally takes precedence: repeatedly, the analogy of speech to a child is used. Calvin's *Institutes* (1536) provides a definitive statement of the reformation attitude, that as a principle of exegesis, we must take scriptural corporeal descriptions as fitted to the wits of children:

For what man, yea though he be slenderly witted, doth not understand that God doth so with us speake as it were childishly, as nurses doe with their babes. Therefore such maner of speeches doe not so plainly express what God is, as they doe apply the understanding of him to our slender capacitie. Which to doe, it behooved of necessitie that he descended a great way beneath his owne height.[17]

Calvin's statement does not unequivocally address, however, the question of *who* these children are, whether it is humanity as a whole that needs these sops to our diluted intelligence, or whether the need for childish speech applied merely to the biblical Israelites.[18] This distinction was to become extremely important to annotators of the seventeenth century. The notion of the "vulgar Israelites" accounted for both the "rude" style of the Bible and its perceived lack of philosophical subtlety. Alexander Ross (1626), for example, wonders, "Why doth not Moses speak distinctly of the creation of angels? Because hee did accommodate himself to the rude capacitie of the Jews."[19] At the same time, the philosophical "gaps" in the text opened up an important terrain, a potential to explore what Moses *would* have said, had his audience consisted, presumably, of early modern scientist-philosophers.[20] Accommodation became the provision by which the scientific lacunae of the Bible are available for re-inscription, for imagining the subtleties that Moses was obliged to leave out.

The imprecision of biblical imagery, its use of anthropomorphism, for example, had in addition a more serious theological consequence. It was also liable to lead to idolatry, that most pernicious and slippery of crimes in the panoply of postreformation ungodliness. Richard Stock (1641), a Puritan preacher familiar at Allhallows, Milton's local childhood church, urges his readers not to be seduced by the Bible's anthropomorphisms, nor even to allow a mental image of God: "We say God hath eies, becaue he is wholly an eie and sees everything . . . this reproves any representation of God, in any Images, whither internall, in the mind, by thoughts, or externall by Pictures."[21] This terror at the potential idolatry in reading Scripture's corporeal metaphors for God elicited an almost obsessive caveat in writers of the period, who were anxious to avoid idolatrous connotations to their exegeses. Such caveats have been usefully compared to postmodern notions of "metafiction," which is continually at pains to point out its own constructedness and artificial nature. Discourse on accommodation is likewise adamant on its own fictive status and compulsively points to the unreality of the biblical metaphors by which God is represented.[22]

Milton insists, however, in a manner quite singular in the literature of accommodation, that the scriptural presentation of God does not require the intricate apologetics that often attend the depiction of a bodily God (YP 6:131–35). Furthermore, the scriptural imagery is not tainted by, nor dependent on, the particular ineptitude of the biblical Israelites. Milton conceives of the biblical images of God as perfectly poised, epistemologically speaking. They are, he tells us in *De Doctrina Christiana*, simply and singularly, right:

It is safest for us to form an image of God in our minds which corresponds to his representation and description of himself in the sacred writings. Admittedly, God is always described or outlined not as he really is but in such a way as will make him conceivable to us. Nevertheless, we ought to form just such a mental image of him as he, in bringing himself within the limits of our understanding, wishes us to form. Indeed he has brought himself down to our level expressly to prevent our being carried beyond the reach of human comprehension and outside the written authority of scripture, into vague subtleties of speculation. (YP 6:133–34)

Biblical images are, for Milton, right, though not complete. They are consummately devised to convey as full a notion of God as humans are able to understand and, moreover, the images contain a kind of epistemological elasticity, adjusted to the intellect of the reader. Milton rejects any idea of "translating" the terms used in the Bible, of trying to ascertain the real meaning behind the metaphor. Any attempt to penetrate the reality of the image is essentially a human production, or "subtle" speculation, and Milton comments, "however you try to tone down these and similar texts about God by an elaborate show of interpretative glosses, it comes to the same thing in the end" (YP 6:135). For Milton, God has consummately epitomized (rather than compromised) himself in his biblical depiction: "We may be certain that God's majesty and glory were so dear to him that he could never say anything about himself which was lower or meaner than his real nature, nor would he ever ascribe to himself any property if he did not wish us to ascribe it to him" (YP 6:136). Moreover, the Scriptures, being so apposite to human capacity, are effectively "authorized" for thinking with. He continues: "Let there be no question about it: they understand best what God is like who adjust their understanding to the word of God, for he has adjusted his word to our understanding, and has shown what kind of an idea of him he wishes us to have. . . . Why does our imagination shy away from a notion of God which he himself does not hesitate to promulgate in unambiguous terms" (YP 6:136). As various critics have noted, Milton's approach is relentlessly loyal to the integrity of the biblical text. William Kolbrenner states that, "In Milton's hermeneutic, there is the insistence that the imagination stay anchored in the text and refuse passage into some allegorical beyond," while William Kerrigan summarizes the approach as "an unusually positive theory of the truth-value of the biblical metaphors for God."[23] God has, it might be said, already done the work necessary to fine-tune the text to our understanding. In the tradition of accommodation, there is always an implicit or explicit onus upon the reader to "decode" the Scriptures, to disinter the metaphor (the "hand" or "anger" of God, for example) from its referent. This process, however, is intrinsically doomed to failure because a second implicit stipulation is that the referent (God) remain fundamentally unknowable. Thus, the use of accommodation, which is often treated as an uncontentious and relatively simple concept, is beset by a conceptual impasse; God's depiction in human terms does not invite, but rather forbids, the application of rhetorical method to the unbridgeable lacuna between human perception and reality.[24] God, Milton tells us, "has brought himself down to our level expressly to *prevent* our being carried beyond the reach of human comprehension and outside the written authority of Scripture, into vague subtleties of speculation" (YP 6:133–34; my italics). Neil Graves summarizes Milton's position usefully, that the biblical image is not "linguistic shorthand for complex metaphysical theories of God's subsistence." Milton halts at the hermeneutic leap from metaphor to referent, insisting instead that the "accommodated image should be the locus of our attention." It is *sufficient* because it constitutes "a divinely sanctioned experience of God."[25] There is, of course, an additional problem in relating Milton's theory of accommodation to *Paradise Lost*. The perception of impropriety in the epic is largely based on Milton's presuming to write an extrabiblical account of God. Scriptural accommodation is, intrinsically, a special case, the divinely proportioned accommodations of holy writ, but it is not usually seen as an authorization to expand and extrapolate on the Bible.[26] Milton's inclusion of an elaborate ontology, grafted on to his retelling of the Fall, is not generally considered within his theory of accommodation. However, the monism of *Paradise Lost* can usefully be viewed in relation to contemporaries' efforts to link their natural philosophy to the accommodated reality of the Bible.

"A NICE AND PHILOSOPHICAL ACCOUNT OF THE ORIGIN OF ALL THINGS":
SCIENCE AND ACCOMMODATION

The function of accommodation changed radically in the late seventeenth century. No longer did it work merely to explicate biblical tropes. Rather, accommodation came to inscribe the explanatory spaces between events, to fill in the gaps, and provide the relation—philosophical, scientific, or historical—among biblical events. In this respect, Milton's inclusion of an elaborate monist philosophy tracing the mechanics of creation is comparable with the set of scientific texts responding to Thomas Burnet's *Telluris theoria sacra* (1681). The collection of geological theories that constitute the sacred earth controversy might seem at first sight unpromising analogues for *Paradise Lost*. The point of comparison, however, is not the fascinating details of their theories, but their methodological similarities. It is not a claim for Milton's affinity with Burnet in natural philosophy; rather, it describes a distinct and short period in the history of hermeneutics, prior to the emergence of the historical critical method, which sought to determine the nature of biblical truth and its relation to scientific or philosophical truth. I cited earlier Gerard Reedy's claim that doctrinal disputes in the post–civil war period become secondary to debates over the nature of biblical truth and the type of exegetical method best suited to discerning the forms of scriptural truth. Like Milton, the sacred earth theorists construct a comprehensive philosophical-scientific scheme upon a biblical narrative of Genesis, placing exegetical questions on a par with philosophical puzzles. The central exegetical dilemma was the manner in which Moses had "compressed," or accommodated, scientific truth in the Pentateuch.[27] In itself, this was not a new exegetical question; what was novel was the scale and complexity of the scientific theories hoisted upon the Scriptures, the idea that the Bible contained the suppressed mechanics of Creation underneath its textual surface. The exegetical dilemma was whether scientific clues were substantially present in the Scriptures, or whether the text functioned by its receptive capacity, that "true" theories would be demonstrable not only from their internal plausibility but also by showing how the theory was in harmony with the biblical narratives.[28]

Thomas Burnet (1635–1715) was a pupil of John Tillotson, and had become master of Charterhouse when he published his account of the deluge.[29] His *Sacred Theory of the Earth* presents a detailed model of geological history, developing his ideas on the Earth's geomorphology from the Creation "data" in Genesis, Psalms, Job, Isaiah, and the New Testament.[30] He argues that the prelapsarian landscape emerging from its liquid chaos was a pristine smooth globe, "as the shell of an Egg is of the like form with the surface of the liquor it lies upon." This was a time when the Earth "had the beauty of Youth and blooming Nature, fresh and fruitful, and not a wrinkle, scar or fracture in all its body; no Rocks nor Mountains, no hollow Caves, nor gaping Chanels, but even and uniform all over."[31] Burnet goes on, however, to contrast this virgin landscape, somewhat ruefully, with the present-day Earth:

> We must therefore be impartial where the Truth requires it, and describe the Earth as it is really in it self; and though it be handsome and regular enough to the eye in certain parts of it, single tracts and single Regions; yet if we consider the whole surface of it, or the whole Exterior Region, 'tis as a broken and confus'd heap of bodies, plac'd in no order to one another, nor with any correspondency or regularity of parts . . . a World lying in its rubbish.[32]

For all the wistful aesthetic of this passage, *The Sacred Theory of the Earth* is most remarkable for the scientific vigor with which it pursues its argument. Roger North (1651–1734), for example, describes the work as "meer Cartesian."[33] Burnet bases his idea of the egg-smooth globe on careful calculations of the volume of water needed to cover the Earth, and he proposes that the deluge could only be total—and the scriptural account therefore be true—if the world had been level in this fashion; a mountainous surface would entail an impossibly high waterline. Furthermore, he calculates that the volume of water necessary to cover the face of even a smooth, globular Earth could not have come from precipitation, from circulating rainwater. Thus, taking his cue from Genesis 7:1, Burnet argues that the Earth must have been ripped open to release its internal waters: "Moses directs us to no other for the causes of the deluge. The fountains (he saith) of the *great Abysse* were broken up or burst asunder," and Burnet points further to biblical clues that the ante- and postdiluvian landscapes of the Earth differed (2 Pet. 3:5–7). He concludes that the water must have been contained within the Earth. The entire terrestrial landscape as we know it is attributable to the ruinous effects of this water from the depths, which flowed back into the gaps following the flood.[34]

Burnet's theory, while it is premised on biblical creation narratives, hardly strikes a modern reader as scripturally based, any more than it resonates as a model of proper scientific procedure. He seems, one would think, to be making it up, fancifully speculating. Indeed, many of the early responses accuse him of just such invention. However, the grounds on which we might deem it incoherent—its incongruous medley of Scripture and crude scientific speculation—are fundamentally different from Burnet's contemporary critics. The appearance of *The Sacred Theory of the Earth*, translated at the behest of Charles II, prompted a flow of detailed scientific responses and counterarguments.[35] These replies work, almost without exception, on dual levels; they propose alternative models for the geological history of the Earth while simultaneously debating the nature of Burnet's exegetical procedure. It was not the speculative nature of his theory, in itself, that was objectionable. Nor was it the application of the principles of Cartesian philosophy to the biblical scenes of Creation. Both of these were widely deemed licit; at least the replies utilized similar "scientific" criteria. Rather, the objections centered on perceived faults in his exegesis, and in particular his ideas on accommodation and Burnet's working presumption that Moses had nothing but disdain for his Israelite audience.

William Whiston's *New Theory of the Earth* (1696) devotes a ninety-five-page introduction to biblical interpretation, "to discourse of the nature of that Sacred History, the Stile in which it is Writ, and how far it is to be Extended." This lengthy discussion of accommodation signals its importance to the scientific thought involved in the controversy. Whiston's core objection to *The Sacred Theory of the Earth* is exegetical, that "The Mosaick Creation is not a Nice and Philosophical account of the Origin of All Things; but an Historical and True Representation of the formation of our single Earth out of a confused Chaos, and of the successive and visible changes therof each day, till it became the habitation of Mankind."[36] For Whiston, Burnet both fails to take the "historical" aspect of Genesis seriously enough and expects too detailed a "philosophical account." This is not, however, an objection in principle to the use of natural philosophy to explain the mechanisms of the Creation and flood. On the contrary, Whiston proposes in its place a model of comet disturbance that, he argues, does less damage to the Genesis narrative. Similarly, John Woodward in *An Essay towards a Natural History of the Earth* (1695) introduces fossil evidence as a problematic that Burnet had failed to consider.[37] The range of and nature of these counterconjectures suggest that, in theory, the application of mechanical hypotheses to Scripture was held to be proper, but that in practice Burnet had failed to produce a plausible fusion. His primary fault for Whiston is imagining that Moses had nothing but scorn for his audience. Burnet's *Archælogiæ philosophicæ,* the second part of the sacred theory, is particularly blunt, arguing that Genesis is "only spoken popularly, to comply with the dull Israelites, lately slavish Brickmakers and smelling strong of the Garlick and Onions of *Egypt.* To humour these ignorant Blockheads that were newly broke loose from the Egyptian Taskmasters, and had no Sense nor Reason in their thick Sculls, *Moses* talks after this rate; but not a Syllable of Truth is in all that he saith."[38] This passage is quoted and translated from its Latin by John Edwards and is, Peter Harrison notes, far "less delicate" than Burnet's own English version, in the second part of his *Sacred Theory of the Earth.*[39] Edwards is one of Burnet's least "scientific" respondents, objecting on theological grounds and altogether unhappy that Burnet's theory gives ammunition to atheists; he has "abundantly gratified the whole Tribe of Atheists and Deists . . . more pleasing to them than Mr. Hobbs."[40] I earlier drew a distinction between epistemological accommodation (based on human limitations) and social accommodation (based on the "childish" first audience of Scripture). Burnet is an extreme example of the latter. The marvelously irate Burnet displays an intense irritation with the "vulgar Israelites," because of whose limitations Moses had chosen to deliver a mere sketch of Creation, depriving the more sophisticated scientific minds of posterity of all the philosophical information he might have delivered.

Burnet's credentials as a serious scientific thinker are lent support by his detailed correspondence with Isaac Newton on the issue. Again, where they disagree, the issue is not that Newton objects to the conjunction of Scripture and science. On the contrary, both accept implicitly the rightness of testing a scientific theory upon the Bible, and they engage in a detailed assessment of Burnet's ideas in terms of both Cartesian mechanics and biblical interpretation. Newton posits a Cartesian-based vortex theory, that the speed of the spinning Earth might centrifugally "conglobe" the waters away from the poles, toward a central equatorial band, thus needing a lesser volume of water to accomplish the covering of the Earth to the letter of Genesis.[41] But of equal importance is their dispute on the use of accommodation. It is noteworthy that Newton's disagreement does not rest on what might seem to us a primary objection to the egg theory—the simple fact that it is absent from the Bible. There seems to be an assumption of "workable" space in the Bible, in which it is safe to theorize, and it is likewise presumed that the absence of a full and ornate theory from Genesis is explicable simply in terms of Moses' choosing to accommodate his explanations. Burnet claims that Moses wrote of his *own* postdeluge Earth, rather than its primeval egg-smooth form, simply in order not to confuse his audience:

wherof if Moses had given ye Theory it would have been a thing altogether inaccommodate to ye people & a useless distracting amusemt [*sic*] and therefore instead of it hee gives a short idea & draught of a Terraqueous Earth riseing from a Chaos, not according to ye order of Nature & natural causes, but in yt order wch was most conceivable to ye people, & wherin they could easily imagine an Omnipotent power might forme it, wth respect to ye conveniency of man & animals: Beginning first wth wt was most necessary, & proceeding by steps in ye same order to prepare an habitable world, furnisht wth every thing proper first for animals, & then for man ye Master of all.[42]

The scientific explanation is absent from Scripture, then, because it would be a "distracting amusement" for its audience, who require a simpler intellectual fare. Far from opposing Burnet's ideas on accommodation, Newton's response is in broad agreement that Moses wrote down to the vulgar, though Newton suspects that true philosophical knowledge remains encoded in the Scriptures for those who know how to seek it: "As to Moses I do not think his description of ye creation either Philosophical or feigned, but that he described realities in a language artificially adapted to ye sense of ye vulgar."[43] Moses' descriptions correspond, for Newton, with the "apparent" rather than real nature of things, although he insists that from the terrestrial perspective, the account must have been perceptually true. There can be no sense of Moses having simply muddied the truth. Thus, the sun and moon may not have been physically created on the fourth day, but the description might represent a truth that "the air then first became clear enough for them to shine through it and so put on ye appearance of lights in ye firmament to enlighten the earth."[44] Newton's account of accommodated knowledge denies that the Bible constitutes a regrettable lowest common denominator, and he refutes that idea that the subtlety of scientific thought that Moses chose to hold back from the unfit Israelites was information that would have been readily comprehensible to the more subtle minds of the post-Baconian world. Burnet is part of a wide heritage of disdain for the capacities of the biblical Jews. In contrast, Newton, though he admits the Scriptures are "observer-centred," belongs to a tradition focusing on the encoded nature of the Bible, in which its accommodation consists of multilayered knowledge, for both the vulgar lay reader and the adept.

Milton might seem some distance from the philosophical controversy ignited by Thomas Burnet. Their writings differ in most respects. However, insofar as their philosophical speculation is a product of their exegetical thought, there are important similarities between them. The participants in the discussion over *The Sacred Theory of the Earth* work on the common presumption that the nature of the physical world can in part be determined by establishing the interstices among biblical truths. They aim to ascertain the spaces elided in the Mosaic account, within which one may theorize. This corresponds in many ways with Milton's procedure in schematizing his monist ontology onto a biblical "space," in his retelling of Genesis. The extensive presence of monism in *Paradise Lost,* traced by Fallon and others, will not be replicated here. Its importance can be traced in the depiction of hell, in the fallen angels who "harden more" as they rebel—both physically and spiritually—and in the physical alterations to Adam and Eve by which their material nature becomes incommensurable with the purity of Eden. Most famously, monism is explicated in Raphael's creedal statement of the matter, explaining the idea of "one first matter all, / Indued with various forms, various degrees / Of substance, and in things that live, of life" (5.472–74). The basis of the comparison is that, first, Milton's monism is derived from

Scripture, in his idiosyncratic statement of *ex Deo* creation in *De Doctrina Christiana*, and, second, that the monist philosophy is deemed to provide a coherence to Scripture (YP 6:305–15). It is, of course, neither an ontological nor a geological parallel I wish to draw between the sacred earth theorists and *Paradise Lost*. They are comparable, rather, in the similar methodological presumptions that underlie the works. Just as Milton offers an intricate physical theory of substance, which he suggests is implicit in the Bible, so too Burnet and the responses to his work produce detailed accounts of the physical world, which argue that they are implied within the Mosaic account of Creation.[45] In two important aspects, the epic shadows the sacred earth debates: first, *Paradise Lost* similarly interrogates the notion of how the Bible is true and the extent to which ulterior truths are contained within Scripture. Secondly, it also bases its philosophical enquiries on an enhanced use of accommodation. These parallels suggest that Milton's practice constituted less a theological impropriety than a properly *full* and rounded approach to reading the Bible, interstices and all.

As a model for the interaction of science and theology, the practices of Milton and Burnet can be contrasted usefully with "physico-theology," an idea propounded by thinkers as diverse as Walter Charlton, Robert Boyle, and John Ray.[46] Physico-theology (in its "depths and banalities," as Catherine Wilson puts it) sought to discover tangible traces of God, or God's evident design, in the natural world.[47] It was a study of the minutiae of nature, from the design of birds' nests to the arrangement of petals on flowers, from the human body to celestial systems. It was, one might say, a set of studies that continually concluded the same point—that it was God's providence, not chance, which brought about such sophisticated design. The set of questions raised by the sacred earth theorists and by Milton, however, addresses the interaction of religion and science on quite a different level: it attends to a correlation of scriptural text and the natural world to discover what latent truths might be contained within its narratives. As such, it involves a directly hermeneutic approach to the "discovery" of the natural world. This resolutely textual focus begins with the Scriptures and applies sophisticated criteria of physical plausibility to explain biblical phenomena. The two approaches are not mutually incompatible as scientific stances, but they are nevertheless distinct, and Milton is resolutely in the latter group—his philosophical and scientific stance, such as it is, is scriptural, but not, for all that, backward and out of date. On the contrary, it is distinctly of its time.

Milton's early and notorious editor, Richard Bentley, complains about the intrusion of Scripture into *Paradise Lost:* "Why should *Raphael* be so tied up to the Letter in *Genesis*, who makes this Narrative thousands of Years before *Genesis* was writ."[48] Bentley asks how Raphael could preempt so precisely the words that Moses would use long after. But the point is precisely this: that the biblical description is no haphazard approximation of the matter, nor a vague equivalence of the truth. Raphael quotes the future scriptural words because they are *right*. He elaborates monist detail in the interstices of the six days because Scripture permits this expository space. What is unique in this exegetical-scientific position illustrated by Milton and Burnet is the scope expected of this space, and the presumption that essentially hermeneutic questions, deciphering what happened in the Bible, in the flood or Creation, for example, might be answered retrospectively by natural philosophy. The sacred earth theorists likewise work under the presumption that the words of Scripture are "right" and must be read literally. The nature of this literal reading, however, is such that it demands sophisticated and detailed elaboration, indeed corroboration, as it deliberates on the relation of the Bible to other forms of truth. Accommodation provides the set of protocols for how this was to be achieved.

University of Reading

NOTES

1. *The Complete Prose Works of John Milton*, 8 vols., ed. Don M. Wolfe et al. (New Haven, 1953–1982), 8:419, hereafter designated YP and cited by volume and page number. Deut. 4:2, "Ye shall not add unto the word which I command you, neither shall ye diminish *ought* from it"; compare similar statements, Josh. 1:7, Rev. 22:18.

2. Peter Harrison, *The Bible, Protestantism and the Rise of Natural Science* (Cambridge, 1999), 129–38

3. John Wilkins, *A Discourse concerning a new Planet, Tending to prove, That 'tis probably our Earth is one of the Planets. Second book of The Discovery of a New World* (1640), 30–35; Joseph Glanvill, *Philosophia pia; or, A discourse of the religious temper and tendencies of the experimental philosophy which is profest by the Royal Society* (1671), 119–20; Robert Boyle, *Usefulness of Experimental Natural Philosophy* (1663), in *Works*, ed. Thomas Birch (1772), 2:19.

4. For a statement of its traditional function, see, for example, Augustine, *The City of God* (London, 1972), 15.25, pp. 642–43.

5. Samuel Johnson, *Samuel Johnson: Oxford Authors*, ed. Donald Green (Oxford, 1984), 711. William Riley Parker, *Milton: A Biographical Commentary*, 2 vols. (Oxford, 1968), delivers an equally caustic assessment: "Let me say it plainly: Milton was simply not a profound or an original thinker" (1:641). Similarly, attacking Milton's philosophical competence, see Lawrence Babb, *The Moral Cosmos of Paradise Lost* (Michigan, 1970), 24–26; William Kerrigan, *The Sacred Complex: On the Psychogenesis of "Paradise Lost"* (Cambridge, Mass., 1983), 200.

6. See *Paradise Lost*, ed. Alastair Fowler (Harlow, 1998), 11.52–53. All subsequent quotations are from this edition.

7. Stephen Fallon, *Milton Among the Philosophers: Poetry and Materialism in Seventeenth Century England* (Ithaca, N.Y., 1991), 241. See also D. Bentley Hart, "Matter, Monism and Narrative: An Essay on the Metaphysics of *Paradise Lost*," *MQ* 30, no. 1 (1996): 16–27; Philip J.

Donnelly, " 'Matter' versus Body: The Character of Milton's Monism," *MQ* 33, no. 3 (1999): 79–85; Neil Davis, " 'The Whole Fulness of the Godhead Dwells in Him Bodily': The Materiality of Milton's God, *Christianity and Literature* 52, no. 4 (2003): 497–522; John Rogers, *The Matter of Revolution: Science, Poetry and Politics in the Age of Milton* (Ithaca, N.Y., 1996); Kerrigan, *Sacred Complex*, 193–262; Harinder Singh Marjara, *Contemplation of Created Things: Science in "Paradise Lost"* (Toronto, 1992), 220–48; Walter Clyde Curry, *Milton's Ontology, Cosmogony and Physics* (Kentucky, 1957), 22–47.

8. Gerald Reedy, *The Bible and Reason* (Philadelphia, 1985), 20.

9. Georgia Christopher, *Milton and the Science of the Saints* (Princeton, 1982), 15.

10. Karen Edwards, *Milton and the Natural World: Science and Poetry in "Paradise Lost"* (Cambridge, 1999), 42, 66.

11. Diane Kelsey McColley, *A Gust for Paradise: Milton's Eden and the Visual Arts* (Urbana, Ill., 1993), 107.

12. Dayton Haskin, *Milton's Burden of Interpretation* (Philadelphia, 1994), 226.

13. General studies of the notion include Stephen D. Benin, *The Footprints of God: Divine Accommodation in Jewish and Christian Thought* (New York, 1993); Amos Funkenstein, *Theology and the Scientific Imagination from the Middle Ages to the Seventeenth Century* (Princeton, 1986), 213–71.

14. John Wollebius, *The Abridgement of Christian Divinity*, trans. Alexander Ross (London, 1650), 15.

15. Walter Charleton, *The Darkness of Atheism Dispelled by the Light of Nature. A Physico-Theologicall Treatise* (London, 1652), 24–25. See also Neil D. Graves, "Milton and the Theory of Accommodation," *SP* 98, no. 2 (Spring 2001): 251–72; quotation from 263.

16. The double nature of accommodation is pointed out by Kathleen Swaim, "The Mimesis of Accommodation in Book III of *Paradise Lost*," *PQ* 63 (1984): 463, 471.

17. John Calvin, *The Institution of Christian Religion* (1536), trans. Thomas Norton (London, 1611), 1.13.1, p. 43. See also Origen, *Contra Celsum*, Ante-Nicene Christian Library, vol. 23, ed. Alexander Roberts and James Donaldson (Edinburgh, 1872), 236; Aquinas, *Summa Theologiae*, 40 vols., ed. Thomas Gilby (London, 1964–1976), 1.33, art. 10, p. 41; John Calvin, *A Commentarie of John Calvine, Upon the First Booke of Moses called Genesis*, trans. Thomas Tymme (London, 1578), commentary on Genesis 6:6.

18. The lack of Israelite sophistication is cited, for example, by Origen, *Contra Celsum*, 237, and Luther, *Works*, vol. 1, *Lectures on Genesis* (1535), ed. Jaroslav Pelikan (Saint Louis, 1958), 23.

19. Alexander Ross, *An Exposition on the Fourteene first Chapters of Genesis, by way of Question and Answere* (London, 1626), 32.

20. H. R. MacCallum, "Milton and Figurative Interpretation of the Bible," *UTQ* 31, no. 3 (1962): 402–3. See also Swaim, "Mimesis," 463.

21. Richard Stock, *A Stock of Divine Knowledge, Being a Lively Description of Divine Nature* (London, 1641), 74–75. On Stock and Milton, see Peter Fiore, *Milton and Augustine: Patterns of Augustinian Thought in "Paradise Lost"* (London, 1981), 5–6.

22. Michael H. Keefer, "Accommodation and Synecdoche: Calvin's God in *King Lear*," *Shakespeare Studies* 20 (1987): 149.

23. William Kolbrenner, *Milton's Warring Angels: A Study of Critical Engagements* (Cambridge, 1997), 75; William Kerrigan, *The Sacred Complex*, 237. Also see John Reichert, *Milton's Wisdom: Nature and Scripture in "Paradise Lost"* (Ann Arbor, 1992), 36–37.

24. Critics who believe Milton's use of accommodation is straightforward and unproblematic include Roland M. Frye, *"Paradise Lost." God, Man and Satan: Patterns of Christian Thought and Life in "Paradise Lost," "Pilgrim's Progress" and the Great Theologians* (Princeton,

1960), 14; C. A. Patrides, *"Paradise Lost* and the Theory of Accommodation," *TSLL* 5 (1963–1964): 58–63; Walter R. Davis, "The Languages of Accommodation and the Styles of *Paradise Lost,"* in *Milton Studies* 18, ed. James D. Simmonds (Pittsburgh, 1985), 105; Purvis E. Boyette, "Accommodation, Theory of," in *A Milton Encyclopedia*, ed. William B. Hunter et al. (London, 1978), 1:13.

25. Neil D. Graves, "Milton and the Theory of Accommodation," *SP* 98, no. 2 (Spring 2001): 267, 257. A useful account also appears in Michael Lieb, "Reading God: Milton and the Anthropopathetic Tradition," in *Milton Studies* 25, ed. James D. Simmonds (Pittsburgh, 1985), 213–43.

26. See William G. Madsen, *From Shadowy Types to Truth: Studies in Milton's Symbolism* (New Haven, 1968), 73–74; Michael Lieb, "Reading God," 232; MacCallum, "Figurative Interpretation," 311.

27. See on this point Kenneth J. Howell, *God's Two Books: Copernican Cosmology and Biblical Interpretation in Early Modern Science* (Notre Dame, Ind., 2002).

28. An earlier example is Lambert Daneau, *The Wonderfull Woorkmanship of the World,* trans. Thomas Twyne (London, 1578), fol. 7^v: "For Moses . . . is either a vaine fellowe or a lier, if that knowledge of Natural Philosophie be not conteined in the holy Scripture."

29. See Ralph Heathcote, "Life of Burnet," preface to *Sacred Theory,* 7th ed. (1759); Scott Mandelbrote, *Dictionary of National Biography* (Oxford: Oxford University Press, 2004), entry for Burnet; Joseph Warton, *An Essay on the Writings and Genius of Pope* (1756), 118.

30. Thomas Burnet, *Telluris theoria sacra* (1681), translated as *Sacred Theory of the Earth* (1684). This work, dealing largely with the flood and its effects on the Earth, was followed by a similarly theorized account of the final conflagration of the world, Thomas Burnet, *Archælogiæ philosophicæ* (1692). Quotation from John Edwards, *A Discourse Concerning the Authority, Stile and Perfection of the Books of the Old and New Testament,* 3 vols. (London, 1689), 2:35. See also Burnet, *The Sacred Theory of the Earth,* ed. Basil Willey (1690; reprint, London, 1965).

31. Burnet, *Sacred Theory of the Earth* (1684), 51, 67.

32. Ibid., 110.

33. Roger North, BL, Add. MS 32546, fol. 22v.

34. Burnet, *Sacred Theory of the Earth,* 13–15 (Gen. 1:7), 45–46 (2 Pet. 3:5–7).

35. For example, William Whiston, *A New Theory of the Earth from its Original to the Consummation of all Things* (London, 1696); John Woodward, *An Essay Towards a Natural History of the Earth* (1695); John Keill, *An Examination of Dr. Burnet's Theory of the Earth, Together with Some Remarks on Mr. Whiston's New Theory of the Earth* (Oxford, 1698); John Arbuthnot, *An Examination of Dr. Woodward's Account of the Deluge* (1697); Thomas Robinson, *New Observations on the Natural History of the World of Matter* (1696); John Edwards, *Brief Remarks upon Mr Whiston's New Theory of the Earth* (London, 1697); Erasmus Warren, *Geologia; or, A Discourse Concerning the Earth Before the Deluge* (London, 1690).

36. Whiston, *A New Theory of the Earth,* 1, 3. A good account of the controversy is given in James E. Force, *William Whiston, Honest Newtonian* (Cambridge, 1985), 32–63. See also Marjorie Hope Nicolson, *Mountain Gloom and Mountain Glory: The Development of the Aesthetics of the Infinite* (Ithaca, N.Y., 1959); Harrison, *The Bible, Protestantism,* chap. 4; George Davies, *The Earth in Decay: A History of British Geomorphology, 1578–1878* (London, 1969); John Anthony Smith, *Sacred Earth: Metaphysical Poetry and the Advance of Science* (Oxford, 1986).

37. Woodward, *An Essay.* See also Joseph M. Levine, *Dr. Woodward's Shield* (Berkeley and Los Angeles, 1977).

38. Burnet, *Archælogiæ philosophicæ.* Edwards, *A Discourse Concerning the Authority,* 2:35.

39. Harrison, *The Bible, Protestantism*, 135.

40. Edwards, *Discourse*, 2:37. See also John Le Clerc, *Twelve Dissertations out of Monsieur Le Clerc's Genesis* (London, 1696), who decries the entire controversy: "What a monstrous Mosaick dress have we in Whiston's *Theory* with a train of comets . . . in Woodward's *Essay* with all the mountains down about his heels" (preface).

41. Isaac Newton, *The Correspondence of Isaac Newton*, vol. 2, 1667–1687, ed. H. W. Turnbull (Cambridge, 1960), 319. On the correspondence, see Scott Mandelbrote, "Isaac Newton and Thomas Burnet: Biblical Criticism and the Crisis of Late Seventeenth-Century England," in *The Books of Nature and Scripture*, ed. James E. Force and Richard H. Popkin (Dordrecht, 1994), 149–78.

42. Newton, *Correspondence*, 2:323 (Burnet to Newton, January 13, 1680–1681).

43. Ibid., 2:331 (Newton to Burnet, January 1680–1681).

44. Ibid., 333.

45. The purported biblical roots of Milton's monist arguments are given in *DDC* 1.7, in YP 6:299–323.

46. See, for example, Walter Charleton, *The Darkness of Atheism Dispelled by the Light of Nature. A Physico-Theologicall Treatise* (London, 1652); Robert Boyle, *Some Physico-Theological Considerations about the Possibility of the Resurrection* (1675); John Ray, *The Wisdom of God Manifested in the Works of the Creation* (London, 1691); John Ray, *Three Physico-Theological Discourses* (1693).

47. See Catherine Wilson, *The Invisible World, Early Modern Philosophy and the Invention of the Microscope* (Princeton, 1995), 176. See also Harrison, *The Bible, Protestantism*, 161–205.

48. *Dr. Bentley's Emendations on the Twelve Books of Milton's "Paradise Lost"* (London, 1732), comment on *PL* 7.391–98.

ROYAL SAMSON

Clay Daniel

R EADINGS OF *Samson Agonistes* as a political document identify
Samson in some way with the defeated "good old cause"—either as the
subject of Milton's critique, or exhortation, or consolation.[1] These criticisms,
even those arguing Milton's political unease, are at odds with contentions that
Samson is a deeply flawed protagonist who sharply contrasts with Milton's
concept of Christian heroism, embodied in Christ in *Paradise Regained,*
which was published in the same volume as the dramatic poem (1671).[2]
Reading Samson as a profoundly flawed character suggests some important
revaluations of the politics of *Samson Agonistes.* Though Samson does at
times evoke Milton's causes and even Milton himself, a more resonant political identity for Samson is the most tragic, betrayed figure of the civil war era,
a "league-breaker gave up bound" (*SA* 1209) by his people to their "Masters"
(1215), deprived of his "part from Heav'n assign'd" (1217), "cut off / Quite
from his people" (1157–58): Charles I.[3] Indeed, Milton's political experience
clearly is evident in the uncanny resemblance between his dramatic version
of Samson and the bloody, weak-minded, thick-headed king that Milton
creates in his prose.[4] This identification is critical to understanding the marriage of Samson and Dalila, which is structured by Milton's use of the husband and wife, king and state metaphors. Samson's defense of his actions,
especially in relation to his marriage(s), repeatedly resounds with the king's
rhetoric of divine right. And Dalila's defense of her betrayal of Samson
echoes the Presbyterians and parliamentarians who claimed that they fought
against the king in order to save him from unwise actions and policies. The
Philistines, believing that they indeed have succeeded in prevailing over
Samson, restore him to the public sphere as "a public servant" (*SA* 1615).
The ensuing climactic carnage, heavily informed by the events of regicide
and restoration, reveals that brutal political circumstances have been obscured by "a civil kinde of Idolatry in idolizing . . . Kings."[5]

Not that the work is a consistent political allegory. Yet, as we examine the
profound ways in which the dramatic poem is informed by Milton's political
experience, we must ask why it is not. My answer to this question strongly
supports—and to an extent relies upon—an early dating of the poem's incep-

tion. Roy Flannagan, commenting on "the thorny question of dating" the poem, states, "the consensus now favors a late date, largely because of the kinds of evidence critics have advanced about the politics of the dramatic poem."[6] However, again, these critics almost unanimously identify Samson in some way with Milton's defeated "good old cause." And many of them read the play as expressing Milton's disillusionment and bitterness as he witnessed the monarchical restoration. I will argue that Samson is a royal figure and that the dramatic poem's strongest political messages warn against restoring the monarchy. Milton, as suggested by his avowal that the "work never was intended" for the stage, apparently composed his dramatic poem over many years, under changing political circumstances, perhaps beginning it when the parliamentarians had closed the theaters (and Puritan "theater" would have been limited to print), and certainly publishing it when royalists had re-opened them.[7] At the time that was perhaps most opportune to publish *Samson Agonistes* as a warning against monarchical restoration (1659–1660), Milton was busy with *Paradise Lost* or preferred to use, in a readier and easier way, his left hand. After 1660, Milton would have wanted to revise his political allegory for two reasons. First, the work's antiroyalist imagery would have alerted the censor (sensitive to eclipse imagery, if to nothing else), unless perhaps it were cloaked with the revered name of Samson. And successfully cloaked it was, as apparently no one—except for perhaps those who had seen earlier versions of the work—discerned at work in the dramatic poem a "Poet blind, yet bold" who was attempting to "ruin . . . / The Sacred Truths to Fable and old Song."[8] And second, Milton's warning would not have had much urgency in Restoration England. The tragedy's bloody climax indicates that a monarchical restoration will produce the kind of recriminatory slaughter of English citizens that Milton believed to have occurred in Ireland. This did not happen. The tragedy, then, ultimately functions as a warning about the consequences of having restored the monarchy, charting the cultural priorities that led to this relatively peaceful restoration and, just as significantly, indicating the consequences of those priorities. If this had been Milton's initial purpose, I do not think he would have selected the sensational, violent story of Samson, which does not readily adapt to this charting or even to an analysis of the violence experienced by persecuted sectarians. On the other hand, the Samson saga readily interlocks with the bloody years of the civil wars. Indeed, Milton's royal Samson echoes not his limited assessments of Charles II but his extensive characterization of Charles I. Any bitterness or disillusionment that is in the work reflects political attitudes that characterized Milton as he, long before 1660, strove to avert a restoration.[9]

As early as 1649 Milton had attempted to awaken "prudent foresight" to what could be expected from a "restorement" of monarchy in *Eikonoklastes* (1649) (YP 3:360, 568), and this warning was repeated in his first two *Defenses* (1651, 1654), *Likeliest Means* (1659), *The Readie and Easie Way* (1660), and *Brief Notes upon a Late Sermon* (1660). But Milton's prose warnings were of doubtful effect. Though Milton was pleased with the international successes of the Latin defenses, the English *Eikonoklastes* went through only two editions to the thirty-five English editions of the King's Book, in England alone, in its first year. Milton has appeared not to respond to this failure, other than perhaps reassailing the king's image, again with his left hand, in his *Defenses*. But we should keep in mind Milton's statements about Aquinas and Spenser, about poetry and the pulpit, especially in *The Reason of Church-Government* (1642), in which he argues for a Puritan theater to counteract the "writings and interludes of libidinous and ignorant" royalists (YP 1:818). It would seem probable that Milton, in light of his book's poor success, at least considered turning to his right hand at a time when "both Royalists and non-Royalists aggressively appropriated dramatic terminology to promulgate their version of the act of regicide."[10] Milton himself is a vivid example of this appropriation in his prose, countering royalists like Salmasius, who fashioned "wondrous tragedies" from the king's demise (*First Defense*, YP 4:312). But *Samson Agonistes* also is layered with political elements that suggest it as Milton's attempt to accomplish in verse what he had failed to do in *Eikonoklastes:* steel his country against a restoration of monarchy by shattering the image of the martyr king.

I. THE KING AND SAMSON

During the civil war era, "the Samson legend was the property of no single political party."[11] Both Milton and Cromwell were compared to Samson, but the primary political identity for Samson was Charles I. Though Samson was a judge, scholars such as Salmasius, defending patriarchal monarchy, argued that "the Judges of the Hebrews could with better right be called kings: there was one of them at a time and they held the power [for] life."[12] Moreover, Samson's judgeship represented what Milton often attacked in explaining why "war has followed war throughout our Christian world for so many years" (*First Defense*, YP 4:321): sacral monarchy. Charles I's "sacral monarchy" was often praised for its combination of secular and priestly power.[13] As part of this praise, in the years of personal rule, the irresistible Charles I often "had been flatteringly compared with Samson by his courtiers" (YP 3:461n).

Throughout the 1640s the king's troubles infused these comparisons with fresh significance. According to John Gauden, Cromwell and his hench-men had acted the *"Dalilah* to bring the *Philistines* upon our *Sampson.*"[14] The cult of the martyr-king then exploited the arguments and images that identified Samson with Christ: Charles was a divine man who had been betrayed by those who should have loved him, abandoned by a vacillating people. But through his heroic death, he had avenged himself on his hypo-critical, scheming enemies.[15] Though rejecting this interpretation, Milton accepts the basic comparison of the king to Samson. In *Eikonoklastes,* the "English Silver" that purchased the king from "an hireling Army of Scots" (YP 3:545) jingles to the same tune as the *"Philistian* gold" that buys Samson (*SA* 831), "thee whose strength, while virtue was her mate, / Might have subdu'd the Earth, / Universally crown'd with highest praises" (173–75).[16] Milton writes that *"the words of a King,* as they are *full of power,* in the authority and strength of Law, so like *Sampson,* without the strength of that *Nazarites* lock, they have no more power in them then the words of another man" (YP 3:545–46). Though the king's short chapter in *Eikon Basilike* (1649) on his betrayal by the Scots does not allude to Samson, Milton would not have cited this powerful political metaphor carelessly. Indeed, Milton could not "better liken the state and person of a King then to that mighty Nazarite *Samson;* who being disciplin'd from his birth in the precepts and the practice of Temperance and Sobriety . . . grows up to a noble strength and perfection with those his illustrious and sunny locks the laws waving and curling about his god like shoulders" (*The Reason of Church-Government,* YP 1:858). Adorned with "the golden beames of Law and Right," a king is like a mighty Samson. Violating the law, he is a shorn Samson punished by God for "laying down his head among the strumpet flatteries of Prelats" (YP 1:859).[17] In 1649, Milton believed this to be what had happened.

The dramatic poem's opening lines suggest that it is Milton's verse "des-cant on the misfortunes of a person fall'n from so high a dignity" (first sen-tence of *Eikonoklastes* [YP 3:337]). Samson has been defeated by a religious culture that he identifies with "the people" (*SA* 12), upheld by "popular noise" (16) and "Superstition" (15). The king similarly insisted that his en-emies' claims were characterized by "the greatest noise and ostentations of religion," which had dazzled "the seduced train of the vulgar."[18] Samson has recovered from having his cavalier locks shorn, but his physical change is marked. The semidivine figure emerges from "air imprison'd . . . close and damp, / Unwholesome draught" (*SA* 8–9), not unlike the "'nauseous, pesti-lential Air'" of Hurst Castle, where the king was incarcerated by the army in December 1648.[19] There the king reportedly was reduced to beggary, isola-tion, and "melancholy apprehensions" under the grim eye of Lieutenant-Colonel Ewer and other lower-class rebels:[20]

O change beyond report, thought, or belief!
See how he lies at random, carelessly diffus'd,
With languish't head unpropt,
As one past hope, abandon'd,
And by himself given over;
In slavish habit, ill-fitted weeds
O'erworn and soil'd.   (117–23)

Such a description would hardly, at any time, have been "beyond . . . belief" in regard to New Model Army soldiers or politicized sectarians. These often appeared to be "a poor and contemptible company of men, neither versed in military affairs nor having much natural propensity to them." They had succeeded beyond anyone's expectations, seeking the latest divine revelation—"those strange windings and turnings of providence"—to guide them through the cultural kaleidoscope of civil war.[21] The incredible outcome was that their defeat had been averted. Samson's plight instead points to accounts of the king's captivities, during which he suffered "infinite reproaches, injuries and indignities" as he was reduced to being "the very shadow and bare name of a king."[22] The king "had his hair cut short" to disguise himself as he rode out from Oxford to surrender in April 1646, and by December he had become "disillusioned" and "strangely apathetic."[23] At Newport (autumn 1648) the king infamously suffered "from that load of sorrows, under which he laboured": "When the king presented himself to this company [Parliament's commissioners], a great and sensible alteration was remarked in his aspect. . . . he had laid aside all care of his person, and had allowed his beard and hair to grow, and to hang disheveled and neglected. . . . His friends beheld with compassion."[24]

But appearances are deceiving, especially to idolaters. Milton consistently assails this dejected image as he creates a king that reflects his intense hostility for monarchy. In *Eikonoklastes* Milton emphasizes the king's ridicule of his enemies as "swine" and *"Beasts"* and "Slaves" (YP 3:396–97, 412). The king even dismisses his "Friends" (that is, the Oxford Parliament) as "a *Mungrill Parlament*," incurring his royal displeasure for having *"vext"* Henrietta Maria (YP 3:396–97). The captive Samson too, despite his representations of himself as the victim of abuse, insults his enemies as well as the meeker Israelites (who purportedly "despise, or envy, or suspect" him [272]). Samson's fierce response to Harapha indicates that Samson's violent capacities extend far beyond the Philistine's. Similarly, the king and his "trusty *Myrmidons*" had provoked the violence that the sovereign attributes to the parliamentarians (YP 3:387). The king claimed he feared to walk the streets of rioting London. Milton demands,

Did he not the very next day after his irruption into the House of Commons, then which nothing had more exasperated the people, goe in his Coach unguarded into the City? did hee receave the least affront, much less violence in any of the Streets, but rather humble demeanours, and supplications? Hence may be gather'd, that however in his own guiltiness hee might have justly fear'd, yet that hee knew the people so full of aw and reverence to his Person, as to dare commit himself single among the thickest of them, at a time when he had most provok'd them. (YP 3:394)

Not unlike the passage cited immediately above, the Chorus recounts its vivid memory of Samson:

> That invincible *Samson,* far renown'd,
> The dread of *Israel's* foes, who with a strength
> Equivalent to Angels' walk'd thir streets,
> None offering fight; who single combatant
> Duell'd thir Armies rank't in proud array,
> Himself an Army.   (341–46)

Samson eloquently poses the question so often asked by defeated royalists and even victorious parliamentarians: how could God have allowed his anointed to be defeated? Samson asks,

> O wherefore was my birth from Heaven foretold
> Twice by an angel, who at last in sight
> Of both my Parents all in flames ascended
> From off the Altar, where an Off'ring burn'd
> As in a fiery column charioting
> His Godlike presence . . . ?   (23–28)

This passage strongly suggests Milton's view of royalist panegyrists who had transformed the king's despotic actions, failed political strategies, and military defeats into the legend of the saintly, wise, martyred king. The scriptural angel instructs Samson's mother in a field. Manoah, apparently incredulous, prays to the Lord to send "the man of God" again (Judg. 13:8). The angel then descends again and repeats his instructions to Manoah. Nevertheless, Manoah is told less than his unnamed, barren wife, who remains the human focus of the angelic visit ("let her beware . . . let her observe" [Judg. 13:13–14]). The angel declines to reveal his name or to dine with the couple. The two are finally dazzled into comprehending their guest's true identity when the "Godlike presence" suddenly departs in the flames produced by the "burnt offering" of the couple's hastily contrived altar (Judg. 13:16). And then Manoah fears for their lives.[25] The biblical author stresses that "the angel of the Lord" (who dominates the narrative) "did no more appear to Manoah and to his wife" (Judg. 13:21).

Milton's Samson clearly "aggrandizes" his birth.[26] He suppresses the humbler facts to create the kind of a description—"popish," idolatrous—that Milton had emphatically rejected when representing the birth of Jesus, which was often compared to Samson's. Samson particularly echoes royalist panegyrists who used the imagery of fire, sun, and light to link royal births with Christ's Nativity as a "birth from Heaven" (*SA* 23). Charles II's birth had been exceptionally spectacular: "A whole myth had grown around the appearance of a star at midday on Charles's birth."[27] According to Auerilian Cook, this star indicated that, "as soon as Born, Heaven took notice of him . . . that his life should be continued with Miracles, as it began with one; or that his Glory shou'd shine like a star."[28]

Samson too is "destin'd from the womb" (*SA* 634) ("destin'd" is rarely a good word with Milton), the subject of "ordain'd . . . nurture, holy," "solemnly elected" by God, "crown'd with highest praises" (362, 678, 175). Samson, "full of divine instinct . . . like a petty God . . . walk'd about admir'd of all and dreaded / On hostile ground" (526, 529–31). These lines strongly evoke the idolatry of the king that Milton rejected in his tracts, a king who, "Ador'd like a Demigod," would "pageant himself up and down in progress among the perpetual bowings and cringings of an abject people, on either side deifying and adoring him" (*The Readie and Easie Way*, YP 7:425–26). Even more illuminating are Milton's remarks in *Observations on the Articles of Peace:* "we gladly would be instructed why any mortal man for the good and wellfare of his own brethren beeing made a King, should by a clean contrary motion make himself a God, exalted above Law: the readiest way to become utterly unsensible, both of his human condition, and his own duty" (YP 3:307–8).

Though Samson is not empowered by "long descent of birth" (*SA* 171), he acts as one of Milton's "unsensible" monarchs. He claims that he only appears to be a "private person" (1208) that is subject to law. He actually has been "appointed to office before his birth."[29] Samson insists that he "was no private but a person rais'd / With strength sufficient and command from Heav'n" (*SA* 1211–12) to execute such shady legal and political maneuvers as killing and robbing the Askolonites. This strength is deployed like that of Milton's Charles I, as the royal lion that combats "force with force" (*SA* 1206). Samson's strength emphatically is not intellect. He is not once in the poem called a judge. Though there was a strong tradition that the riddling Samson was in most things wise, Milton insists on his "wisdom nothing more than mean" (*SA* 207). Charles I, like kings generally, was also popularly reputed to be wise, especially after the publication of *Eikon Basilike*.[30] However, for Milton he was "a man neither by nature nor by nurture wise" and as such was a typical king (*Eikonoklastes*, YP 3:416).

A royal Samson is further developed by the numerous citations of Fortune, and later of "necessity," as the sources for Samson's woes. Providence is cited only twice in the work, once ironically (1545). "Crowned Fortune" (*Sonnet XVI*, 5), baffling and inscrutable, was antipathetic for many Puritans, including Milton. Did Milton in 1660 (or 1649?) experience a crisis of religious faith? No such crisis informs *Paradise Lost*, which is, after all, a Restoration poem. Furthermore, whatever the quietism of *Paradise Regained* (another sharp contrast with the dramatic poem), its emphasis on a providential overview of the human condition prevails. Nor is it likely that many English citizens abandoned their sectarian views of God to embrace classical Fortuna. On the other hand, royalist civil war writers evaded the issue of providence by representing the king as an unfortunate prince who had been ruined by the "Sterne Fates."[31] The king in "ecliptic condition" was "a sorrowful spectacle, and great example of fortune's inconstancy."[32] Samson too is in eclipse and "to lowest pitch of abject fortune . . . fallen" (*SA* 169), "in low dejected state, / As erst in highest" (338–39). He is a compelling example of "our fickle"—mortal and political—"state" (163). Samson searches for his "own default" (45) in the shadow of the ludicrously phrased "Divine Prediction" (44), perplexed by the "heavenly disposition" (373) of a purportedly "contrarious" God (669).

The fault to which Samson ascribes his woes similarly jars with Milton's priorities. Samson the violator of commandment and law laments his propensity to be a "blab" (495). He has, because of Dalila's importunity, "publish'd, impiously, / Weakly at least, and shamefully" God's "holy secret" (497–99). Milton brashly published religious truth that royal and parliamentary government had attempted to silence. Furthermore, Milton's profoundly spiritual concept of marriage does not readily allow for one spouse to keep secrets from another, especially in matters of religion. Samson's confession again recalls the king's circumstances. "Publish'd," along with Dalila's publishing of Samson's secrets (*SA* 777), glances at the disastrous consequences for a king whose correspondence with his queen was illicitly published; the letters "to summ up all . . . shewd him govern'd by a Woman" (*Eikonoklastes*, YP 3:538). Royalists decried the publication as "'barbarous'" (YP 3:537 n. 1), yet the turpitude of this act is slight in relation to the king's violences: "What he feares not by Warr and slaughter, should we feare *to make desperate* by op'ning his Letters?" (YP 3:542–43).

II. SAMSON'S ROYAL MARRIAGE

Samson's marriage to a foreign idolater, Dalila, creates his royal identity in several ways. First, it suggests the controversy caused by the projected Spanish match, which may also parallel Samson's earlier marriage to the woman of Timna. More emphatically, Samson's relationship with Dalila recalls the enormous problems that swirled around the French Catholic Henrietta Maria, including her supposed domination, especially in matters of religion, of her husband (*Eikonoklastes*, YP 3:421). Samson's marriage to Dalila also evokes the "carnal metaphor" of the king being " 'seduced by wicked Counsell.' "[33] In the words of Mildmay Fane, the king "by the seducement of a few evil Counsailers" ("Those Dalila Respects") had worked "his own ruine."[34] But more importantly, the relationship between "vanquisht" (*SA* 235) Samson and the "Traitress" (725) Dalila, who "treacherously" deprives him of the "fatal harvest of" his "head" (1023–24), embodies the political imagery so vital to Stuart patriarchy for which the significance of the king as head of state and as husband parallels the metaphor of the kingdom as the king's body and also his spouse.[35]

A political context is quickly established when Dalila arrives to reclaim her husband. Significantly, Dalila is Samson's wife, which she is not in the Bible. The Chorus describes her as "a stately Ship" (714). The robust and satiric mercantile imagery identifies Dalila (and her "Sea-Idol" [*SA* 13]) with Parliament as an embodiment of the English ship of state. Parliament, like Dalila, emerges triumphant from her rebellion against her pilot, to be "courted by all the winds" of international commerce and diplomacy (*SA* 719). Samson, like the king, fares otherwise. With lowered head, the "foolish Pilot" rues the wreckage caused by his own unskillful navigation of the ship of state given to him by authority "from above" (198–99). Commiserating with Samson, the Chorus significantly modifies this metaphor: "What Pilot so expert but needs must wreck / Embark'd with such a Steers-mate at the Helm?" (1044–45). Though they were often identified with ships, women (as wives) were not commonly accorded "steers-mate" status. This metaphor more readily points to allegations of Parliament's "usurpation" (1060) in commandeering the ship of state, launching the ensuing wreck of civil war and regicide. The Chorus adds that since man—identified with the "Favor'd of Heav'n—rarely finds such a mate," "peace" would not exist except "God's universal Law / Gave to the man despotic power / Over his female in due awe" to prevent her "usurpation" (1046, 1049, 1053–54, 1060). This "despotic power" is a "right" that should never be compromised (1056). The Chorus's insistence on the subordination of women to men, within the political context, is not so much Miltonically sexist as wrongly royalist.

The ship-of-state metaphor is especially calculated to represent the political misfortunes of Charles I. The king's collection of the tax known as "ship money" was unpopular, as was his attempt to use the fleet built with this money to protect the interests of the land of Tarsus and Gadire. With the outbreak of civil war, the fleet was commandeered to the services of Parliament when "all but five captains" of the fleet accepted Parliament's appointee as lord admiral, and "those five were overborne by their own crews": "When the mariners had joined the demonstrations against him [Charles I] in January [1642] they had offered a petition which contained significant phrases: 'That great vessel the Parliament House which is so richly fraught with no less than the price of a kingdom is fearfully shaken and in great danger. Rome has rocks and Spain quicksands to swallow her up.'"[36] Moreover, "the imagery of fire and storm" were, "thanks to the *Eikon Basilike,* commonplaces for Charles's sufferings."[37] The book's frontispiece pictures the king against the background of a stormy sea.[38] In his book the king claims that he was "forced to sea by a storm," the "shame" of the "tumults" (*Eikon Basilike,* 24–25). He then explains, "the uprightness of his intentions will excuse the possible failings of his understanding. If a pilot at sea cannot see the polestar, it can be no fault in him to steer his course by such stars as do best appear to him" (27). The foolish pilot Samson practices similar erroneous reasoning. He marries Dalila, violating Hebrew marriage law as well as the fifth commandment, with the best of intentions: under divine supervision, he will kill Philistines (a violation, perhaps, of the sixth commandment). Milton clearly rejects the king's defense and, it would seem, Samson's: "He alleges the uprightness of his intentions to excuse his possible failings; a position fals both in Law and Divinity" (*Eikonoklastes,* YP 3:416). Milton denies that "the small skill of him who undertakes to be a *Pilot,* will excuse him to be misledd by any wandring Starr mistak'n for the Pole" (416).

Royalist elegists combined shipwreck with an even more pervasive image of royal misfortune, eclipse: "Night makes the day, & darkness gilds the Sun. . . . we are tost / Upon a sea of woes; our Pilot lost; / Driven by th'winds and waves, distrest, forlorn."[39] Samson experiences "total eclipse" in perhaps the work's most well-known lines (*SA* 80–82). His name is associated with *shemesh,* the Hebrew word for "sun": "*the Sun,* which in all figurative use, and significance beares allusion to a King, not to a Subject" (*Eikonoklastes,* YP 3:372). Not surprisingly, "Charles himself hidden in a cloud" becomes a common theme of civil war literature. Royalists and nonroyalists used "eclipse" to characterize the royalist cause generally and the regicide in particular: "Our SUN went down at *Noon*"; "Accursed day that blotted'st out our Light!"[40] The king writes at length of his "enforced darkness and eclipse" in *Eikon Basilike* (49). He attributes his "eclipse of outward fortune" to the "riddle of their [the rebellious Scots'] loyalty" (134–36). Milton satirically calls it "a fatal Riddle" in the same chapter of *Eikonoklastes* in which he compares the king to Samson (YP 3:545).

Scholars have documented "the eroticism which figures so strangely in the literary treatment of Charles, the fact that the king is often seen as the husband or lover rather than as the father of the kingdom."[41] Indeed, the king's "fatal riddle" could in many ways be characterized as a "love riddle," which is especially true in relation to the Scots, who were fearful of the strength of their beloved king. Charles and the Scots had "not only common ties of nature," but they shared "bonds of nature and conscience." In dealing with the Scots, the king admittedly succumbed to the temptation to violate his own maxim that there are "some things . . . to be denied to some men lest he [Charles I] should seem not to dare to deny anything and give too much encouragement to unreasonable demands or importunities" (*Eikon Basilike*, 59, 74, 53): "For although I can be content to eclipse my own beams to satisfy their fears, who think they must needs be scorched or blinded if I should shine in the full luster of kingly power wherewith God and the laws have invested me, yet I will never consent to put out the sun of sovereignty to all posterity and succeeding kings" (49). Charles explains that to derogate from his authority, "were as if Samson should have consented not only to bind his own hands and cut off his hair but to put out his own eyes, that the Philistines might with the more safety mock and abuse him, which they chose to do than quite destroy him when he was become so tame an object and fit occasion for their sport and scorn" (53–54). Examining "the riddle of their loyalty," the king protests that his betrayers often excused their treasons, especially when attempting to reconcile with their king, as the actions of those who "fought not against . . . but for" him (*Eikon Basilike*, 134–35). Milton's complaint is even more vivid. Many Presbyterians and parliamentarians, Scots and English, filled "mens ears continually with the noise of thir conscientious Loyaltie and Allegeance to the King," though their "profess'd Loyalty and Allegeance led them to direct Arms against the Kings Person" (*Eikonoklastes*, YP 3:346). Despite Charles's and Milton's skepticism, the argument was repeatedly made: "This was the argument of Pym, Hampden, Essex, and all the leaders of the Parliamentary party: they reverenced the person of the King and fought to restore him to his Parliament and to reintegrate the threatened state." Wedgwood adds, "A satirical parody of the Roundhead contention was crystallised in a piece of Cavalier ballad mockery: ' 'Tis to Preserve His Majesty / That we against him fight.' "[42] Parliament's army in August 1642 sought "to release His Majesty from the 'malignants' and bring him home to his faithful Parliament"; and "the Assembly of the Scottish Church—as particular in this as the Parliament of England—sent a message to the King assuring him that the Scots were entering the war entirely in his own best interest." Leading troops raised by writs "gone out under the King's official signet," Argyll "composed a manifesto to the English Royalists in the North, urging them to join with the incoming Scots . . . to rescue 'His Majesty's person and honour' " from those who counseled " 'popery and tyranny.' "[43]

Dalila makes a very similar noise as she seeks "pardon" (*SA* 738, 771,

814), a politically charged term during the Restoration. She says that Samson had been too powerful, too busy. She had desired an enhanced relationship based on her gaining his "key of strength and safety" (799). She betrayed him not to destroy him but to limit him. She wanted Samson as Argyll had wanted the king: " 'rather reformed than ruined' and the monarchy 'rather regulated than destroyed.' "[44] To achieve Samson's reformation, Dalila sought his return to the "safe custody" of her house as "Love's prisoner" (*SA* 802, 808). Samson's scorn prompts her to rehearse something like the rise of Parliament's hard-liners. "Solicited, commanded, threaten'd, urg'd / Adjur'd" by the "Magistrates / And Princes" of her country (*SA* 852–53, 850–51), she was thundered at about "the bonds of civil Duty / And of Religion" (853–54) that demanded she act against one "who had destroy'd / Such numbers of our Nation . . . an irreligious / Dishonourer of Dagon" (856–61). Samson was the regal, irreligious man of blood who must be punished, "against whom God had witnessed for shedding the blood of thousands."[45] She pleads, "Hear what assaults I had, what snares besides, / What sieges girt me round, ere I consented" (*SA* 845–46). Samson also uses political and military vocabulary to describe the unsuccessful defense of his "sacred trust" (1001). Recalling the king's explanation for abandoning London, Samson laments the consequences of divulging his "capital secret" to Dalila: "pledge / Of vow," "betray," "Spies," "Treason against me," "Traitor," "parleys," "must'ring," "batteries," "storm me," "snares," "o blot / To Honor and Religion" (391–412). Samson, "over-watch't, and wearied out" (405), at length succumbs to the "foul effeminacy" (410) that Milton identified with the cavaliers.

According to many, and "not least by Charles himself," the Scots sell their king to the English.[46] Separated by a paragraph from his citation of Samson, the Latin secretary slyly scorns the "English Silver" that purchased the king from "an hireling Army of Scots" (*Eikonoklastes,* YP 3:545):[47] "That the Scots in *England* should *sell thir King,* as he himself here affirmes, and for a *price so much above that,* which the covetousness of *Judas* was contented to sell *our Saviour,* is so foule an infamy and dishonour cast upon them, as befitts none to vindicate but themselves" (YP 3:546). Yet, after selling the king, many covenanting Scots worked for his release from the New Model Army. Dalila similarly negotiates for the welfare of the man whom she has helped to destroy by accepting "the gold / Of Matrimonial treason" (*SA* 958–59). Dalila reasons with Samson, the two of them having been confounded by a common opponent, "let weakness then with weakness come to parle" (785). The defeated Samson with the help of "the Lords" (920) even now could be kept "at home in leisure and domestic ease, / Exempt from many a care" (917–18). Manoa also negotiates:

Some much averse I found and wondrous harsh,
Contemptuous, proud, set on revenge and spite;
That part most reverenc'd *Dagon* and his Priests;
Others more moderate seeming, but thir aim
Private reward, for which both God and State
They easily would set to sale: a third
More generous far and civil, who confess'd
They had enough reveng'd, having reduc't
Thir foe to misery beneath thir fears.   (1461–69).

This assessment vividly configures the factions, allegiances, and al-
liances that swirled around the attempts to gain control of the king in the later
1640s. "Others more moderate seeming," especially when read with an eye
on Dalila, recall Milton's view of the Parliament that sought "to Hucster the
Common-wealth" (YP 5:444). Of course, few were as "wondrous harsh" in
defending regicide as Milton, who would not have accused himself of "spite."
But Milton's lack of spite might have been exceptional. Indeed, Manoa's
assessment suggests that Milton's attitude toward the regicides is perhaps
more complex than scholars have realized. Who, for example, would have
believed without reading the digression how bitterly Milton viewed the Long
Parliament? Or how the New Model Army had tamely yielded, like Harapha
to Samson, to the restoration of the monarchy? Or, without the testimony of
his widow, how Milton had been invited to join the restored Stuart court? In
any case, in 1660 the English authorities were almost united in their persecution of regicides and sectaries, a persecution often led by powerful Presbyterians who were as "moderate seeming" on this issue as they were in their use
of public office to reap private rewards. On the other hand, Manoa does
succeed in negotiating a "restoration" of his son with Philistines who believed
Samson to be "beneath thir fears."

Samson's response to these negotiations is thoroughly Caroline. Samson
prefers death to capitulation. If Dalila could "sell" him in his "flower of youth
and strength, when all men / Lov'd, honor'd, fear'd" him, how will she
"betray" him in his "perfect thraldom" (938–40, 946)? Dalila has violated
"the law of nature, law of nations" (890) that subjugate the wife to the
husband and, according to political theorists such as Salmasius, the nation to
the monarch. If she is allowed to retain authority, she will continue to subvert
the "the law of nature, the law of nations": "how again betray me, / Bearing
my words and doings to the Lords / To gloss upon" (946–48).

Since the biblical narrative lacks any such references, their inclusion by
Milton may suggest contemporary English political culture. Similarly suggestive are Samson's claims to liberty: "This Gaol I count the house of Liberty"

(949). The king repeatedly claimed that he was the true defender of "the just rights of Parliament against a conspiracy of rogues at Westminster."[48] Samson charges that "zeal mov'd" Dalila and "an impious crew / Of men conspiring to uphold thir state" to violate "the ends / For which our country is a name so dear" (*SA* 891–95). Cavaliers and Puritans, of course, often cited Puritan zeal as the source of the rebellion. And Samson's ridicule of Dalila's "feign'd Religion, smooth hypocrisy" (*SA* 872) resounds with the king's invective against his enemies' "soft and smooth pretensions of religion, reformation, and liberty" (*Eikon Basilike*, 165). In his chapter on the "Jealousies . . . Cast Upon the King," Charles denounces the rogues who had disguised their ambition and jealousies—their "zealous adventures" and "seductions"—with "great professions of singular piety." "Stratagems and conflicts of malice" are more dangerous than "open hostility" (*Eikon Basilike*, 84, 87; "by worse than hostile deeds" [*SA* 893]).

Yet Milton insists that the primary source of the king's woes is neither royal lenience toward his people, nor Scots' treachery, nor Fortune's whims; rather, it is the king's claims that because of his divine right he was above English law. This is perhaps the most significant political connection of Milton's king to Milton's Samson. "Divinely call'd" Samson (*SA* 226) repeatedly cites his special status to excuse his violation not only of Philistine law, but of several commandments (1, 2, 5, 6, 8), Hebrew marriage law, and even his Nazarite oath ("All the days that he separateth himself unto the Lord he shall come upon no dead body" [Num. 6:6]). The Chorus endorses this perspective (*SA* 315–21), arguing a God

> Who made our Laws to bind us, not himself,
> And hath full right to exempt
> Whom so it pleases him by choice
> From National obstriction, without taint
> Of sin, or legal debt;
> For with his own Laws he can best dispense.   (309–14)

As Hebrew judges emphatically were not exempted from "National obstriction," this circumstance may be more readily related to contemporary England. England had fought, or was fighting, a civil war over whether a purportedly divinely elected king, when performing "what was needful for the general welfare . . . was not bound by law" and "could, in certain matters, break law."[49] Royalists had supported their argument "through formulating and endorsing a patriarchal philosophy of government."[50] One of the most prominent formulations was *Defensio regia*. Citing Psalm 51, Salmasius argues, "a king can be judged by no one but God and is obliged to account for his acts to no one but God. For if the one who is and is called king can be summoned before another authority, then this must, by definition, be superior to kingly authority."[51] Milton derides this position as a "masterpiece of our courtiers": "Did he [David] believe that all God's people, his own brothers, were so contemptible in comparison with him that to murder, defile, rob them could be no crime for him? Far be such arrogance and unseemly ignorance of himself or his kindred from so revered a ruler" (*First Defense*, YP 4:361–62). He adds that, "to punish all others while granting one man impunity for every crime, despite the fact that the law allows no exceptions, is the height of injustice": "May kings also steal, kill, and commit adultery with impunity?" (YP 4:365, 352). Milton clearly refuses to excuse those who claim a religious-legal sanction for their unjust actions. Instead, he cites "natural law" to condemn them: "Reason, justice, and morality command the punishment of all sinners without distinction": "the attribution of infallibility and omnipotence to a human being [significantly singular] is the root of all evils" (YP 4:397, 398). Yet, disguising their evil with divine claims, kings "in the midst of all their wickedness" are "honored and adored and treated as next to God himself even" (YP 4:426). Such are worse than more common criminals: "Which is the greater criminal, he who sins against the law or he who attempts to make the law itself his accomplice in crime, and even does away with the law to avoid the appearance of crime?" (*Second Defense*, YP 4:529).

Milton foregrounds this legal debate in *Eikonoklastes*. He excoriates the king for citing his conscience and reason to justify "the extortions, the oppressions, the public robberies, and rapines" of his policies (YP 3:435). A nation that accepts this argument is allowing itself to be "ty'd and chain'd to the conscience, judgement, and reason of one Man; as if those gifts had been only his peculiar and Prerogative, instal'd upon him with his fortune to be a King" (YP 3:359). Milton refuses to make the English people's "general good and safety . . . depend upon the privat and overweening Reason of one obstinat Man; who against all the Kingdom, if he list, will interpret both the Law and his Oath of Coronation by the tenor of his own will" (YP 3:416). The basis for public action is "the autority of Law onely" (YP 3:529). He specifically rejects the plea of "one kind of Magistrat" (the king) that "the Anointment of God, should be as it were a charme against Law; and give them privilege who punish others, to sin themselves unpunishably": "And by that ancient and universal Law, *whoever sheddeth mans blood, by man shall his blood be shed;* we find heer no exception. If a king therfore doe this, to a King, and that by men also, the same shall be don. This is the Law of *Moses*" (YP 3:586–87). King Charles was no exception—and no martyr: "if to die for the *testimony of his* [the King's] *own conscience,*" such as many "Romish priests" purportedly have done, "be enough to make him Martyr, what Heretic dying for direct blasphemie, . . . may not boast a Martyrdom?" (YP 3:575–76). This, of course, throws a lurid light over a Samson who was not inspired by God but who "was persuaded inwardly that this [his martyrdom] was from God" (*SA*, Argument). The passage that condemns the king would seem to condemn Samson: "It is no new, or unwonted thing for bad men to claim as much part in God as his best servants; to usurp and imitate thir words, and appropriate to themselves those properties which belong onely to the good and righteous. This not only in Scripture is familiarly to be found, but heer also in this Chapter of *Apocrypha*" (YP 3:528).

III. The Philistines' Festival: Regicide and Restoration

For most English citizens the king was Charles the Martyr. And with the publication of *Eikon Basilike*, he was perceived to be an emphatically Protestant martyr. The "pieties and providences" of the "saints" are clearly voiced throughout that book, especially in the enormously popular "Meditations upon Death."[52] Charles, like Samson, eloquently and poignantly meditates on the "few steps between the prisons and graves" of God's chosen ones: "The assaults of affliction may be terrible like Samson's lion, but they yield much sweetness to those that dare to encounter and overcome them" (*Eikon Basilike*, 172–73). But the king's death revealed to Milton that he resembled Samson in more than a search for sweetness. Samson's enemies were harmed more by his death than by all of his previous exploits combined (Judg. 16:30). Something similar can be said of the king's death and of the King's Book. The regicide intensified the popular appeal of divine right. *Eikon Basilike*, "in a word, . . . was an army, and did vanquish more than any sword could."[53] The events of 1660 confirmed that Stuart kings did not prefer martyrdom. They preferred thrones. Just as clearly, their people preferred enthroned Stuart kings. Milton anticipates these attitudes and their consequences, countering them in his dramatic poem. The English people's imagined deliverance from the uncertainties of republican experiment, the problems of economic stagnation, and the gloom of Puritan morality is enacted in Samson's attendance at the festival that celebrates his subjection to Philistine authority. This subjection proves to be a fatal illusion for the Philistines. The English people's belief in the restoration of a chastened, compliant king will prove to be similarly fatal. In a country where political beliefs have been determined by the "theater" of the king's martyrdom, the national political theater will turn slaughterhouse, as the king acts the part of Samson in a way not staged by royalist propagandists.

A Public Officer approaches Samson with "a Scepter or quaint staff" to bring Samson "before th' illustrious Lords" (*SA* 1303, 1318). English royal officers do not bear scepters, and it is unlikely Milton was familiar with the

Philistines' royal procedures. The "quaint staff," perhaps glancing at Cromwell's "bauble," points to the persistent negotiations and intrigues with Charles II to restore the monarchy. And, destroyed in 1649, two royal scepters were remade for the coronation of Charles II. Samson's enumeration of those that would compromise his dignity—"Gymnic Artists, Wrestlers, Riders, Runners, / Jugglers and Dancers, Antics, Mummers, Mimics" (1324–25)—suggests that this passage was written after Milton had witnessed the festive culture that was restored with the merry monarch, who at this point becomes a political identity for Samson. As Samson in "state Livery" (1616) is restored to public life, all are pleased: Manoa, his fellow citizens, the Philistine people, and above all "th' illustrious Lords." A triumphal shout "tore the Sky" (1472). A similar shout was heard at Charles II's coronation in April 1661: "Whereupon, all the *People,* with loud and repeated shouts, cryed, *God save the King;* and, by a Signal then given, the great *Ordinance* from the *Tower* were also shot off."[54] The Philistines' triumphal shout is followed by the "hideous noise" (1509) that reveals the true nature of Samson's return as a public figure, performer, servant. Similarly unsettling, the loud rejoicings of coronation day were followed by the terrific, ominous storm that began when the "King and his Traine" sat down to the coronation banquet.[55]

Milton conflates the coronation and the banquet, as Samson appears in a "spacious Theater" (1605), where the Philistine lords "had fill'd thir hearts with mirth, high cheer, and wine" (1613). "Theater" is Milton's interpolation. In most translations of Scripture, Samson appears in a "house" (Judg. 16:26–27). Yet "Theater" deftly points to Milton's work itself, which as a dramatic poem was never intended to be performed in a theater. More obviously, the "spacious Theater" images Charles II's reopening of the theaters, a return to frivolity heightened by a glance at *The Book of Sports:* "They only set on sport and play" (*SA* 1679). "Theater" also suggests the "*Theatre* (erected close to the four high *Pillars*) . . . upon which the *Throne of Estate* was placed" during the coronation in Westminster Abbey.[56] Samson significantly is placed between "two massy pillars / That to the arched roof gave main support" (*SA* 1633–34). Four massive triumphal arches marked the route of the royal cavalcade as it passed among the cheering throngs on its way to Westminster. As part of this rejoicing, one of the arches was inscribed with that paragon of royal (and, for the Chorus at least, secular) birds, the Arabian phoenix. The phoenix often was used to reaffirm the enduring fame of the Stuarts, especially in 1660.[57] Milton aptly describes this tumultuous progress, which he likely heard: "the City rings, / And numbers thither flock" (*SA* 1449–50).

However, the trial and execution of Charles I remain the dominant political context for the ominous violence that concludes Milton's dramatic poem. Samson initially refuses to obey the summons to attend the festival.

Citing the importance of Hebrew "Law" and of his own "Consecrated gift" (1320, 1354), he argues that his attendance would be "venturing to displease / God for the fear of Man, and Man prefer" (1373–74). Charles had similarly defended his refusal to return to govern with Parliament, asserting his "constancy as to fear Him more than man" (*Eikon Basilike,* 38). Returning to London as a prisoner, the king still refused to acknowledge the "legal authority" of the Rump's High Court of Justice: "I cannot submit to your pretended authority without violating the trust which I have from God for the welfare and liberty of my people" (*Eikon Basilike,* 191). He was charged with being a "tyrant, traitor, and murderer . . . a public and implacable enemy" who had "traitorously and maliciously levied war against the present Parliament and the people therein represented . . . much innocent blood of the free people of this nation hath been spilt, many families have been undone, the public treasure wasted and exhausted."[58] "A Murderer, a Revolter, and a Robber" (*SA* 1180) are the charges leveled by Harapha at Samson for his "notorious murder" (1186) of the Askolonites and his subsequent robbery to discharge a perceived unfair debt. Samson insists that in fact he "was no private but a person rais'd / With strength sufficient and command from Heav'n" (1211–12). The king, "no ordinary prisoner," informed the court, "I shall not betray my trust. I have a trust committed to me by God, by old and lawful descent."[59] For many English citizens (including Milton), this argument was discredited by the king's deposition and execution, an attitude clearly expressed in Harapha's derision of Samson: "Presume not on thy God, whate'er he be, / Thee he regards not, owns not, hath cut off / Quite from his people, and deliver'd up" (1156–58).

Milton's "Theater" deftly critiques the theatricality of royalist regicide literature. For one final performance, the royal actor had entered and exited the scene of so many other idolatrous performances, the colonnaded Banqueting House with its painted deification of James I. Court masks had presented a "Vitruvian apotheosis, celebrating through architecture and engineering the triumph that history was to deny the Stuart monarchy."[60] These "solemn feasts" had been in the tradition that Milton creates for the "solemn Feast" of the Philistines (*SA* 1311), which suggests a court mask or Restoration play rather than any religious service.[61] Indeed, this inappropriately theatrical atmosphere pervaded the regicide. On the scaffold were "two grotesquely garbed and disguised executioners" (their disguises consisting of elaborate "vizards" and beards) amid "staples, ropes and pulleys, the cheap pine coffin made of planks and covered by a black velvet cloth and, finally, the axe resting against the block." When the solemn event concluded, the soldiers acted as antimaskers on the scaffold-stage, charging admission, bargaining for relics, garnering souvenirs. The severed head retained hair "barely an inch long."[62]

Other descriptions similarly evoke the regicide. "The throng / On banks and scaffolds" jostle for a glimpse of a purportedly divine figure reduced to being a condemned "public servant" (*SA* 1609–10, 1615). The demigod appears among "armed guards, / Both horse and foot before him and behind, / Archers, and Slingers, Cataphracts and Spears" (*SA* 1617–19). The streets near Banqueting House and adjoining scaffold were "lined with soldiers, standing so thick that they [Fairfax and diplomats] had great difficulty in driving back to their own quarters."[63] The better views of the execution were for those "who thronged the upper windows and roofs of the surrounding buildings."[64] The king stepped from a window of the Banqueting House onto a scaffold that was placed between the pillars of the neoclassical, colonnaded Banqueting House: "And where's the Slaughter-House? *White-Hall* must bee, / Lately His Palace, now His *Calvarie*."[65] "Pillars of state," of course, characterizes many royal Stuart portraits, and royalists often had condemned the damage caused by those who had attempted to "use our Sampson (as it were)" to subvert "the Pillars of his Kingdom (the just Laws of our Church & State)."[66] During an "intermission" (*SA* 1629), Samson appears between "two massy pillars," not praying but "as one who pray'd" (1633, 37). This glances at Milton's generally negative view of public prayers, such as those of the king in *Eikon Basilike*. On his scaffold, "The King stood for a moment, raising his hands and eyes to heaven and praying in silence."[67] The king's last speech had been inaudible to all except those on and around the scaffold. However, in Samson's speech, the king is heard much more clearly than the Hebrew judge.[68] In another ironic hit at *Eikon Basilike,* Samson says that he has "perform'd, as reason was" what he has been requested to perform (*SA* 1641), but now, of his "own accord," he intends to stage one "other trial" (*SA* 1643). In this "trial," Samson seeks his death, spurning the hopes presented by Manoa's negotiations for a private, limited status. Believing in his divine rights, Charles at his trial made little effort to preserve his life, despite the many persons in power, including some of the commissioners of the High Court of Justice, who were desperately searching for a way to avoid his execution.

Samson then acts as one who, as Milton describes Charles I, "sits and watches when any thing will dropp, that might solace him with the likeness of a punishment from Heav'n" (*Eikonoklastes,* YP 3:563). Royalists had warned that when "the *Church* and *State* do shake; that Building must / Expect to fall, whose *Prop* is turn'd to *Dust.*"[69] Determined that the prop will be turned to dust, the king usurps the function of providence to ensure the destruction of "that Building." The king uses his only remaining weapon—"his own fraile cogitations"—to enact, with terrific effect, this destruction through his post-humously published book. Milton's comments illuminate the carnage of Samson's last desperate act:

But to counterfet the hand of God is the boldest of all Forgery: And he, who without warrant but his own fantastic surmise, takes upon him perpetually to unfold the secret and unsearchable Mysteries of high Providence, is likely for the most part to mistake and slander them; and approaches to the madness of those reprobate thoughts, that would wrest the Sword of Justice out of Gods own hand, and imploy it more justly in thir own conceit. (YP 3:564)

Milton adds, "Although if ever *fatal blindness* did both *attend and punish* wilfulness, if ever any *enjoy'd not comforts*, for *neglecting counsel belonging to thir peace*, it was in none more conspicuously brought to pass then in himself: and his predictions against the Parlament and thir adherents have for the most part bin verify'd upon his own head, and upon his cheif Coun-selors" (YP 3:567). This too is Samson's fatal blindness, and Samson similarly suffers "the same penalty he would have inflicted on any other man" (*First Defense*, YP 4:304–5).

Yet the king's "frail cogitations" powerfully further a monarchical resto-ration that will appear miraculous to many English people in 1660, as mirac-ulous as Samson's triumph to many of Milton's readers in 1671. The royal actor, as Milton describes Samson, brings ruin "upon the heads of all who sat beneath" (*SA* 1652) his scaffold. The "horrid spectacle" (*SA* 1542) at the "place of horror . . . sad event" (*SA* 1550–51) elicits a "universal groan / As if the whole inhabitation perish'd" (*SA* 1511–12): "This Bloody Stroke being struck upon the Royal Neck . . . it seemed rather to fall upon the People than the King; for as soon as it fell upon his Neck, the People cryed out with so grievous and doleful a cry, as I never heard before."[70] This cry purportedly indicated that the state had been destroyed. The regicides had "severed the *Royal Head* of King *Charles* from his *own Body natural*, and *our* [England's] *body Politick*."[71] One author lamented, "we lost our King, / And in Him lost our selves."[72] According to the political cliché, the groan signaled that En-gland had become forever a monarchy.

Milton, ever watchful for signs of the perhaps inevitable return to Egypt, seems immediately to have understood this signal. His dramatic response suggests a terrible irony. Groans at tragic theater might signal success, but in the "Theater" of politics they mark disaster. The state indeed had suffered catastrophe on January 30, 1649, because of the failure of the English to understand what they had seen. The implications of this failure were clear to Milton: "They only set on sport and play / Unwittingly importun'd / Thir own destruction to come speedy upon them" (*SA* 1679–81). "With blindness internal struck" (*SA* 1686), the English perceive the highly theatrical death of the king not as an ignominious shame but as a moral triumph. And those who cannot distinguish between a murderer and a martyr, a killer and a saint, in a theater or on the throne—or between a theater and a throne—will almost certainly "invite" a killer to sit on the throne. Then the ironic groan of regicide will be heard again, but louder, and with more conviction.

Despite this prediction, Charles II does not "over heaps of slaughter'd walk his way" (*SA* 1530) to the throne. Nevertheless, perhaps reflecting the millenarian malaise of the later 1660s during which he would have revised his dramatic poem, Milton's ominous political theme in many ways intensifies. Samson's climactic carnage ceases to comment on a single, specific political act, only to chart the cultural values that predetermine such acts and their catastrophic consequences. Intoxicated by their idolatry of the king, the English people have negotiated an immensely popular restoration of a monarchy based (according to Milton) upon violence, licentiousness, and powerlust. Just as Hebrew and Philistine unite in endorsing Samson's appearance at the theater, royalist and Presbyterian (and many sectaries and many more Independents) have merged into a single admiration for Charles I on the scaffold and, less uniformly of course, Charles II on the throne. Blind to the spectacular evils of revenge, treachery, lying, mass slaughter, and easy assumptions of divine status, the English have sought convenient, simplistic answers to deep errors. The profound evils that Milton perceived in the Stuart monarchy have been located in the king's unfortunate marriage (if only he had married a Protestant woman). Similarly simplistic, the tragedy of Samson is his conjugal blabbing: "only bewailing / His lot unfortunate in nuptial choice, / From whence captivity and loss of eyes" (1742–44).

This culture that has created Charles the Martyr and indeed the Restoration itself will transform the sin of Milton's Samson into his heroism. This transformation is what the published dramatic poem anticipates, enacts, and even "prophesies," and what readings of the poem for the last three hundred years confirm. Within this context, the significance of Samson's climactic violence shifts, from the practical political counsel that Milton had offered to his fellow citizens in the 1650s, to inspired religious prophecy for the fit and future reader. The political disaster to be suffered by the chosen people at the hands of the reprobate gives way to a gloomier cultural scenario. No such significant opposition exists in 1671 England. Royalists and parliamentarians interact in a single political culture, moving toward catastrophe, an eventual retribution of all—except for perhaps the most extreme dissenters: "the vulgar . . . who stood without" (*SA* 1659). Whatever their political troubles, these dissenters will be spared the apocalyptic woe that haunts Milton's tragedy, in which destruction is no longer visited on a faction, or its persecutors, in a specific event of England's civil war era. Instead, it waits, as an end judgment, to punish an image-doting, imperial culture that has chosen to enshrine men such as Milton's Samson and, as 1660 clearly indicated, Milton's king.

University of Texas–Pan American

NOTES

1. For a recent summary of interpretations, see Alan Rudrum, "Milton Scholarship and the *Agon* over *Samson Agonistes*," *HLQ* 65 (2003): 465–88.

2. See especially Joseph Wittreich, *Interpreting "Samson Agonistes"* (Princeton, 1987), and *Shifting Contexts: Re-Interpreting "Samson Agonistes"* (Pittsburgh, 2002).

3. All quotations from Milton's poetry are from *John Milton: Complete Poems and Major Prose*, ed. Merritt Y. Hughes (New York, 1957). Poetry from this edition will be cited parenthetically by line number in the text.

4. Joan Bennett similarly argues Milton's fictional King Charles in "Satan and King Charles: Milton's Royal Portraits," *Reviving Liberty: Radical Christian Humanism in Milton's Great Poems* (Cambridge, Mass., 1989), 33–58. The strongest connection between Milton's Satan and his king is "their claims of divine right to power" (35). I will argue this connection between Samson and Charles.

5. *Eikonoklastes*, in *The Complete Prose Works of John Milton*, 8 vols., ed. Don M. Wolfe et al. (New Haven, 1953–82), 3:343. Subsequent references to Milton's prose are from this edition, hereafter designated YP and cited parenthetically by volume and page number in the text.

6. *The Riverside Milton*, ed. Roy Flannagan (New York, 1998), 792. Adding that "the dating game quickly becomes a futile exercise," Flannagan writes that "Parker's arguments remain forceful and difficult to refute." William Riley Parker, "The Date of *Samson Agonistes*," *PQ* 28 (1949): 145–66, argues for "the pertinence of the Samson story 1647–1653" (164). For another discussion of the poem's dating, see *Milton: Complete Shorter Poems*, 2nd ed., ed. John Carey (London, 1998), 349–50.

7. John Milton, "Of That Sort of Dramatic Poem Which is Call'd Tragedy," in Hughes, *Complete Poems and Major Prose*, 550.

8. Andrew Marvell, "On *Paradise Lost*," 1, 7–8, in Hughes, *Complete Poems and Major Prose*, 209. Had Marvell read the tragedy in its earliest stages, understood its political implications, and feared similar arguments in *Paradise Lost*? A positive answer would at least partially resolve the "bewildering array of contradictory observation" that Marvell's allusion has elicited (Wittreich, *Interpreting "Samson Agonistes*," 266). Within a political context, a royal Samson has been largely unobserved. Nicholas Jose, *Ideas of the Restoration in English Literature 1660–1671* (Cambridge, Mass., 1984), comments, "Samson takes over the role of monarch in Milton's drama" (161). Jose points out that his name is "etymologically associated with the sun"; his staff is oaken, and the "royal oak" was often used to represent monarchs, especially Charles II, because of his hiding in an oak tree during his escape after the battle of Worcester.

9. William Riley Parker, *Milton: A Biography*, 2 vols., 2nd ed., ed. Gordon Campbell (Oxford, 1996), comments, "Milton took a cynical and disillusioned view of the national character, a view unquestionably influenced by the confusion of his own times and the general atmosphere of

pessimism in 1648" (1:327). For Milton's pessimism, see especially David Loewenstein, *Milton and the Drama of History: Historical Vision, Iconoclasm, and the Literary Imagination* (New York, 1990), and Nicholas von Maltzahn, *Milton's "History of Britain": Republican Historiography in the English Revolution* (Oxford, 1991).

10. Nancy Maguire, "The Theatrical Mask/Masque of Politics: The Case of Charles I," *Journal of British Studies* 28 (1989): 8. Maguire adds that royalist playwrights most frequently rewrote the king's execution as tragedy, "thus changing political defeat into theatrical (and ultimately political) success" (11).

11. Wittreich, *Interpreting "Samson Agonistes,"* 215. In *Shifting Contexts*, Wittreich argues that *Samson* is a critique of Cromwell's "claims to providential favor, intervention, and inspiration" (115). That this argument is not incompatible with a royal Samson suggests much about Milton's view of England's "short but scandalous night of interruption" (*Considerations Touching the Likeliest Means*, YP 7:274).

12. Salmasius, *Defensio Pro Regia*, in YP 4:1008.

13. For "Charles's sacral monarchy," see James Loxley, *Royalism and Poetry in the English Civil Wars: The Drawn Sword* (New York, 1997), 177.

14. John Gauden, *Cromwell's Bloody Slaughter-house* (London, 1660), 22; accessed through "Early English Books Online," wwwlib.umi.com/eebo; hereafter cited as EEBO. Gauden explains that the regicides murdered the "Husband of the Kingdome" although they "pretended to fight for him, and preserve him" (17, 50).

15. Andrew Lacey, *The Cult of King Charles the Martyr* (Woodbridge, Suffolk, 2003), 29–33; F. Michael Krouse, *Milton's Samson and the Christian Tradition* (Princeton, 1949), 67–69.

16. Dennis Kezar examines the intertextuality of *Eikonoklastes, Eikon Basilike,* and *Samson Agonistes* in "Samson's Death by Theater and Milton's Art of Dying," *ELH* 66 (1999): 295–336. His cultural argument anticipates many of the points highlighted by my present political argument: Charles's and Milton's textual references to Samson, Samson's and the king's claims to conscience and their "published" secrets, Milton's use of eclipse imagery, and the theme of betrayal. Except for the textual references—examined within the *ars moriendi* tradition—these points are not developed in Kezar's essay.

17. Milton's only explicit citation of Samson that would support an identification of Samson with the rebels appears in his *First Defense* (YP 4:402). Yet there, where Milton cites Samson's actions as a precedent for rebellion, "even the heroic Samson" suggests a possible disjunction between this exemplary action and Samson's usual conduct, and his valor is set in striking opposition to divine prompting.

18. Charles I, *Eikon Basilike: The Portraiture of His Sacred Majesty in His Solitudes and Sufferings,* ed. Philip Knachel, Folger Shakespeare Library (Ithaca, N.Y., 1966), 165. Subsequent references to this work will be cited in the text.

19. Sir Richard Bulstrode, *Memoirs and Reflections on the Reign of Kings Charles I and II* (Tonbridge, Kent, 1997), 176.

20. Sir Thomas Herbert, *Memoirs of the Two last Years of the Reign of the Unparallel'd Prince, of Ever Blessed Memory, King Charles I,* in *Charles I in Captivity from Contemporary Sources,* ed. Gertrude Stevenson (London, 1927), 165, 167. The mill also perhaps recalls the humiliations of the newly crowned Charles II at the hands of the Scots. One contemporary cartoon represented "The Scots Holding Their Young Kinges Nose To Ye Grinstone" (depicted in Ronald Hutton, *Charles II: King of England, Scotland, and Ireland* [Oxford, 1989]).

21. Oliver Cromwell, *Speeches of Oliver Cromwell: 1644–1658,* ed. Charles L. Stainer (London, 1901), 87.

22. EEBO, 30. Gauden comments on "this Tragedy of Tragedies carried on to such bloody conclusions."

23. C. V. Wedgwood, *The King's War 1641–47* (London, 1966), 554, 607.

24. David Hume, *The History of England from the Invasion of Julius Caesar to the Revolution in 1688*, 7 vols. (Baltimore, 1810), 6:147.

25. For commentary on this passage, see especially *The Jerome Biblical Commentary*, 2 vols., gen. ed. Raymond Brown (Englewood Cliffs, N.J., 1968), 1:159; *Harper's Bible Commentary*, gen. ed. James Mays (San Francisco, 1988), 257; Jo Cheryl Exum, "Literary Patterns in the Samson Saga: An Investigation of Rhetorical Style in Biblical Prose" (Ph.D. diss., Columbia University, 1976), 93–115. Citations of Scripture included within the text refer to the King James Version.

26. Wittreich, *Interpreting "Samson Agonistes,"* 158.

27. Ronald Knowles, introduction to *The Entertainment of His Most Excellent Majestie Charles II in His Passage through the City of London to His Coronation*, by John Ogilby (Binghamton, N.Y., 1988), 14.

28. Quoted in Gerard Reedy, "Mystical Politics: The Imagery of Charles II's Restoration," in *Studies in Change and Revolution: Aspects of English Intellectual History 1640–1800*, ed. Paul Korshin (Menston, Yorkshire, 1972), 28.

29. Wittreich, *Interpreting "Samson Agonistes,"* 67.

30. Kevin Sharpe, *Remapping Early Modern England: The Culture of Seventeenth-Century Politics* (New York, 2000), 177–98, discusses "the king as the reason of the body politic" (183).

31. "To the Sacred Majestie of Great *Britain, France* and *Ireland,* King Charls II" (line 1), dedication to *The Famous Tragedie of King Charles I* (London, 1649) (accessed through EEBO).

32. Herbert, *Memoirs of the Two Last Years,* 161–65.

33. Joad Raymond, "Popular Representations of Charles I," in *The Royal Image: Representations of Charles I,* ed. Thomas Corns (New York, 1999), 61. Sir Benjamin Rudyerd, in a parliamentary speech (November 1640), states that evil counselors "have eclipsed him [the king] by their interposition"; from *Images of English Puritanism: A Collection of Contemporary Sources 1589–1646,* ed. Lawrence Sasek (Baton Rouge, 1989), 124. Sasek writes that Rudyerd "uses one common way of resolving the dilemma of the parliamentary royalists who eventually fought against Charles" (121).

34. Quoted in Tom Cain, "'A Sad Intestine War': Mildmay Fane and the Poetry of Civil Strife," in *The English Civil Wars in the Literary Imagination,* ed. Claude Summers and Ted-Larry Pebworth (Columbia, 1999), 36.

35. Samson's marriage with Dalila is also characterized by Milton's view of the union of church and state, "two powers, utterly diverse, the civil and the ecclesiastical, to make harlots of each other and while appearing to strengthten, [*sic*] by their mingled and spurious riches, actually to undermine and at length destroy each other" (*Second Defense,* YP 4:678).

36. Wedgwood, *The King's War,* 103–4.

37. Annabel Patterson, *Marvell and the Civic Crown* (Princeton, 1978), 24–25.

38. In 1659, Charles I's writings had been published as *Bibliotheca Regia,* and, according to Lois Potter, *Secret Rites and Secret Writing: Royalist Literature, 1641–1660* (New York, 1989), "it is not surprising that the two illustrations commissioned for the volume should depict a young, active and successful ruler on his throne or at the helm of the ship of state" (202).

39. Thomas Forde, "An Anniversary on Charls the First, 1657," lines 43, 49–51, in *Virtus Rediviva; or, A Panegyrick on the Late K Charls I. Second Monarch of Great Britain* (London, 1660) (accessed through EEBO).

40. George Wither, "On the Martyrdom of His Late Majestie," in *Vaticinium Votivum; or, Palaemon's Prophetick Prayer with Several Elegies,* Spenser Society Publications, vol. 41, Burt Franklin Research & Source Works Series, no. 150 (New York, 1967), 79; John Cleveland, "A

Deep Groan Fetch'd at the Funerall of that Incomparable and Glorious Monarch Charles the First," in *Monumentum Regale; or, A Tombe, Erected for that Incomparable and Glorious Monarch, Charles the First King of Great Britiane, France and Ireland, &c. In Select Elegies, Epitaphs, and Poems* (London, 1649), 32 (accessed through EEBO).

41. Potter, *Secret Rites and Secret Writing*, 211.

42. Wedgwood, *The King's War*, 130; also see 164–65 for the ballad on the "the clean contrary way" as an example of "a hundred ribald ballads" that commented on the war. Milton might have had this ballad in mind when he commented on the king's "clean contrary motion" (YP 3:308).

43. Ibid., 198, 258, 287–88.

44. Ibid., 567.

45. Austin Woolrych, *Britain in Revolution 1625–1660* (Oxford, 2002), 433, 391.

46. Ibid., 349.

47. Hume, *History of England*, laments, "Thus the Scottish nation underwent, and still undergo (for such grievous stains are not easily wiped off), the reproach of selling their king, and betraying their prince for money" (111).

48. Wedgwood, *The King's War*, 128.

49. Perez Zagorin, *A History of Political Thought in the English Revolution* (London, 1954), 193–94.

50. Kristen Poole, *Radical Religion from Shakespeare to Milton: Figures of Nonconformity in Early Modern England* (New York, 2000), 125.

51. Salmasius, *Defensio regia*, in YP 4:986. "Princes are not bound to give account of their actions, but to God alone," stated a proclamation after the dissolution of Parliament in 1629. See *The Letters, Speeches, and Proclamations of King Charles I*, ed. Sir Charles Petrie (London: Cassell, 1935), 63. In the speech he was unable to deliver at his trial, he emphasized the legal maxim "that the King can do no wrong" (259–60).

52. Steven Zwicker, *Lines of Authority: Politics and English Literary Culture 1649–1689* (Ithaca, N.Y., 1993), 38.

53. Gauden, quoted in the introduction to *Eikon Basilike*, xxxii.

54. Elias Ashmole, *A Briefe Narrative of His Majestie's Solemn Coronation with His Magnificent Proceeding, and Royal Feast in Westminster-Hall*, in John Ogilby, *The Entertainment of His Most Excellent Majestie Charles II in His Passage through the City of London to His Coronation* (Binghamton, N.Y., 1988), 180.

55. Reedy, "Mystical Politics," 33–39; N. H. Keeble, *The Restoration: England in the 1660s* (London, 2002), 53.

56. Ashmole, *A Briefe Narrative*, 173.

57. A few examples would include John Quarles, "An Elegy upon that Never to be Forgotten Charles the First," in *Regale Lectum Miseriae; or, A Kingly Bed of Misery* (London, 1660), 44 (accessed through EEBO); George Wither, "To the Sacred Memorie of that late High and Mightie Monarch, CHARLS the FIRST; Hee who fell Jan. 30. 1648. The Princelie Proto-Martyr of *Great* Britain, &c.," in *Vaticinium Votivum*, 46–47; John Crouch, "A Mixt Poem" (London, 1660), 1 (accessed through EEBO); Ben Jonson, "Another Epigram on the Birth of the Prince," 1, in *Ben Jonson: Poems*, ed. Ian Donaldson (London, 1975); Richard Crashaw, "To the Queen Upon Her Numerous Progenie," 140, in *The Complete Works of Richard Crashaw*, 2 vols., ed. Rev. Alexander Grossart (London, 1872), 2:265. The image is also significant to the visual arts, such as in Wenceslas Hollar's engraving of Charles II's escape from the battle of Worcester.

58. Quoted in Graham Edwards, *The Last Days of Charles I* (Phoenix Mill, Gloucestershire, 1999), 131.

59. Quoted in ibid., 139, 133.

60. Stephen Orgel and Roy Strong, *Inigo Jones: The Theatre of the Stuart Court,* 2 vols. (Berkeley and Los Angeles, 1973), 1:75.

61. DuMoulin describes court masks as "solemn feasts" in *Cry of the King's Blood,* in YP 4:1063.

62. Edwards, *The Last Days of Charles I,* 177, 184.

63. C. V. Wedgwood, *A Coffin for King Charles: The Trial and Execution of Charles I* (New York, 1964), 216.

64. Edwards, *The Last Days of Charles I,* 178.

65. Wither, "On the Martyrdom of His Late Majestie," 79.

66. *The Faithful, yet Imperfect, Character of a Glorious King, King Charles I. His Country's & Religions Martyr* (London, 1660), 23 (accessed through EEBO).

67. Wedgwood, *A Coffin for King Charles,* 223.

68. As Wittreich, *Interpreting "Samson Agonistes,"* points out, "What was in Judges a prayer is here a thinly veiled threat" (74).

69. Wither, "On the Martyrdom of His Late Majestie," 81.

70. John Gauden, *The Bloody Court; or, The Fatall Tribunall* (London, 1649), 14 (accessed through EEBO).

71. John Paradise, *Hadadrimmon, sive Threnodia Anglicana ob Regicidium* (London, 1661), 2 (accessed through EEBO).

72. Quoted in Maguire, "The Theatrical Mask," 4.

READING *SAMSON* IN
THE NEW AMERICAN CENTURY

Feisal G. Mohamed

"Nation-states have the capacity to enforce their truth games, and universities, their critical distance notwithstanding, are part of the battery of institutions complicit in this process"

Dipesh Chakrabarty, *Provincializing Europe*

"Freedom is on the march."

George W. Bush, second presidential debate, October 8, 2004

EORGE W. BUSH'S yoking together of the language of liberty and militarism in his second debate with John Kerry is characteristic of his notion of "freedom," an ideal given fullest expression in his second inaugural address, where he claimed that the "force of human freedom . . . is not *primarily* the task of arms."[1] In what Bush apologist David Brooks beamingly described on PBS's *NewsHour* as "a very liberal speech," Bush held up as "America's ideal of freedom" Abraham Lincoln's Homestead Act, FDR's Social Security Act, and Harry Truman's G. I. Bill of Rights, and evoked along the way George Washington's "fire of liberty" from the very first inaugural address, Roosevelt's Four Freedoms, and John F. Kennedy's promise to "pay any price" in defense of freedom. Even Peter Beinart has been led to wonder in the ninetieth anniversary issue of the *New Republic*, titled "To Liberalism!" whether Bush is "the new champion of the liberal foreign policy tradition" and concedes the "moral power of Bush's words."[2]

Only fools should be fooled by this president's ostensibly liberal rhetoric, though not for the reasons that have been offered. Bush's second inaugural address is not simple dissembling at odds with his policy; it transforms the liberalism it evokes into the expansionist rhetoric of "freedom" characteristic of this policy. This is revealed in the language of godliness pervasive in the speech, which makes reliance on "the truths of Sinai, the Sermon on the Mount, [and] the words of the Koran" a shibboleth of "the governing of the self."[3] Bush's address is thus a plea for the political ascendancy of the enlightened. The pervasiveness of such a notion of positive liberty across the American political spectrum is suggested by the reaction of left-leaning commentators to the president's speech who have not interrogated its values but rather have claimed that the American Left's actions best suit Bush's "lofty" words.[4]

Such rhetoric reflects a notion of liberty quite at odds with the liberal tradition, and will evoke for scholars of the seventeenth century Quentin Skinner's and Paul A. Rahe's arguments on the classical republicanism of Milton and his contemporaries, which is concerned less with the civil and political rights of all individuals than with the right of the virtuous to govern.[5] Indeed, the "governing of the self" that Bush renders as the hallmark of American freedom evokes directly Milton's typical opposition of liberty to license as expressed in the opening sentences of *The Tenure of Kings and Magistrates:* "being slaves within doors, no wonder that they strive so much to have the public State conformably govern'd to the inward vitious rule, by which they govern themselves. For indeed none can love freedom heartilie, but good men; the rest love not freedom, but licence; which never hath more scope or more indulgence then under Tyrants" (YP 3:190).[6] In the terms of the Bush inaugural address and of *Tenure,* the development of civil institutions that seek broad consensus and guarantee the rights of dissenting individuals is less desirable than a condition where "good men" exercise political authority. This authority takes for granted the necessity of suppressing the political rights of the morally benighted, no matter how numerous and thus democratically legitimate they might be. "Nothing is more natural, nothing more just, nothing more useful or more advantageous to the human race," Milton claims in *A Second Defense,* "than that the lesser obey the greater, not the lesser number the greater number, but the lesser virtue the greater virtue, the lesser wisdom the greater wisdom" (YP 4:636).

The misprision of the term *liberty* that allows it to be divorced from its liberal signification and to become instead a moral defense of expansionism and interventionism finds a parallel in current response to *Samson Agonistes.* Rather than refining our understanding of various cultures of violence—of the seventeenth century and of today, of Christianity and of Islam—this response has sought instead to oppose Milton's dramatic poem to current religious radicalism, and thus tacitly to affirm a sense of Western moral superiority. The most obvious expression of this tendency has come from England—perhaps fittingly given the recent behavior of Tony Blair, Margaret Thatcher, Bernard Lewis, and Niall Ferguson—in the form of John Carey's now infamous brief article in the *Time Literary Supplement.* "September 11," Carey claims, "has changed *Samson Agonistes,* because it has changed the readings we *can* derive from it while still celebrating it as an achievement of the human imagination."[7] If Milton's brief tragedy endorses Samson's actions, he wonders, "should it not be withdrawn from schools and colleges and, indeed, banned more generally as an incitement to terrorism?" Not only do these comments presuppose that educational curricula should suppress dissenting views on terrorism, but they also claim that a right-thinking community cannot attribute aesthetic value to a work that presents a heroic Samson: we can, Carey claims, celebrate *Samson Agonistes* as an achievement of the human imagination if and only if we derive readings from it that show the text's opposition to religious violence.

The participation of this response in the rhetoric of the political dominant is fully revealed in Carey's oversimplification of Arab reaction to the terrorist attacks on New York and Washington: he likens the Danite Chorus celebrating Samson's slaughter of the Philistine lords to "the pictures screened on British television in the immediate aftermath of September 11, which showed people in Arab dress dancing for joy in the streets."[8] In Carey's terminology these are not real-life Arabs with a religion and culture of their own, not to mention valid objections to American foreign policy, but rather "murderous bigots" entirely removed from the realm of "human imagination" in which we must place Milton. This is something of an update of the reading of Samson as "outmoded hero" that Carey mounted over thirty-five years ago: where his 1969 book on Milton is informed by mid-twentieth-century subordination of Judaism to Christianity, he now supports his arguments by raising the bogey of the sons of Shem currently in ill repute.[9] The supposed "change" that 9/11 creates in reading *Samson Agonistes* is used here as cover for the advancement of a preexisting argument. This after-the-fact justification recalls the way that 9/11 served after the fact to justify the desire voiced one year before by Donald Rumsfeld and Paul Wolfowitz's Project for the New American Century that "some catastrophic and catalyzing event like a new Pearl Harbor" might galvanize public support for increased defense spending.[10] Like Rumsfeld and Wolfowitz, Carey seems to see 9/11 as a "catalyzing event" in that history has provided a convenient device—terrorists now occupy the rhetorical space where communists, papists, and Anabaptists have tread before—with which one can dismiss out of hand arguments that have posed a legitimate and longstanding challenge to one's views.

Carey's brief article is in some respects an extreme example of literary criticism's duplication of the logic of American dominance. In many respects, however, it only makes explicit an anxiety implicit in many critiques of *Samson Agonistes*. Though, as Mark R. Kelley and Joseph Wittreich have recently described it, this text is "the major site of contestation within Milton studies," several of its agonists have united in their desire to distance it from religious violence, either by arguing for its opposition to the events it displays or by contrasting its radicalism to that of the present day.[11]

This tendency displays itself in the ostensibly divergent readings of Stanley Fish, Joseph Wittreich, and David Loewenstein. In their positions on *Samson* a broad range of Miltonists display parallels to Gayatri Spivak's theorization of the Native Informants of postcolonial studies who seek to legitimize disciplinary work by providing a token representation of alien culture that confirms the presuppositions of the dominant culture. A more inclusive approach to *Samson* would challenge the borders of Western humanist nonviolence that current readings buttress, and complicate the relationship between this text's performative iconoclasm and the "performance violence," to use Mark Juergensmeyer's phrase, of modern terrorism.[12]

Carey's desire to dissociate Milton from religious violence is also subtly evinced in the reading of *Samson* to which he objects, that of Stanley Fish. In Fish's reading, two plots are resolved at the end of Milton's dramatic poem: that of Samson's internal regeneration and that of his external revenge on the Philistines, with the violence of the latter calling into question its relationship to the former. Thus, Milton's Samson takes his place alongside the heroes of faith of Hebrews, chapter 11, who, Fish claims, are praised for taking "provisional actions . . . in the name of a certain faith."[13] This is an entirely valid point if this provisionalness refers only to Samson's lack of foreknowledge regarding the actions his "rousing motions" will impel (*SA* 1382). Fish, however, extends the uncertainty of this moment to include doubt over the divine source of Samson's actions, claiming that we can only say "that God has willed or permitted (the distinction is unimportant) what the Chorus terms Samson's glorious revenge."[14]

The distinction dismissed in Fish's parentheses is, in fact, of utmost importance: though God allows his champion to sin and despair, it is Samson's ability to rise from this condition and become attuned to divine will that marks him as a hero of faith. To say that the worthies of Hebrews 11 are valued only for taking "*provisional* actions in the *name* of a certain faith" is to set the bar of spiritual heroism rather lower than Milton would allow, and especially to ignore the divine favor and reward fundamental to such heroism. This is what Milton emphasizes in his portrayals of other worthies of Hebrews 11: Michael reassures Adam in *Paradise Lost* that Abel's faith will be "approv'd" by God and that he will "Lose no reward" (11.458–59); that Enoch is removed from harm's way, "Rapt in a balmy Cloud . . . to walk with God / High in Salvation" (11.706–8); that Noah is observed by God to be "The one just Man alive" (11.818); and that in Moses we see what "wondrous power God to his Saint will lend" (12.200). Jesus tells us in *Paradise Regained* that the godly general Gideon shall enjoy the celestial reward of "reign in *Israel* without end" (2.442).[15] Most pertinently, Abraham follows his "Faith" not to ambiguous action but to the execution of God's plan for his elect: "[God] from him will raise / A mighty Nation, and upon him show'r / His benediction" (12.123–25). Though he does not see the future of Israel clearly before him, Abraham is not praised, as Fish claims, simply for his "resolution to keep moving, to see what happens, take a chance";[16] his heroism is predicated upon the special calling granted to him by God as a reward for his faith. Though they may see their actions as provisional, we are told over and again that what makes the men of Hebrews 11 exemplary is their ability to "hear [God] call" (*PL* 3.185), a sensitivity to divine prompting that always and necessarily produces justified external action.

To say otherwise is to attribute to Milton what Fish describes in his *Harper's* article as the "light-as-air [modern] spirituality" in which "the sorting out of big theological questions" is left to "God and eternity," and to engage in precisely the forgetfulness against which Fish himself warns: "it is only if the first principle of Milton's thought—that God is God and not one of a number of contending forces—is denied or forgotten that his poetry can be seen as conflicted or tragic or inconclusive or polysemous or paradoxical, words that name literary qualities most of us have been taught to admire. They are not, I will argue, qualities Milton admires."[17] By this claim, to see Samson's final slaughter of the Philistines as a provisional action divorced from divine agency is to impose a sense of tragic outcome informed more by current definitions of literary value than by Milton's views on spiritual heroism and Christian tragedy. The reading of *Samson Agonistes* offered in *How Milton Works* tends, as Michael Lieb observes, to undermine much of the argument of Fish's book by introducing doubt in the divine procession and return that it describes as the Miltonic master plot.[18]

Carey thus misrepresents Fish in two significant ways. First, he all but ignores the emphasis on uncertainty in Fish's reading of *Samson Agonistes*. Fish quite clearly claims that Milton makes the divine impetus of Samson's final act more mysterious than do such antecedents as Marcus Andreas Wunstius, Theodorus Rhodius, Hieronymus Zieglerus, and Joost van den Vondel: "it is that act which in every other version is the dramatic and interpretive centerpiece; and by surrounding it with circumstances that obscure rather than clarify its significance, Milton departs from the tradition he inherits in ways that can only be deliberate."[19] Second, and much more egregiously, Carey deploys *How Milton Works* in an entirely unfair and unreasonable way: the events of September 11, Carey claims, "seem like a devilish implementation of [Fish's] arguments."[20] In his recent address to the International Milton Congress at Duquesne University, Fish was tetchy on this point—"I am not a terrorist, *I am a literary critic*"—and with good reason, for there is positively no rational way in which the terrorist attacks of September 11,

2001, can seem like an implementation of his arguments on *Samson Agonistes*.

Fish's arguments can be seen, however, as consistent with liberal anxiety over the violence of *Samson Agonistes*. He makes an exception to his arguments on Miltonic antinomianism in order to introduce in *Samson* literary values of inconclusiveness, polysemy, and paradox, and to downplay the dramatic poem's theme of divinely inspired violence—an echo in its own way of Carey's sentiment that we cannot posit the text's approval of religious violence while celebrating it as an achievement of the human imagination. Rather than seeing *Samson* as a religious poem where, as Fish puts it in his *Harper's* article, "identification of the actions that may or may not be taken" is an *"internal* matter" unconcerned with the fate of those "poor lost souls" who "are in the grip of error and too blind to see,"[21] he argues that it displays concern with the fate of the Philistine lords, implicitly associating Milton's dramatic poem with liberal humanist nonviolence.

This comes despite Fish's recent criticism in these pages of the tendency among liberal academics to find in Milton a poet who has "the right political values—their values," a claim made in an argument skeptical of historicism and in favor of a formalist valuation of "aesthetic achievement."[22] Though Fish avoids the absurdity of New Criticism by recognizing that literary form is itself underwritten by history and politics—and that Milton's period especially is one where debates on literary genre are "unintelligible apart from the issues of nationalism, political authority, and public morality"[23]—he revives this absurdity to the extent that there is no room in his thesis for consideration of Milton's prose as illuminating the poetry. Once we admit in our examination of the poetry the significance of the antiprelatical tracts or the defenses, we must also admit the significance of Joseph Hall, James Ussher, Claude Saumaise, Alexander More, and a host of others whose influence on Milton does not reside primarily in the field of poetic aesthetics. In the terms of Fish's essay, this is impermissible; we must consider each form as having its own independent history: "you have to attend to the specificity of the discourse that has solicited your attention, and that means attending to its history, not to history in general (there is no such thing) but to the history of a form."[24] Fish thus renders a Milton who "matters" only insofar as we recognize the poet's aesthetic achievement and ignore the polemicist's sometimes unseemly political views. Though this is not a Milton marching in the cause of modern liberalism, it is nonetheless a Milton whose status within the liberal tradition remains largely uncomplicated by the unsettling aspects of his political and religious thought.

If Fish implicitly displays liberal values in his reading of *Samson,* Joseph Wittreich does so explicitly in his claim that "Milton *matters* because, in facing tragedy, he forces us to reach beyond an axis of good and evil in the world to a more ambiguous reality." "Poetry," Wittreich tells us, "repeals traditions and voids conventions"—a claim difficult to reconcile with the Renaissance repristination of traditions and conventions, literary and religious, in which *Samson Agonistes* is deeply engaged.[25] In *Shifting Contexts*, he has described the relationship between Samson and Christ as a "typology of difference" where "Samson's slaying . . . sets him at odds with Christ's saving" and even from the "moral bearing" and "heroic character" of Hercules.[26] As he is aware, this is an extension of the readings of Samson most often associated with John Carey and Irene Samuel, though, he argues, this view received "major articulation" in J. H. B. Masterman's 1897 *Age of Milton*, which "sought to free *Samson Agonistes* from a politics of violence and religion of retaliation." Finding such precedents for the Carey and Samuel readings would seem a worthwhile project in light of Alan Rudrum's recent review article, which saddles their interpretation with that dismissive tag of newfangledness, "revisionist."[27] A second look at Masterman, however, reveals that this is not at all the portrait he paints of *Samson:*

When, therefore, Milton issued his last two poems together, he laid before the vanquished adherents of the Commonwealth a great alternative. On the one side was the victory of patience and self-repression—the Divine overcoming of evil with good; on the other hand was *the triumph of revenge*—swift, merciless, irresistible; *and though the poet leaves the scales balanced between the two,* his own old age testified that he had chosen the better part—to obey, to be patient, and to hope.[28]

In Masterman's reading, the text registers the desire of "the Puritan party" to "strike one more blow for freedom," and though Milton does not strike such a blow himself in his final years, the 1671 edition shows equal valuation of patience and of resistance. If Masterman is objecting to an interpretation of *Samson,* it is the straightforward autobiographical reading pervasive in the late nineteenth and early twentieth centuries; in so doing, he argues for the dramatic poem's theme of violent retribution with greater force than do his contemporaries.[29]

If this extension of the authority of the "outmoded hero" reading of *Samson* is suspect, the deployment of Milton to criticize current conservative politics is rather more so. This is evinced in Wittreich's commentary on Margaret Thatcher's evocation of the Samson image of *Areopagitica* in her argument that America should respond to its moment of crisis with vigorous militarism: "Thatcher herself uses Milton differently than he would be used, far differently than he (and others) had used Euripides against those who would reduce a city to ruin and desolation and therefore as part of an appeal not to tear down—to create rather than destroy and thereby revive 'expiring libertie.' "[30] Although this portrait of Milton is inviting, its closing reference to *The Readie and Easie Way* points to complications arising from an association of Milton's libertarianism with current liberalism: the comment on "expiring libertie" to which Wittreich directs attention describes the inevitability of God's defense of an enlightened few in a tract advocating the suspension of the rights of the majority—which suspension, we learn in Milton's *Letter to a Friend,* was to be implemented and sustained by military force, if necessary (YP 7:330).[31] In this sense, Milton's revival of "expiring libertie" does share some of the spirit of Margaret Thatcher's and of Tony Blair's encouragement of American unilateralism. Wittreich's position, like Carey's and Fish's, thus forecloses discussion of Milton's radicalism in an effort to present him as a poet sympathetic to the values of modern humanism.

Wittreich's comments are, however, animated by a timely and important concern that we not consider ourselves members of an enlightened age that has outgrown "revenge fantasy." If, he claims, we see Samson's heroism as Milton's imagined tearing down of the "pillars of [Restoration] church and state," then we posit that his "excellence is his relevance to the seventeenth century and irrelevance to our own—with Milton, then, seeming to embrace the very values that, having outgrown them, we now oppose."[32] This presents a valid criticism of the increasingly specific location of *Samson* in its moment of publication—the branch of scholarship that has seen Samson as part of Milton's larger political resistance to the restored Stuart monarchy, or as hero of London Nonconformity, or as stand-in for a martyr of the Good Old Cause like Sir Henry Vane.[33] Even when such historicist readings are temporally widened beyond the text's immediate Restoration context, they tend to look to *Samson* as artifact of abandoned ideas. In this vein a reviewer of Derek Wood's *Exiled from Light* claims that Milton's tragic hero is an unsettling portrait of the poet's "powerfully anti-Semitic . . . understanding of the Hebrew Bible," showing "what Christians in the seventeenth century really thought about Judaism," a reading that would turn Samson into a Miltonic Shylock.[34]

Interpreting the seventeenth-century values identified by historicism in light of current politics has furthermore created instances of discomfort. In his review of David Loewenstein's *Representing Revolution in Milton and His Contemporaries,* Michael Mendle involves this significant piece of scholarship in the confusion and fear surrounding 9/11:

Unlike Loewenstein, I write in the wake of the terrorist attacks, which confirm in their way the full hideousness of Milton's fantasy of exterminatory hatred upon "all who sat beneath" (line 1652). . . . Like the modern terrorist "martyrs" who deny their deaths constitute the sin of suicide, Milton's Samson's death is only "by accident" . . . the consequence of "dire necessity" (line 1666). One can only wonder whether Milton (and Loewenstein) recalled at this juncture the lines of *Paradise Lost* (Book IV, ll. 393–4): "So spake the Fiend, and with necessity, / The tyrant's plea, excus'd his devilish deeds."[35]

Faced with the prospect that Milton's dramatic poem "confirms" the values animating terrorism, Mendle retreats to a quotation of *Paradise Lost* with the soothing ring of moral aphorism. The comfort derived from these lines, which seem to capture liberal objection to both jihadist and Bush culture, is, however, entirely fallacious: they are not at all at odds with Samson's divinely appointed slaughter, which is impelled by Providence rather than by political necessity and is thus fundamentally opposed to the demonic tyranny represented by the idol-worshipping Philistines.

Loewenstein has recently reiterated the parallels between *Samson* and Quaker polemics for which he argues in *Representing Revolution,* but, perhaps to prevent such alarmed objection, he adds that while Milton's dramatic poem displays "religious terror" it does not present us with "terrorism," a term that arises only after the French Revolution. "We need," Loewenstein claims, "to make crucial distinctions, informed particularly by an understanding of religious terror in the tumultuous world of seventeenth-century England, before branding Milton's Samson with the pejorative name 'terrorist,' a word unknown to Milton and his contemporaries."[36] These include Milton's removal of the vengeful prayer in Judges and his stipulation that Samson's death is not a suicide, as well as the fact that Samson does not plan his attack upon the Philistines or even actively seek Dagon's temple. Such distinctions call into question the parallel between Samson and the 9/11 hijackers that Carey describes as "obvious" but tend to skirt around a central similarity: that Samson, in Carey's words, "destroys many innocent victims, whose lives, hopes and loves are all quite unknown to him personally."[37] By emphasizing differences between Milton's Samson and the modern terrorist, Loewenstein's reading generates a comfortable distance between seventeenth-century radicalism and that of today. This gesture allows us to explore Milton's radical religion without raising unsettling parallels to the violence of its current counterpart; in the process, it avoids subjecting the modern term "terrorism" to the kind of "discriminating analysis" and "rational argument" that Loewenstein identifies as absent in "political and cultural discourse."[38]

Each side of the great divide on *Samson* thus operates to cleanse Milton of association with present-day religious violence, either by vaccinating him with current liberal ideals or by consigning him to a distant and irrelevant past. We can see in this process Milton studies showing the tendency identified by poststructuralists of intellectual work to support the presuppositions of the political dominant. As Pierre Bourdieu claims, the critic's "only hope of producing scientific knowledge—rather than weapons to advance a particular class of specific interests—is to make explicit to oneself one's position in the sub-field of the producers of discourse about art."[39] In a similar vein, Michel Foucault observes in a conversation with Gilles Deleuze that the intellectual must "struggle against the forms of power that transform him into its object and instrument in the sphere of 'knowledge,' 'truth,' 'consciousness,' and 'discourse.' "[40]

This certainly holds a valuable lesson for Milton studies as it turns its attention to the issue of terrorism: criticism should beware of the potential of perpetuating a discourse that has employed global terrorism to solidify its own power. The teleology of Bourdieu's and Foucault's statements, however, must come under suspicion: the hope of producing a "scientific knowledge" that is not a weapon of specific interests, and the creation of a class of intellectuals engaged in a genuine struggle against "power" are aspirations employed to legitimize the theories of the practitioners who voice them. The very voices that these intellectuals would claim to make heard are marginalized and subordinated to an a priori narrative of class struggle—one is consistently aware that the workers on whose behalf the signs must burn have their desires and aspirations assumed and articulated for them by the poststructuralist theorist.

Attuned to such complications is Gayatri Spivak's theorization of the Native Informant. Commenting on the above-cited conversation between Foucault and Delueze, Spivak observes, "the ventriloquism of the speaking subaltern is the left intellectual's stock-in-trade."[41] In the terms of her argument, academic postcolonialism is a discipline especially fraught with the contradiction of making a show of resistance to the cultural dominant while operating within its terms. "Postcolonial informants" take professional advantage of an "aura of identification with . . . distant objects of oppression," and "at worst, they . . . play the native informant uncontaminated by disavowed involvement with the machinery of the production of knowledge." In order to be more "effective," then, postcolonialism must acknowledge its complicity in the silencing of subaltern voices and the perpetuation of colonial relationships between the Western metropolis and the "third world."[42]

This may seem a far cry from *Samson Agonistes,* but it is not. If early modern studies shares a quality with postcolonial studies, it is that it offers an aura of authority on a culture foreign to the uninitiated. Like the postcolonial informant Spivak identifies, Miltonists in their current response to *Samson* have deployed an aura of identification with a distant culture in a way that silently affirms, and gains legitimacy by affirming, presuppositions of the current cultural dominant. Either by declaring Milton's sympathy with horror over religious violence or by asserting the irrelevance of his radicalism to the present day, such intellectual work declares its allegiance with Western values of nonviolence and liberty and its uncomplicated cultural superiority to the religious violence of the Other.

This can be seen as only the latest episode in the long history of politically charged interpretation of Milton, and especially of *Samson*. It is no coincidence, as Sharon Achinstein has suggested, that the "notorious missing middle is blotted out by the conservative Tory Samuel Johnson," a gesture that radicalizes the text by shifting focus to its conclusion and supports Johnson's estimation of it as "the tragedy which ignorance has admired and bigotry applauded."[43] Achinstein's observation on Johnson's politicized aesthetic is borne out by Richard Cumberland's Whig rescue of the tragedy's middle in *The Observer* (1791).[44] What I am suggesting here is in some ways an extension of the brand of inquiry evinced in Joan S. Bennett's reading of Milton in light of current liberation theology. Drawing on Loewenstein's description of *Samson* as "iconoclastic weapon," Bennett concludes that "Milton's biblical story-making is performative discourse and that iconoclasm is a very important part of the work being done. . . . The modern revolutionary identity more appropriately comparable to Milton than 'terrorist' is perhaps, in a broad sense, 'educator.' "[45] This view of Milton as educator in resistance is undoubtedly true and is suggestive in its relationship to all of Milton's Restoration publications, not only the three major poems but also the *Artis Logicae*, the *Accedence Commenc't Grammar*, *The History of Britain*, and *Of True Religion*. One of the strengths of Bennett's (pre–9/11) argument, however, is that rather than dismissing terrorism as a context significant to *Samson*, it invites broadened consideration of contexts that might allow " 'first world' academics and students today" better to imagine "someone with Milton's deep religiosity and profound humanism maintaining a revolutionary political commitment."[46]

Surely one of the contexts that must now obtain is what Mark Juergensmeyer has described as the "performance violence" of modern terrorism, where "explosive scenarios are not *tactics* directed toward an immediate, earthly, or strategic goal, but *dramatic events* intended to impress for their symbolic significance." When viewers of such attacks "take them seriously" and "begin to distrust the peacefulness of the world around [them,] the purposes of this theater are achieved."[47]

Though it must be stressed that the performance violence of *Samson Agonistes* remains fictive, this aspect of modern terrorism finds a ready parallel to the text's intervention in Restoration culture. In its every sinew *Samson Agonistes* strains against Restoration triumphalism and reminds its readers

that a defeated and ridiculed blind guide can carry within him the larger—
and, in the chiliastic terms the text invites, the more menacing—triumph of
divine illumination. It is in this sense, *pace* Wittreich, that the dramatic poem
is consistent with the statement in the *Readie and Easie Way* that the Father
and Son will not allow Milton's "to be the last words of our expiring libertie"
(YP 7:463): it unsettles as illusory the peacefulness of restored monarchy and
affirms as irresistible the cosmic progress toward human liberty—a liberty
equivalent in Milton's terms to the defeat of the ungodly and the justification
of the elect.

This recognition of the text's performance violence is no new account of
Samson, for it evokes the reading that Sir Walter Raleigh advanced over a
century ago with his typical sensitivity and verve:

Milton was thinking not very remotely of his own case when he wrote that jubilant
semi-chorus, with the marvellous fugal succession of figures, wherein Samson, and by
inference Milton himself, is compared to a smouldering fire revived, to a serpent
attacking a hen-roost, to an eagle swooping on his helpless prey, and last, his enemies
now silent for ever, to the phoenix, self-begotten and self-perpetuating. The Philistian
nobility (or the Restoration notables) are described, with huge scorn, as ranged along
the tiers of their theatre, like barnyard fowl blinking on their perch, watching, not
without a flutter of apprehension, the vain attempts made on their safety by the reptile
groveling in the dust below.[48]

In Raleigh's reading, literary complexity is not at all at odds with a revenge
ethic. This need not be married to the autobiographical element emphasized
here, as it is not in Douglas Bush's account of Samson's "triumphant martyrdom," which describes the tragedy as "the most deeply humanized treatment
of Milton's perennial theme."[49] *Samson's* imaginative achievements are in-
eluctably a part of its effectiveness as an "iconoclastic weapon": the text's
literary complexity, religious piety, and virtuoso humanist adherence to ancient models are all necessary to its arraignment of the lesser achievements of
a Dryden or a Davenant. That Milton's humanized treatment of Samson
simultaneously dehumanizes the Philistian nobility, or the Restoration notables, serves as a reminder of the inherent consequences of choosing sides in a
clash of civilizations.

The lesson here must be to resist operation within the logic of today's
equally dehumanizing clash of civilizations. What is most necessary is to
refrain from precisely the change in our appreciation of achievements of the
human imagination that Carey advocates in his post–9/11 reading of *Samson
Agonistes*. Indeed, the "change" in the way we read *Samson* evinced thus far
after 9/11 has been no change at all, but rather has produced new language to
justify preexisting conclusions: the terrorist attacks on New York and Wash-

ington have not prevented John Carey and Joseph Wittreich from seeing in the text a fundamental objection to violence, nor have they prevented Alan Rudrum and Michael Lieb from seeing otherwise. Historical events have, however, raised the stakes of a heated literary debate; justifying conclusions suggested by literary criticism has become a process more fraught with the possibility of unsettling real world implications.

The great irony in this change is that in seeking to avoid the conclusion unsettling within the discipline of Milton studies—that there was a place in Milton's view of Providence for a brand of religious violence analogous to that of our own day—critics have tended toward positions a good deal more unsettling in their coincidence with current discourses of domination. By taking as their chief task the disassociation of Milton from current religious extremism, they have implicitly advanced narrativization of the moral enlightenment of Western liberal humanism. As in President Bush's second inaugural address, this view functions as an ideological handmaiden to a militarist imposition of freedom: once an elite arrogates to itself the right to define the course of human liberty and to oppose by force the irrationality of the Other, the moral high ground of cultural expansionism is affirmed.

More desirable is a position informed by Gilbert Achcar's recent observation that "each civilization has its own barbarism."[50] If Milton matters it is because he so clearly reminds us that even while we relish the greatest intellectual and artistic achievements of the Western tradition, we would be remiss not also to recognize its barbarisms. If Milton prompts us to look beyond an axis of good and evil, it is because of, not despite, the unsettling parallels between *Samson* and modern terrorism or *The Tenure of Kings and Magistrates* and American expansionism; in these parallels we see that even a subtle-minded poet energetic in his defense of liberty can promulgate an exceptionalist discourse privileging the rights of the elect. And if we will take a critical position that looks beyond our own disciplinary and national borders —an aim that can never be successful but is worthwhile in the attempt—it will be neither by consigning Milton to the distant past nor by obfuscating his political and religious views.

Texas Tech University

NOTES

For their generous commentary on an earlier draft of this essay, I am very grateful to Paul Stevens, Nicholas von Maltzahn, and the anonymous reader for *Milton Studies*.
Epigraphs are from Dipesh Chakrabarty, *Provincializing Europe* (Princeton, 2000), 41;

George W. Bush, "October 8, 2004: The Second Bush-Kerry Presidential Debate," Commission on Presidential Debates, transcript, available at www.debates.org/pages/trans2004c.html (accessed October 11, 2004).

1. The White House, "President Sworn-In to Second Term" (Washington, January 20, 2005, 1 (emphasis mine), available at www.whitehouse.gov/news /releases/2005/01/print/20050120–1.html (accessed January 20, 2005).

2. *The NewsHour with Jim Lehrer,* PBS, January 20, 2005; Peter Beinart, "More than Words," *New Republic,* February 28, 2005, 6. See also David Kusnet, "Stumped: Well Disguised," *New Republic Online,* January 21, 2005, available at www.tnr.com/docprint.mhtml?i=stumped&s=kusneto12105 (accessed January 22, 2005); John F. Harris, "An Ambitious President Advances his Idealism," *Washington Post,* January 21, 2005, A1.

3. White House, "President Sworn-In," 3.

4. For this brand of liberal commentary, see Beinart, "More than Words," 6.

5. See Quentin Skinner, *Liberty before Liberalism* (Oxford, 1998), 82, 87; Paul A. Rahe, "The Classical Republicanism of John Milton," *History of Political Thought* 25 (2004): 247–48. Though Skinner and Rahe differ in their characterization of Milton's republicanism, particularly in its relationship to Machiavelli, both point to its classical emphasis on, as Rahe puts it, "the aristocratic principle of differential moral and political rationality that had underpinned both theory and practice in ancient Greece and Rome" (251).

6. See also *The Doctrine and Discipline of Divorce,* YP 2:225, and *A Second Defense of the English People,* YP 4:552, 680. All citations of Milton's prose are to *The Complete Prose Works,* 8 vols., ed. Don M. Wolfe et al. (New Haven, 1953–1982), designated YP and cited parenthetically by volume and page number; all citations of Milton's poetry refer to *Complete Poems and Major Prose,* ed. Merritt Y. Hughes (New York, 1957).

7. John Carey, "A Work in Praise of Terrorism? September 11 and *Samson Agonistes,*" *TLS,* September 6, 2002, 15; on this comment, see also Alan Rudrum, "Milton Scholarship and the Agon over *Samson Agonistes,*" *HLQ* 65 (2002): 466.

8. Carey, "A Work in Praise of Terrorism," 16; for further discussion of Carey's *TLS* piece and his reading of *Samson,* see my "Confronting Religious Violence: Milton's *Samson Agonistes,*" *PMLA* 120 (2005): 327–40, and the ensuing exchange between myself, Joseph Wittreich, and Peter C. Herman in the "Forum," *PMLA* 120 (2005): 1641–44.

9. See John Carey, *Milton* (1969; reprint, New York, 1970), 138–46.

10. *Rebuilding America's Defenses: Strategy, Forces, and Resources for a New Century,* The Project for the New American Century, September 2000, available at www.newamericancentury.org/RebuildingAmericasDefenses.pdf (accessed October 11, 2004).

11. Mark R. Kelley and Joseph Wittreich, eds., *Altering Eyes: New Perspectives on "Samson Agonistes"* (Newark, 2002), 11.

12. See Mark Juergensmeyer, *Terror in the Mind of God* (Berkeley and Los Angeles, 2000), 122–26.

13. Stanley Fish, *How Milton Works* (Cambridge, Mass., 2001), 417.

14. Ibid., 425.

15. Also relevant is the divine sanction of violence in Milton's plan for a Phineas tragedy, which concludes with "the word of the lord . . . acquitting & approving phineas" (YP 8:560). For an astute analysis of the relevance of Milton's plans for tragedies to Samson's spiritual heroism, see Norman T. Burns, " 'Then Stood up Phinehas': Milton's Antinomianism, and Samson's," in *Milton Studies* 33, *The Miltonic Samson,* ed. Albert C. Labriola and Michael Lieb (Pittsburgh, 1996), 27–46.

16. Fish, *How Milton Works,* 465.

17. Stanley Fish, "Postmodern Warfare: The Ignorance of Our Warrior Intellectuals," *Harper's Magazine,* July 2002, 37, 36; *How Milton Works,* 14.

18. Michael Lieb, "Returning the Gorgon Medusa's Gaze: Terror and Annihilation in Milton," in forthcoming collection, edited by Albert C. Labriola and Michael Lieb (Pittsburgh, 2006).

19. Fish, *How Milton Works,* 454.

20. Carey, "A Work in Praise of Terrorism," 15.

21. Fish, "Postmodern Warfare," 35.

22. Stanley Fish, "Why Milton Matters; or, Against Historicism," in *Milton Studies* 44, ed. Albert C. Labriola (Pittsburgh, 2005), 10.

23. Ibid., 8.

24. Ibid., 8.

25. Joseph Wittreich, "Joseph Wittreich on Why Milton Matters," in *Milton Studies* 44, ed. Albert C. Labriola (Pittsburgh, 2005), 30–31, 34.

26. Joseph Wittreich, *Shifting Contexts: Reinterpreting "Samson Agonistes"* (Pittsburgh, 2002), 49, 55.

27. Wittreich, "Why Milton Matters," 34; Rudrum, "Milton Scholarship," 465, 470.

28. J. Howard B. Masterman, *The Age of Milton* (London, 1911), 72; my italics.

29. For examples of this nineteenth-century tendency, see John Churton Collins, ed., *Samson Agonistes* (1883; reprint, Oxford, 1925), 8–9; H. M. Percival, ed., *Samson Agonistes* (1890; reprint, London, 1960), xxv; and A. W. Verity, ed., *Milton's "Samson Agonistes"* (1892; reprint, Cambridge, 1925), lviii–lix.

30. Wittreich, "Why Milton Matters," 24; see Margaret Thatcher, "Advice to a Superpower," *New York Times,* Monday, February 11, 2002, A27.

31. Barbara Lewalski, "Barbara K. Lewalski on Why Milton Matters," in *Milton Studies* 44, ed. Albert C. Labriola (Pittsburgh, 2005), 16–17, also tends to ignore these aspects of *The Readie and Easie Way,* seeing it only as a courageous defense of the republican cause.

32. Wittreich, "Why Milton Matters," 23.

33. I refer here to the compelling readings of *Samson Agonistes* found in the following: Barbara Lewalski, " 'To try and teach the Erring Soul': Milton's Last Seven Years," in *Milton and the Terms of Liberty,* ed. Graham Parry and Joad Raymond, Studies in Renaissance Literature 7 (Cambridge, 2002), 175–90; Janel Mueller, "The Figure and the Ground: Samson as Hero of London Nonconformity, 1662–1667," in Parry and Raymond, *Milton and the Terms of Liberty,* 137–62; Sharon Achinstein, "*Samson Agonistes* and the Drama of Dissent," in *Milton Studies* 33, *The Miltonic Samson,* ed. Albert C. Labriola and Michael Lieb (Pittsburgh, 1996), 133–58; and Blair Worden, "Milton, *Samson Agonistes,* and the Restoration," in *Culture and Society in the Stuart Restoration,* ed. Gerald MacLean (Cambridge, 1995), 111–36.

34. Andrew Barnaby, review of *'Exiled from Light': Divine Law, Morality, and Violence in Milton's "Samson Agonistes,"* by Derek N. C. Wood, *Renaissance Quarterly* 56 (2003): 1342; for criticism of Wood's use of biblical material, see Rudrum, "Milton Scholarship," 485, and David Urban, review of *'Exiled from Light,'* MQ 37 (2003): 43–46.

35. Michael Mendle, review of *Representing Revolution in Milton and His Contemporaries,* by David Loewenstein, *Renaissance Quarterly* 55 (2002): 778–79.

36. David Loewenstein, "*Samson Agonistes* and the Culture of Religious Terror," in forthcoming collection, edited by Albert C. Labriola and Michael Lieb (Pittsburgh, 2006), [6].

37. Carey, "A Work in Praise of Terrorism," 15.

38. Loewenstein, "*Samson Agonistes* and the Culture of Religious Terror," [4].

39. Pierre Bourdieu, "The Field of Cultural Production; or, The Economic World Reversed," trans. Richard Nice, *Poetics* 12 (1983): 317.

40. Michel Foucault, "Intellectuals and Power: A Conversation between Michel Foucault and Gilles Deleuze," in *Language, Counter-Memory, Practice,* ed. Donald F. Bouchard (Ithaca, N.Y., 1977), 207–8.

41. Gayatri C. Spivak, *A Critique of Postcolonial Reason: Toward a History of the Vanishing Present* (Cambridge, Mass., 1999), 255.

42. Ibid., 358, 360, xii, 309.

43. Achinstein, "*Samson Agonistes* and the Drama of Dissent," 135; Samuel Johnson, "*Rambler* 139," in *Milton's "Samson Agonistes": The Poem and Materials for Analysis,* ed. Ralph E. Hone (San Francisco, 1966), 103.

44. See Richard Cumberland, *The Observer: Being a Collection of Moral, Literary, and Familiar Essays* (Dublin, 1791), 3:262 [no. 111]: "Aristotle has said *that every whole hath not amplitude enough for the construction of a tragic fable; now by a whole,* (adds he in the way of illustration) *I mean that, which hath beginning, middle and end.* This and no more is what he says upon beginning, middle and end; and this, which the author of the Rambler conceives to be a rule for tragedy, turns out to be merely an explanation of the word *whole.*"

45. Joan S. Bennett, "Asserting Eternal Providence: John Milton through the Window of Liberation Theology," in *Milton and Heresy,* ed. Stephen B. Dobranski and John P. Rumrich (Cambridge, 1998), 237; see Loewenstein, *Milton and the Drama of History* (Cambridge, 1990), 145.

46. Bennett, "Asserting Eternal Providence," 220.

47. Juergensmeyer, *Terror in the Mind of God,* 123, 126.

48. Sir Walter Raleigh, *Milton* (1900; reprint, New York, 1967), 28–29.

49. Douglas Bush, *The Renaissance and English Humanism* (1939; reprint, Toronto, 1965), 121.

50. Gilbert Achcar, *The Clash of Barbarisms [Choc des barbaries],* trans. Peter Drucker (New York, 2002), 64.

AREOPAGITICA AND THE
TOLERATIONIST RHETORICS OF THE 1640s

James Egan

I

AREOPAGITICA CONTAINS ONE of the most ingenious mixtures of rhetorical persuasion and poetic enhancement in all of Milton's prose and surely among the early revolutionary pamphlets. *Areopagitica's* rhetoric has been familiar for over three hundred years, whether in the form of the oratorical structure Milton favors, the composition of his renowned arguments, or the identity and placement of the three styles identified by classical rhetoricians, "lofty, mean, or lowly."[1] His relationship to the oratorical legacy of Aristotle, Cicero, and Quintilian has been extensively documented.[2] These same authorities considered poetry the close companion of rhetoric, a conceptual linkage postulated in Aristotle's *Rhetoric* and *Poetics,* elaborated in Cicero's *Orator* and *De Oratore* and in Quintilian's *Institutio Oratoria,* and then continued in the Renaissance critical tradition of George Puttenham, Philip Sidney, and Ben Jonson.[3] Milton participated in this tradition of cultivating the synergistic relationship between the two mediums.[4] The aesthetic configuration of *Areopagitica* becomes most apparent when one measures Milton's effort against the adjacent rhetorics of his pamphleteering contemporaries in the toleration controversy of 1643–1644, contemporaries who have been identified in the historical scholarship of the twentieth century: William Walwyn, Henry Robinson, John Goodwin, Thomas Goodwin, Roger Williams, and Robert Greville, Lord Brooke.[5] Specific connections between their views on toleration and Milton's in *Areopagitica* have been charted in the annotations to the Yale edition of the *Complete Prose Works of John Milton.* I propose that Milton's association with this influential group of tract writers and several others extends beyond the intellectual nexus theorized by William Haller, the Yale editors, and Christopher Hill, among others, to an equally intricate network of structural, stylistic, and aesthetic relationships. *Areopagitica* may be read, then, as an implicit, but measurable, dialogue with adjacent prose structures and modes of the early 1640s. Recent criticism has begun to examine the processes and exterior mechanics of such dialogues, and I have shown elsewhere how Milton's exchanges in the antiprelatical, divorce, and regicide tracts are fashioned to define him in opposition to his polemical foes.[6] Moreover, if a rhetorical and aesthetic colloquy between Milton and contemporary tolerationists can be demonstrated, that colloquy will, in turn, initiate one between the formalist hermeneutics of this essay and the hermeneutics of several other recent readings of *Areopagitica*.

Historians have detailed Milton's borrowing from the intellectual ferment of the early 1640s by situating his plea for freedom of the press in the larger context of freedom of conscience and increased toleration of the sects. Arthur Barker suggested that "the reader of the *Areopagitica* [recognizes] the arguments from Christian liberty and reason as the common property of the pamphleteers for toleration." Christopher Hill seconded the early conclusions of Barker and Don M. Wolfe when he graphed sectarian theories of toleration in existence before *Areopagitica*. In her review of this historical evidence, Abbe Blum likened Milton's position to that of "a number of anonymous and unlicensed tracts such as *Queries of highest consideration, Proposed to the five Holland Ministers*" (February 1644) and confirmed the publication sequence of the pamphlets most probably available to Milton before and during his own process of composition. As this conceptual network has been refined in postmodern scholarship, it has widened, so much so that Michael Wilding could justifiably contend that to "see *Areopagitica* only in the context of the arguments of the freedom of the press is to limit it." By the same token, to contextualize the oration's ideational relationships alone amounts to another arbitrary limitation. Reviewing Milton's stance in the regicide tracts, Quentin Skinner has concluded that Milton restated, "in defense of the regicide, a series of arguments already made familiar by Parker and other Parliamentary theorists at the outbreak of the civil war. To leave the story there, however, would be to overlook one important way in which Milton was able at the same time to supplement and transform these earlier presentations." What Skinner has claimed for *The Tenure of Kings and Magistrates* (1649) and *Eikonoklastes* (1650) can profitably be extended to *Areopagitica* by examining Milton's network of structural, stylistic, and mimetic relationships to the texts that passed before him in late 1643 and throughout 1644.[7]

Haller's view that Milton "cannot be said [to have contributed] much that was new" to the toleration controversy still has considerable validity, but if Milton's rhetorical-aesthetic strategies are taken into account, his "contributions" assume a singular, substantial importance.[8] A small cluster of adjacent pamphlets has been named by Haller, Hill, and others, and local parallels to Milton's position have been cited by the Yale editors:

Robert Greville, Lord Brooke, A *Discourse opening the Nature of that Epis-copacie, which is Exercised in England* (1642)

Thomas Goodwin, Philip Nye, Sidrach Simpson, Jeremiah Burroughes, and William Bridge, *An Apologeticall Narration* (January 1644)

Roger Williams, *Queries of Highest Consideration, Proposed to the five Hol-land Ministers* (February 1644)

Henry Robinson, *Liberty of Conscience* (March 1644)

William Walwyn, *The Compassionate Samaritane* (June or July 1644)

Henry Robinson, *John the Baptist* (September 1644)

John Goodwin, *Theomachia* (October 1644)

In addition to this core group, all related directly to the toleration debate of 1643–1644 by virtue of their main arguments, two other texts have been linked to Milton's rhetoric or imagery in *Areopagitica:*

William Sedgwick, *Scripture a Perfect Rule* (December 1643)

Clement Walker, *An Answer to Col: Nathaniel Fiennes Relation concerning his Surrender of the City and Castle of Bristol* (September 1643) (YP 2:50 n. 226; YP 2:505 n. 68)

Collectively, these nine pamphlets constitute a rhetorical-polemic template available to Milton as he immersed himself in the toleration debate. The ideological connections already demonstrated between these adjacent tracts and *Areopagitica* remain secure, but Milton's reaction to the toleration dis-pute can be assessed more accurately when assessment includes the rhetori-cal forms the ideology assumed.

Illustrations are abundant throughout the canon of Milton's lifelong, acute sensitivity to the structures, styles, and genres of whatever he read. Joseph Wittreich has documented Milton's "interest in literary form," de-scribing "all of Milton's poems, and many of his orations" as "gatherings of forms," and outlining the contest of modes and styles.[9] Wittreich's thesis can be corroborated in *Areopagitica* when attention is paid to the rhetorical and aesthetic dialogue that occurs between Milton and his fellow tolerationists, a dialogue that implicates style, structure, and genre. Joad Raymond has begun to categorize such dialogues as a whole during the civil war and interregnum, and Elizabeth Skerpan Wheeler has theorized a metaphysics of form and devices of self-presentation in Milton's public verbal exchanges; both provide preliminary criteria for addressing the internal characteristics of Milton's interactions with adjacent rhetorics.[10] If these rhetorics are to be read as a template known to Milton when he wrote *Areopagitica,* they must be classi-fied and evaluated for their potential usefulness to him. It will be assumed here that Milton's own measurement of the rhetorics of his contemporaries would at least match any postmodern reconstruction of them. Some of Raymond's descriptions of seventeenth-century pamphlet literature offer a broad overview. He finds several discrete genres and many overlapping modes, all of them bound together by a process of "response, counter-response, and anti-counter-response," and calls attention to pamphleteering's defining "capacity to multiply by repetition, recycling, and splitting—of words, pages, books, voices, genres." He notes as well the proliferation of occasional tracts on such topics as accounts of battles, travel writing, supernatural manifestations, and reports of trade or disaster, in addition to minor prose genres (for instance, the satirical character and utopia), some of them corresponding roughly to canonical literary forms of poetry and drama.[11]

II

The texts specified as intellectual influences on, or at least as prominent participants in, the ideational environment of *Areopagitica* fall into the erudite category of writing alluded to by Raymond, the most prominent subgroups being the sermon and the scholarly exegesis or learned commentary.[12] The rhetorical conventions of the sermon can be illustrated in two fast day sermons preached before Commons: William Sedgwick's *Scripture a Perfect Rule* (December 1643) and Thomas Goodwin's *Zerubbabels encouragement to finish the temple* (April 1642). *Scripture a Perfect Rule* has been cited in the Yale edition for providing an imagistic parallel to Milton's mentioning of the new "light" of Reformation (YP 2:550 n. 226). Goodwin was one of the five authors of *An Apologeticall Narration,* widely regarded as the pamphlet that triggered the toleration controversy. Both were prominent preachers before the Long Parliament and regular contributors to the fast day tradition of the 1640s.[13] John F. Wilson's definitive study of these sermons demonstrates their favored rhetorical method: "The initial text was 'divided,' so as to yield a suitable number of 'doctrines.' This act was regarded as an 'opening' of the text for the purpose of extracting principles or general rules from biblical materials. . . . The final section of the sermon was generally termed 'use' or 'application.' Its purpose was to manifest the contemporary relevance of the 'doctrine,' the cogency and truth of which had already been demonstrated."[14] The overwhelming majority of such sermons employed not only this structure, but also an emphatically plain style, on the assumption that scriptural truths did not require figurative enhancement.[15]

The sermons of Sedgwick and Goodwin exemplify the format Wilson has documented. Taking Isaiah 9:6 ("The Government shall be upon his shoulders") as its text, *Scripture a Perfect Rule* maintains that "Christ hath left . . . a government in externalls for the Church under the Gospell" (3). Sedgwick aggressively parses Isaiah 9:6, breaking down the text into words and commenting on each in detail. Proofs are often listed or itemized numerically so that every nuance of an argument can be articulated (see, for example, proofs 9, 17). After "opening" his text, he moves to a series of "propositions" or "doctrines" that derive from Isaiah 9:6 as direct corollaries, Proposition 2 being a typical case in point: "It is necessary that [rules of church government] should be laid downe by Christ, none else can be the author of them" (12). By means of this internal scaffolding of logic, Sedgwick links doctrines to "reasons" and uses and orders the minute details of his overall exposition. A summarily direct prose style also implements the order of his presentation, as in the following: "['Externalls' of church government] are such as none but Christ can be the Author of them. The Apostle gives a right character of worship, *Rom.* 12[:] 1–2. That is it is meant of service or worship, the last word of the first verse shewes. That it is externall, we see in the sequell of the chapter: the Apostle is upon Church-officers, and their manners of administration" (13). Sedgwick intends to speed the comprehension of Scripture by limiting the ambiguity of his own reading, an intention reinforced by his short, linear, declarative sentence structures, simple diction (with "is" as the predominant verb), and avoidance of figurative indulgence or any other species of rhetorical display. John F. Wilson characterizes this plain style as the "universal mode of puritan sermons" delivered before Parliament in the fast day tradition.[16] With Zechariah 4:6–9 as its text, Thomas Goodwin's *Zerubbabels encouragement* provides another incitement to "Church-Reformation," this time in the prophetic, typological framework of the fall of Babylon. Intricate textual splitting and parsing; a discursive movement toward explicating ever-smaller fragments of the sacred text; a traditional dialectical arrangement of premises, corollaries, and rebuttals supported by the normative divisions into doctrines, reasons, and uses; the same affectively neutral, tropally bare prose style Sedgwick had preferred—these features mark *Zerubbabels encouragement* as altogether formulaic.

The jeremiad can also be included in the template available to Milton. Commonly defined as a "prophetic lament over the decline of a covenanted nation," the jeremiad might assume a variety of forms, including the sermon, the proclamation, and the miscellaneous political tract.[17] Speakers of jeremiads typically invoked the prophetic associations of Jeremiah, Hosea, and Ezekiel to sanction their self-depictions as "witnesses" or "watchmen" who reluctantly call attention to national moral error.[18] John Goodwin's *Theomachia: or, The Grand Imprudence of . . . Fighting against God* (1644), a pamphlet with many intellectual affinities to *Areopagitica*, was structured as a sermon and delivered on a Day of Humiliation (its text being Acts 5:38), with the additional themes and conventions of the jeremiad. In the fashion of the jeremiad, Goodwin interprets the recent "sorrowfull [parliamentary] defeat at *Newark*" as a "blow which was reached us from heaven" (4). Like other writers of jeremiads, Goodwin laments moral crisis and forecasts the possibility of God's wrath against the nation.[19]

Several scholarly exegeses and learned commentaries with distinct rhetorical conventions have also been identified as familiar to Milton when he wrote *Areopagitica:* Henry Robinson's *Liberty of Conscience* (March 1644) and *John the Baptist* (September 1644) and Robert Greville, Lord Brooke's *A Discourse . . . of Episcopacie* (1642).[20] A lengthy treatise or compendium of arguments on the origins and historical evolution of episcopacy, *A Discourse* examines the requirements for appointment or election to a bishopric and the relationship of ecclesiastical to civil power in the state. Its mode of argument suggests that *A Discourse* can be categorized as a scholastic disputation, one that takes great care to establish exactness of terminology. The following definition of "the Nature of Indifference" (17) indicates the scholastic rigor of Brooke's tactics:

> Some call, those things *Indifferent* which are neither forbidden, nor commanded: but here they tell us onely what 'tis *not*, and negatives make no *Definition.*

> I must intreat the Reader to remember that we are now upon *Morall beings:* where the Two maine *Ingredients, Matter* and *Forme,* can be but *Metaphysically* Notional, and therefore it will be hard to give an exact *Definition.*
> . . . .

> Before I assay to give the nature of it in a Definition, give me leave to present you with some kind of *Etymology.* (17)

After this etymological framing, complete with intricate qualifications and distinctions, Brooke reviews all of his assumptions, premises, and corollaries before deriving a scholastically valid definition of "Indifference," the process requiring three entire pages. Throughout *A Discourse,* he introduces evidence consistent with these elevated standards of logical proof, commonly quoting or paraphrasing and then refuting opposed positions while presenting a rigorous dialectical cross-examination. The clinical, legalistic nature of *A Discourse,* with its dialectical critique of historical, political, and scriptural sources and its compendiumlike organization, inevitably narrows its audience to erudite readers.

Robinson's *Liberty of Conscience* merges some of the analytical qualities of *A Discourse* with the exegesis typical of the fast day sermon, intending to review scriptural precedents and locate rationales for the freedom-of-conscience argument. This synthetic structure acts as a de facto commonplace book or, in postmodern terms, a casebook of evidence supporting a liberalized church policy. Though his earnest tone recalls that of a sermon, Robinson's arrangement of evidence does not duplicate the conventional format of doctrines, reasons, and uses. Instead, he draws various exegetical conclusions, primarily from Scripture, citing potential objections and rebutting them as he proceeds, without the scholastic detail Brooke had favored. Stylistically, his literal directness does not differ substantially from the formulaic simplicity of the sermons discussed earlier. *John the Baptist* represents an intensified version of Robinson's strategies in *Liberty of Conscience*, and chapter 4 offers a comprehensive example, beginning with a heading, "Christs Instructions, and the Apostles practice concerning Christian Liberty," moving to several broadly interpretative axioms, then to extensive scriptural citations, and finally to ten pages of Robinson's observations upon the citations. As did *Liberty of Conscience,* this tract approximates a commonplace book of arguments and authorities meant to assemble scriptural support for liberty of conscience. Again like its predecessor, *John the Baptist* contains almost no evidence of rhetorical or stylistic embellishment.

Unlike Brooke and Robinson, the authors of *An Apologeticall Narration* (January 1644) elected an informal narrative mode rather than "a more exact and *Scholastique* relation of our judgements in the points of difference about *Church government.*"[21] *An Apologeticall Narration* is the diary of "the Separation," recounting the escape from Laudian persecution by its five authors (Goodwin, Nye, Simpson, Burroughes, and Bridge), their exile in Holland, and the orthodoxy of their church discipline. "We give this briefe and generall account," they write (8), and in so doing, the authors join company with a widespread pamphlet genre of the 1640s, the narrative of personal confession and justification, perhaps best represented by the writings of John Lilburne. As Raymond notes, this genre could easily assume "demotic" forms and lapse into sensationalism, yet *An Apologeticall Narration* achieves intellectual legitimacy and relevance by virtue of its topic—freedom of conscience and the necessity of resistance to religious persecution.[22]

Probably the earliest substantial response to *An Apologeticall Narration,* the *Queries of Highest Consideration, Proposed to the five Holland Ministers* (February 1644), commonly attributed to Roger Williams, is structured as an animadversion, one of the most widespread species of prose controversy in the seventeenth century (YP 2:76). The query-response format approaches a dialectical cross-examination, normally directed to details and particulars, but not necessarily so. As Elizabeth Skerpan Wheeler has shown, the genre of animadversion, with its emphasis on direct-encounter tactics, generates various scenarios for self-presentation, which compete with the mode's established preference for marginal sniping and ad hominem refutation.[23] Indeed, character assassination proves to be the primary modus operandi of Clement Walker's *An Answer to Col*, a document proposed as a possible source for Milton's image of Juno sitting "cros-leg'd over the nativity of any mans intellectual off spring" (505 n. 68). Walker's *Answer* represents the purest form of the animadversion, wherein a confutant quotes, extensively and verbatim, from an adversary's text and then replies.

The final rhetorical paradigm of relevance for Milton's practices in *Areopagitica* occurs in William Walwyn's *The Compassionate Samaritane* (June or July 1644), whose stance on toleration has often been compared to Milton's.[24] Like the dialectical modes of Robinson and Brooke, *The Compassionate Samaritane* incorporates a disputative process of critique—Walwyn makes a claim in the form of a reason, posits hypothetical objections to it, and answers them (for example, 6–8, 43–44), although he avoids both the intricate scholastic rigor of Brooke and the detailed presentation of scriptural evidence preferred by Robinson. Its form does not observe classical criteria precisely, but *The Compassionate Samaritane* nevertheless qualifies as an oration, with an exordium, confirmation, and peroration. One could not reasonably mistake it for Milton's achievement in *Areopagitica,* but Walwyn's prose comes closer than that of any other prominent toleration pamphleteer to having "literary" qualities.[25]

III

As Milton studied the positions of the major writers in the toleration controversy, he would have encountered diverse prose structures and styles, ranging from the sermon and the jeremiad to the scholastic exegesis, the confessional narrative, and the animadversion, along with variations on these primary templates. When Milton's rhetoric and style in *Areopagitica* are measured against the models available to him, his structural and stylistic decision making and poetic shaping can be contextualized more accurately than when *Areopagitica* is detached from its polemical environment. Thomas Corns, Joad Raymond, and others have postulated that Milton, though an active participant in the "rapidly expanding pamphlet culture" of the 1640s, nevertheless "fashioned himself as standing apart from it."[26] The structure and styles of *Areopagitica* provide detailed and disparate evidence, all of it embedded in the text, of how carefully articulated and pervasive was Milton's process of differentiating his statements on freedom of conscience and of the press from those of his contemporaries.

His efforts at uniqueness and differentiation have not passed unnoticed. Don M. Wolfe points out that John Lilburne, Richard Overton, and William Walwyn all regularly complained about censorship, but only Milton devoted an entire tract to it.[27] The same could be said of Henry Robinson, John

Goodwin, and Thomas Goodwin, whose rhetorics were examined earlier: freedom of the press proves no more than an incidental concern of theirs. Milton's strategies prove singular not only among toleration tracts, but in the larger revolutionary context of pamphleteering in the 1640s. Abbe Blum has shown the "deliberately transgressive posture" of Milton's "framing of his own name" on the title page of *Areopagitica*. Unlike Walwyn in *The Compassionate Samaritane,* Milton not only publishes his name, but also conspicuously avoids the imprimatur or any other indicator of registration with the stationer's company.[28] The structure and styles of *Areopagitica* ratify what Wolfe and Blum have suggested. *Areopagitica's* oratorical framework of exordium (486–90), proposition (490–93), historical narration (493–507), confirmation and refutation (507–68), personal digression (537–40), and peroration (568–70) follows the mandates of Cicero in *Orator* and *De Oratore* and Quintilian in *Institutio Oratoria*.[29] Milton's polemical habits in the 1640s and the above rhetorics accentuate the differentiating qualities of this oratorical format. Milton would likely have considered the disputative-exegetical mode of Brooke in *A Discourse . . . of Episcopacie* and Robinson in *Liberty of Conscience* and *John the Baptist* unduly analytical and erudite, best understood by an audience considerably narrower and more scholarly than the parliamentarians he wished to persuade. In providing the intellectual justification for toleration, moreover, Brooke and Robinson had already completed a task Milton would have had no need to repeat: his role would be to urge Parliament to adopt the ideals the exegeses had articulated so elaborately and precisely. That Milton's decision was tactical can be corroborated by his use of the disputative-exegetical format in *Tetrachordon* (1645), published just four months after *Areopagitica*. When the historical moment demanded a learned, scholastic defense of his thesis in *The Doctrine and Discipline of Divorce,* Milton proved himself well qualified to dispute.[30] In *Areopagitica,* Milton's strategic, differentiating choice was to locate his own argument for freedom of the press in the substantially developed humanistic and scriptural context of a more liberal toleration, a context already established by adjacent rhetorics.

As he studied *An Apologeticall Narration,* with its personal, confessional manner of self-justification, Milton would likely have considered its narrative arrangement too limiting, circumstantial, and commonplace for the grand, solemn occasion of his address to Parliament. The rhetorical connotations of informality and topicality attached to *An Apologeticall Narration* would limit the persuasive options and effects of his own plea, which was meant to address a political action (repealing censorship) of national consequence and timeless significance for the realization of Reformation. Milton opted against the animadversion framework of Williams's *Queries of Highest Consideration* and Walker's *An Answer to Col* because of his seasoned awareness of the format's associations of rancorous infighting and ad hominem partisanship. Milton surely had grounds for detesting Parliament's censorship edict, but he would have thought a polemical animadversion too combative and risky to move legislators. Because he had already published his own *Animadversions* (1641) and would animadvert again shortly in *Colasterion* (March 1645) against the anonymous confuter of the 1643 edition of *Doctrine and Discipline*, Milton's decision not to animadvert qualifies as a strategy.[31] Simply put, the historical and rhetorical occasion of *Areopagitica* did not demand, as the occasions of *Animadversions* and *Colasterion* clearly had, a format that emphasized personal reprisal and satiric ridicule.

Nor did circumstances demand a narrow sermonic "eloquence," but rather an ecumenically intellectual one whose connotations evoke the ancient tradition of humanism itself and its rich cultural heritage, an eloquence suggested by the title *Areopagitica* and its etymological link to the seventh oration of Isocrates.[32] Milton's tactical selection of an oratorical structure would signal to a literate reader, and surely to its presumed parliamentary audience, its dramatic, easily recognized difference from both the formulaic sermon mechanism of opening-reasons-uses and the catastrophe-ridden, foreboding tonality of the jeremiad. Despite Milton's emphatic structural message, modern scholarship has occasionally linked *Areopagitica* to the fast day tradition.[33] That this connotation was not his intention can be demonstrated by recalling the political context of the tradition. John F. Wilson has revealed the role of the fast day sermon in announcing, promoting, and "displaying the unity of the parliamentary cause." Not only did their sermons advance the parliamentary agenda, but also many fast day preachers were members of the Westminster Assembly of Divines, so that two of the most potent political forces of the early 1640s held common cause. H. R. Trevor-Roper also labeled the fast day tradition and its signature sermons as "party propaganda" and a "constant sounding-board of parliamentary policy."[34] Studies have likened the propagandistic tendency of early civil war sermons to similar leanings in sermons preached before James I and at Paul's Cross to announce and defend Jacobean political policy.[35]

Milton had reason to be wary of fast day preachers if for no other reason than the denunciation of *Doctrine and Discipline* in a fast sermon by Herbert Palmer on August 13, 1644. His oratorical form reinforces the suggestion of Christopher Hill and others that *Areopagitica* was devised, at least in part, as a rebuttal of this sermon. Milton would have understood the conservative tendency of early fast sermons to support the status quo of Presbyterianism and question the legitimacy of Independency.[36] His own argument, on the other hand, with its defense of the sects, clearly challenged parliamentary decision making as well as clerical authority over censorship. Milton promises to "attend [to the matter of censorship] with such a Homily" (491), but he does so in order to evoke a genre his own mode of composition in *Areopagitica* will easily surpass, a practice omnipresent in his poetry.[37] Instead of making his case for freedom of the press with exclusive, or even extensive, citation of Scripture, as a sermon could be expected to do, Milton draws upon "broadly humanistic" proofs.[38] His election of an oratorical medium underscores the independent, singular nature of his position and its pointed distinction from the fast day tradition's rendering of corporate or collective piety. What better way to counter Palmer's attack on the divorce tracts than to recall the sermon tradition, only to better it at every turn?

Thus, by recovering the template available to Milton in adjacent toleration literature, we can be more historically and rhetorically specific than William Haller and William Riley Parker were in assessing Milton's rationale for addressing Parliament with an oration. It is surely plausible, as Haller proposed, that the oratorical mode was especially "congenial" to Milton, and that he wished to present his arguments in a learned context, as Parker surmised.[39] While accurate, these conclusions are also limiting, failing to account for Milton's intention to display *Areopagitica* as unique, a design best realized by contouring his own dialectic in a manner decisively different from the sermons, jeremiads, exegeses, personal narratives, and animadversions that had contained the major arguments for toleration in 1643–1644. Only Walwyn's *The Compassionate Samaritane*, a hybrid structure (partly exegetical and partly oratorical), bears a plausible resemblance to *Areopagitica*, though the two are more different than alike.

Determining the appropriate style for his magisterial oration would have confronted Milton with the same options he had faced when determining the structure. In the rhetorics of the toleration controversy, he would have detected an undesirable commonality—prose styles with a literal, one-dimensional, tedious and formulaic sameness. This generalization is especially true of the sermon, as both Perry Miller and John F. Wilson have illustrated: Miller studied the sermon manuals, which prescribed an "unrelievedly plain" style, and Wilson documented the pervasive, widely acknowledged failure of the Puritan sermon, such as those preached before the Long Parliament, to "foster elegance of style."[40] In contrast, Milton followed the stylistic advice of Cicero and Quintilian, both of whom had urged a "'wise adaptability' . . . in the use of all the styles," by which they meant the oratorical low, middle, and high styles. Styles, Cicero and Quintilian had suggested, should be judiciously mixed; to avoid satiety and monotony, they cautioned against "Rigid, inappropriate persistence in one style alone."[41] As I have shown elsewhere, *Areopagitica* contains the most persuasive evidence in all of Milton's prose of his mastering of the "fitted [styles] of lofty, mean, or lowly" in English.[42]

Style in *Areopagitica* has several distinct but closely related functions: it clarifies Milton's argument, accentuates his priorities of argument, and is itself a form of affective pleading. The bulk of the oration develops the claim for freedom of the press, a claim that forges the narration, confirmation, and refutation into one. Milton opens with a historical narration, warning that censorship has an unsavory past. The first section of this two-part narration, treating the problem of censorship in classical civilization, employs the oratorical low style singled out in the *Ad Herennium* (attributed to Cicero in the Renaissance) as particularly well adapted for narrative. Milton capitalizes on the classical associations of the low style with the direct, unadorned manner of refined conversation, with examples from Greek and Roman history that epitomize the use or abuse of reason in the matter of censorship.[43] His examples are all specimens of behavior calling for rational analysis and are offered in a plain style virtually devoid of schemes or tropes. In dramatic contrast to its opening, the second part of the narration plays heavily upon pathetic (emotional or affective) appeal when Milton equates the spread of censorship in early Christianity with papal conspiracies. Wishing to implicate Rome in the type of repression currently in practice, he composes in the low style of satire, which blends a logical proposition (Rome conspires against Reformation) with several forms of pathetic proof. When Cicero allows "humour and wit" to the orator who writes in the low style, he identifies this alternate function of the style as a satiric medium.[44] In the narration, then, Milton recounts the vexed history of censorship, and style guides reader responses to this history.

Quintilian's definition of the nature and aims of an exordium describes Milton's procedure in *Areopagitica:* "The style of the Proemium should be different from that of the Proofs, Commonplaces, and Narratives; it must not however always be finely spun or sophisticated, but often simple and apparently effortless, not promising too much either by the words or by the speaker's expression. An unobtrusive delivery . . . often worms its way into the mind better."[45] A masterpiece of stylistic strategy, the exordium portrays Parliament as being comprised of reasonable men capable of responding to a reasonable premise, despite Milton's recognition that these very men had enacted licensing. He presents his case in the middle style, for he could not risk alienating them with an emotional harangue. His subtlety in associating England and Athens renders this appeal witty rather than merely ingratiating. The middle style with which Milton evokes the ideals of classical civilization can be characterized by schemes of repetition and redefinition instead of elaborate tropes, schemes that direct the reader's attention to a significant hypothesis. For example, concerning the man who would speak out against censorship, Milton declares, "His highest praising is not flattery, and his plainest advice is a kinde of praising" (488). Here the *antimetabole* scheme, akin to logical conversion, heightens the distinction between praise and flattery by repeating the terms in converse order.

The climactic argument, that censorship "hinders and retards the importation of our richest Marchandize, Truth" (YP 2:548–68), is presented in the high style. Cicero explains this style as follows: "The style is brilliant if the words employed are chosen for their dignity and used metaphorically and in exaggeration . . . and in harmony with the actual action and the representation of the facts."[46] Abundant, expert deployment of metaphor and simile lends grandeur to the style, while schemes of sound and word order and rhythmic devices afford grace and ornateness. Quintilian's suggestion that the orator raise the tone of his speech by "Amplifications, and rise to Hyperbole" foregrounds the fictive devices, apostrophe and *prosopopoeia*, native to it: the transformation of literal and factual into metaphoric and hyperbolic induces the elaborate emotional reaction desired by the orator.[47] Finally, the tone of the high style should convey a sustained intensity in order to move the audience effectively. By situating the high style in his climactic argument, Milton dissents from classical theory, for both Cicero and Quintilian had suggested the peroration as the most appropriate place for the high style, although it might also be employed in a digression or, less frequently, in the exordium. Milton also adapts classical mandates on the high style to his needs as a Christian orator, shaping his persuasion as an allegorical narrative in which England merges with Zion as the nation chosen to defend Christ's church from its enemies. This visionary scenario represents the metamorphosis of the abundant metaphor and fictive elaboration Cicero and Quintilian had urged for the lofty style into an apocalyptic high style.[48] The wide variety of oratorical styles and their discrete applications evident in *Areopagitica*, then, radically separate Milton's prose from adjacent tolerationist rhetorics, none of which could approach, much less duplicate, his unique stylistic signature.

IV

Even though it is a rhetorical means of persuasion, the apocalyptic high style embeds so many dramatic and allegorical devices, such as *prosopopoeia* and apostrophe, that the style approaches poetic, or at least aesthetic, statement.[49] Milton's most emphatic way of differentiating his case for freedom of the press, I believe, involves the extension of the tropal qualities of this style into several dynamic, implicitly literary processes or movements incorporated into the oration as a whole. He realized that the tolerationist rhetorics he had reviewed, with their overwhelming literality, did not qualify as poetic, and that the uniqueness of his own contribution could be secured by accentuating its aesthetic traits. Milton does so in three ways: by conducting a critical referendum on adjacent rhetorics, by presenting the problem of censorship as a satiric topos, and by eulogizing the emerging movement to reveal the new truths of Reformation. In view of the classical and Renaissance bonding of rhetoric and poetic, Milton's extrapolation of the aesthetics of his position would be not only strategically distinctive, but logical, closely in accordance with the critical tradition he had inherited, so much so that he would have considered poetry as a "higher form of oratory," different in degree rather than function.[50] When Milton surveyed the toleration debate, he implicitly made several critical decisions, the first of which was the appropriateness of the genres and styles of adjacent rhetorics for what he would have considered the momentous historical occasion and the powerful, dignified parliamentary audience he would address. This would be a decision about decorum, in the local and rhetorical sense as well as in the larger, aesthetic sense defined by Thomas Kranidas.[51] Given the fact that his divorce writings had been pilloried in a sermon earlier in 1644, Milton also needed to determine how *Areopagitica* might serve as a rejoinder to what had become an inimical medium to him. Finally, he had to ascertain whether the rhetorics of his contemporaries might further his own design to celebrate toleration as he argued for freedom of the press, whether any polemic templates or individual strategies might be assimilated into his own proposal. The referendum Milton conducted on these issues was resolved by the inclusion of two overt and complementary aesthetic features that complete his process of differentiation.

Milton treats the plague of censorship as a satiric topos, thereby granting himself a creative license to develop a broad range of mimetic improvisations, qualities altogether absent from the tracts of his fellow toleration pamphleteers.[52] Beginning in the narration, Milton's sortie turns on diction, coinages, and wordplay, from his description of "Licensing Books" as *"quadragesimal and matrimonial"* (YP 2:491), to his quip about licensing "under the hands of 2 or 3 glutton Friers" (503), to his allusion to the "fescu of an *Imprimatur"* (531). Satiric diction and verbal association achieve a twofold effect—to redefine licensing as a popish policy recently aped by prelates and to unify the attack by regularly echoing its central motif. Of course, *Areopagitica* functions satirically in far more sophisticated ways as well, again beginning in the narration with the mock "pedigree" of licensing (505). Occasionally Milton amplifies his attack mimetically, as in his sketch of "5 *Imprimaturs* . . . seen together dialogue-wise in the Piatza of one Title page, complementing and ducking each to other with their shav'n reverences, whether the Author, who stands by in perplexity at the foot of his Epistle, shall to the Presse or to the spunge"

(504). This celebrated set-piece acts as a miniature interlude, a mimetic illustration, complete with characters and a setting, of the satiric topos. An integral part of Milton's enactments of the topos is the ironic quality attached to many of them, for example, the anecdote of "that gallant man who thought to pound up the crows by shutting his Parkgate" (520), or the possibility that the "villages also must have their visitors to enquire what lectures the bagpipe and the rebbeck reads ev'n to the ballatry" (524–25). In the second case, Milton speculates that the Laudian system of censorship through official "visitors" could well be reinstituted by Laud's enemies (YP 2:524, 140). His aesthetic perspective, then, extends from overt verbal denunciations to fictive constructions and sophisticated renditions of the self-indicting folly of censorship. At all points, satiric mimesis challenges the imagination of *Areopagitica's* readership, often in elliptical passages that approach poetic conceits in their suggestive brevity—for instance, the observation that censorship might generate the damning, ironic contradiction of "the Pastor of a small unlearned Parish" becoming the "exalted Archbishop over a large dioces of books" (540).

In short, the topos of censorship's all-inclusive folly represents the sustained, carefully linked usage of literary mimesis, whereby Milton's fictive imagination displays itself in a dazzling variety of forms, radically unlike the occasional, literal complaints about censorship voiced in adjacent rhetorics. His incorporation of irony into these satiric improvisations, moreover, adds a witty, urbane, sophisticated tone, again sharply differentiating Milton's fictions of diminution from the exegetical tomes and treatises, melodramatic sermons and jeremiads, and feverish animadversions which had carried the burden of the argument for liberalized toleration before *Areopagitica*. In Milton's hands, mimetic satire dramatizes and insinuates its intention to the reader in the fashion of an aesthetic artifact.

A second literary movement, fully complementary to the satiric enactment of censorship, occurs in the final argument for the unhindered, unlicensed "importation of our richest Marchandize, Truth" (YP 2:543–68), wherein Milton shapes several of the ideational commonplaces about toleration found in adjacent rhetorics into mimetic forms, thus utilizing those rhetorics as raw material for his unique imaginative vision of Reformation. The Yale edition's annotations suggest an uncommonly direct connection to these rhetorics in the climactic "Truth argument."[53] Most of the parallels cited there are circumstantial, part of the large body of intellectual agreement held by Milton and contemporary tolerationists (the rough equivalent of "public domain"), but in several instances they imply a closer relationship, one of aesthetic assimilation, enlargement, and extrapolation. In *Liberty of Conscience,* Robinson serves up a commonplace literal axiom about implicit faith: "there is no *medium* between an implicite faith, and that which a mans

owne judgement and understanding leads him to" (sig. a1; YP 2:543 n. 195).
In *Areopagitica,* Milton regularly converts the ideology of implicit faith into
metaphor and allegory, transforming Robinson's claim into a premise presented as metaphor: "Truth is compar'd in Scripture to a streaming fountain;
if her waters flow not in a perpetuall progression, they sick'n into a muddy
pool of conformity and tradition" (543). William Walwyn also treats implicit
faith and hypocrisy in *The Compassionate Samaritane,* warning about those
who "have yet but the forme and shewe of Religion, but want the inward
sweetnesse and most excellent fruites and effects thereof."[54] This caveat
remains primarily literal, with a mild dependence on scriptural metaphor
("fruites and effects"), whereas in *Areopagitica* the same admonition is re-
written into one of Milton's most familiar literary anecdotes, the character of
the "wealthy man addicted to his pleasure and his profits. . . . [F]ain he would
have the name to be religious, fain he would bear up with his neighbours in
that. What does he therefore, but resolvs to give over toyling, and to find
himself out som factor, to whose care and credit he may commit the whole
managing of his religious affairs; som Divine of note and estimation that must
be" (544).[55] Milton has extrapolated Walwyn's truism on the "forme and
shewe of Religion" into a fictive characterization: a mimetic statement with
an implicit premise (the ease with which some distort religion into conve-
nience and pretension) displaces Walwyn's direct warning about false, untrustworthy divines.[56]

In *Liberty of Conscience,* Robinson cautions about the same moral laxity
and "ease" that had troubled Walwyn, noting that the failure to pursue and
critique new revelations of truth by fully exercising liberty of conscience
must lead inevitably to spiritual regression: "Such will be found carelesse, if
not negligent, in the choice of their Religion, as little troubling themselves to
trie the spirits whether they be of God or no, I John 4.1, or examine the
opinions and doctrine which are taught, [and will] receive them currantly
what ever they be, so they come sealed and delivered by authority of State"
(sig. a1; YP 2:545 n. 206). Milton refashions Robinson's literal statement
about backsliding into what amounts to a coda to his own character of the
wealthy man, an extension of that satiric sketch into the collective:

Another sort there be who when they hear that all things shall be order'd, all things
regulated and setl'd; nothing writt'n but what passes through the custom-house of
certain Publicans that have the tunaging and the poundaging of all free spok'n truth,
will strait give themselves up into your hands, mak'em and cut'em out what religion ye
please; there be delights, there be recreations and jolly pastimes that will fetch the day
about from sun to sun. . . . What need they torture their heads with that which others
have tak'n so strictly, and so unalterably into their own pourveying. (YP 2:545)

A study in irony and blame by means of ostensible praise, the passage reveals how Milton made overtly fictive and imaginative what was literal and implicit in Robinson, and how he multiplied the effects of his earlier character by pluralizing its agenda. Presumably, the wealthy man would recognize his spiritual colleagues in this crowd of the morally complacent. Milton's revision of verbatim claims and concepts from adjacent rhetorics finally occurs not only on the large scale of the character, but in miniature as well. Brooke had proposed in *A Discourse . . . of Episcopacie* that "The Spaniard indeed by his cruell *Inquisition,* hath inclined his Subjects to a kinde of *Unity;* but an Unity of Darknesse and Ignorance; so that the Remedy proves worse than the Disease."[57] The paradoxes and ironies of Brooke's essentially literal statement are intensified in Milton's rewriting: "We doe not see that while we still affect by all means a rigid externall formality, we may as soon fall againe into a grosse conforming stupidity, a stark and and dead congealment of *wood and hay and stubble* forc't and frozen together, which is more to the sudden degenerating of a Church then many *subdichotomies* of petty schisms" (YP 2:564). Milton constructs in this passage the equivalent of a conceit, yoking together Brooke's reference to the Inquisition and his own allusion to the *wood and hay and stubble* of 1 Corinthians 3:10–13 to suggest the paradox of grouping together ("conforming," "congealment"), producing the opposite sensation of what might be anticipated—freezing and death instead of warmth and life (YP 2:564 n. 281). This contradictory yoking yields wit in a form related to that of the aphorism or *sententia,* and again literality and historical reference have been displaced by mimetic ingenuity and display.

Assessing the structure of *Areopagitica,* Keith W. Stavely has concluded that "the oration can thus be summarily described by saying that it moves from proper nouns to local imagery to the more extended metaphors of character, conceit, allegory, and vision."[58] This paradigm offers a valuable internal parallel to Milton's transformative relationship to the external rhetorics he encountered in 1643–1644. As the illustrations have shown, Milton discovered in the idea matrix and languages of those rhetorics material useful for his unique argument, and in several instances he appropriated and reworked this material mimetically, creating literary artifice and wit from what had been doctrinal, polemic, or historical declarations. By assimilating and thus subordinating adjacent rhetorics, Milton transcended them, completing his studied process of differentiation. Considering the Truth argument as a whole, moreover, the process of mimetic assimilation found in the examples from Brooke, Robinson, and Walwyn are writ large in Milton's signature treatment of the grounds for increased toleration. Having secured the uniqueness of his plea for freedom of the press in the ways demonstrated in this essay, Milton then incorporates that plea into the broader context of the search for the shattered body of Osiris. He proceeds from local mimesis and aesthetic transformation in the Truth argument to what Stavely calls allegory and vision. When he presents his climactic appeal for Truth's progress, Milton summarizes and reiterates the core arguments for fuller toleration set out in the pamphlets of Brooke, Walwyn, Robinson, Goodwin, and others, but he does so in narrative fashion, telling the story of Truth's progress toward realization and acting out that story mimetically, through the celebrated allegories, visions, and metaphors that have long held the imagination of the oration's readers.[59] His authorial function has now become poetic. In the Aristotelian conception, poetry provides "imaginative opportunities to test, refine, extend, and perhaps even question."[60] When Milton speaks for what William Haller calls "the nation he thought his countrymen at least had it in them to become," his mimetic intent is to envision Reformation realized, an intention directly congruent with the Aristotelian mandate that the poet recounts, "not the things that have happened, but those that *might* happen, that are possible."[61] Thus, the Truth argument achieves the poetic universal as Aristotle had expressed it, that is, the articulation of the probable.[62] Imaginative poetics in the Renaissance, from Lyly and Sidney to Jonson and Milton, had shared this Aristotelian axiom.[63] Because Milton appreciated that the case for toleration had been well made in the rhetorics he had reviewed, his role became that of advocate of the specific cause of freedom of the press, a cause treated cursorily in those rhetorics. Milton also became the choric celebrant of the heroic quest for freedom of the press by virtue of his aesthetic transformation of the crescendo of the Truth argument into a narrative.[64]

This choric role points to a final aesthetic quality of *Areopagitica,* its likeness to the epic genre of poetry. Locating parallels between various Miltonic tracts and poetic practices has become part of the contemporary critical tradition. Edward S. Le Comte, for example, describes *Paradise Lost* "in phrases taken entirely from *Areopagitica.*" He observes as well that early twentieth-century scholarship, including the studies of Grierson, Hutchinson, and Tillyard, realized that Milton's *Defensio Secunda* (1654) had epic features, a position elaborated by Joan Webber, who theorized that in the *Defensio Secunda* Milton considered the oration an "epic in the making" and "Milton the pamphleteer as an epic hero." Webber's position, in turn, reinforced that of Joseph Wittreich. Laura Lunger Knoppers branches off from this argument, illustrating how in *The Readie and Easie Way* (1660) Milton derives from the genre of the jeremiad a myth whereby England could "interpret the impending doom" of the restoration of Charles II. Examining *Areopagitica* against the intellectual history and rhetorical formats of the toleration debate allows us to foreground several of its traits congruent with the epic mode. E. M. W. Tillyard proposed a "community of formal features" of epic, one of which he named "choric"; that is, the "epic writer must express the feelings of a large group of people living in or near his own time." Milton's appeal for freedom of the press, and his climactic paean to Truth's recovery most of all, incorporate an overview of the positions held by the major proponents of liberalized toleration. Both Joan Webber and Barbara Lewalski have characterized epic as a "comprehensive or encyclopedic" form, a "heterocosm or compendium of subjects, forms, and styles." Given its embedding and summarizing quality, *Areopagitica* functions as a compendium of the entire historical controversy over freedom of the press and clerical-political censorship in the early 1640s. John Shawcross reads the epic as essentially a poem of praise, and Milton's choric celebration of the virtues and benefits of broader toleration fits the definition of praise for a policy he clearly considered of paramount spiritual and historical importance. What is more, the illustrious quality of epic subject matter has been integral to all descriptions of the formal components of the mode. Finally, C. M. Bowra's positioning of epic composition at the close of a historical epoch or at the culminating stage of political or cultural attainment coincides with *Areopagitica*'s publication in November 1644 as the last, most eloquent statement of the need for toleration, the grand recapitulation of a momentous national debate in late 1643 and throughout 1644. Additional parallels between *Areopagitica* and the epic might be cited, but those provided here suggest that partially realized prose approximations of the genre might have been composed well before Milton's formal association of the oration and the epic in *Defensio Secunda*. These analogies between *Areopagitica* and an ancient literary medium, deemed in the Renaissance the "highest" poetic mode, also mark the point of greatest distance between the aesthetic identity of Milton's oration and the adjacent rhetorics of the toleration controversy.[65]

V

My position has been that, when measured against the templates of the toleration pamphlets available to Milton as he wrote *Areopagitica*, the rhetorical and poetic qualities of his own work can be more appropriately contextualized. If studying the policies of major tolerationists was part of Milton's intellectual preparation for debate, it is highly probable, given his lifelong preoccupation with genre and structure, that he carefully noted the rhetorics and styles of these same tracts. In them, he would have discovered a template consisting of exegeses, disputations, sermons, jeremiads, animadversions, and personal narratives, along with a cross-section of plain, utilitarian prose styles. Because of his dialogue with adjacent rhetorics, Milton's own strat-

egies in *Areopagitica* may be read as a process of participating in the toleration controversy while at the same time communicating the uniqueness of his
role. He reiterates and affirms many of the claims of fellow tolerationists, yet
Milton presents his own distinctive petition for freedom of the press with an
oratorical structure and in a variety of styles altogether unlike those found in
his models. This tactic of differentiation extends to incorporating two aesthetic movements, one satiric and the other panegyric, into his own persuasion, movements that explain features of the oration commonly thought of as
poetic. Milton encodes his unique signature, therefore, in the details of his
oratorical structures, Ciceronian styles, and mimetic improvisations, which
include satiric scenarios, the polemic character, the narrative shaping of the
quest for Reformation's unrealized truth, as well as epic recapitulation and
choric celebration.

    These conclusions not only address the longstanding interest in the
arrangement of rhetoric and poetic in *Areopagitica,* they also lend themselves to a critical colloquy with alternative postmodern readings, the most
influential of which will be considered here. Blair Hoxby and Sandra Sherman have framed *Areopagitica* in the context of early modern economic
rhetoric, Hoxby theorizing that Milton's stance on liberty of conscience is co-
involved with economic discourse, specifically free trade arguments, and that
trade serves as an essential metaphor in *Areopagitica.* His interpretation
locates *Areopagitica*'s debt to economic discourse in the forms of antimonop-
oly petitions and pleas for expanding the public sphere, while emphasizing
Milton's awareness of the public sphere as a necessarily open process of
intellectual (and perhaps spiritual) exchange, invention, and experimenta-
tion.[66] Sherman situates the oration "within a . . . discourse of outrage against
the abuses of middlemen, which had been developing in print culture for the
half-century preceding *Areopagitica*"; like Hoxby, she emphasizes the pervasiveness of economic paradigms in the text, connecting Milton's rhetoric to
the "discourse of commodity trading" and to the imagery of the "malign
hands" of intermediaries.[67] The formalist conclusions of this essay parallel
and reinforce those of Hoxby and Sherman by demonstrating the relevance
of adjacent pamphlet rhetorics for understanding Milton's agenda in *Areopagitica.* While both Hoxby and Sherman foreground Milton's agency as a
participant in early modern economic discourse and his sharing of tropes
with that discourse, my reading emphasizes the mechanisms whereby he
converts the literal tolerationist positions of Robinson, Walwyn, Goodwin,
and others into tropes and fictions radically distinct from the rhetorics which
inspired them. Though he may be co-involved with adjacent rhetorics, I
assign equal importance to Milton's deliberate strategy of structural, stylistic,
and mimetic separation from his contemporaries.

The reading of *Areopagitica* proposed here also aligns itself with David Loewenstein's persuasive New Historicist interpretation of Milton's prose. He is concerned with Milton's "figurations of history," his pattern of imaginative responses to historical processes, which implicates literary texts in historical and social actions as agents of change rather than as inert reflectors of events. Loewenstein evaluates the "aesthetic vehicles" for Milton's often millennial visions of history. Despite differences in particulars, the conclusions I have reached about *Areopagitica* are congruent with Loewenstein's assumptions, especially my detailing of Milton's creation of a unique aesthetic signature by refashioning the commonplace genres of the toleration controversy and developing censorship as a satiric topos. Both of these imaginative acts are compatible with what Loewenstein calls *Areopagitica*'s "poetics of history." Moreover, the mythopoetic portraiture Milton delineates in *Defensio Secunda,* which includes his process of interpreting his history as a writer, together with his panegyric rendering of Oliver Cromwell, seems to be anticipated in *Areopagitica*'s choric paean to the sects.[68]

A final nexus between the rhetorical-poetic hermeneutic practiced in this essay and other postmodern readings of Milton's tract involves current efforts to contextualize the republican features of the oration, whether in Milton's privileging of a republic or parliamentary supremacy over kingship, or in his advocacy of a cultural politics that considers the citizen the state's highest resource.[69] Milton proposes London as a new Athens, a cultural center with a revived "public spirit" and a commitment to an expanded, energetic public sphere. David Norbrook advances republican theorizing into a suggestion that *Areopagitica* embeds not only "an implicitly republican politics but also an implicitly republican poetics." *Areopagitica,* he points out, illustrates Milton's ongoing experiment with "restoring classical eloquence."[70] To this claim can be added the evidence gathered here for Milton's sophisticated "Englishing" of the classical lofty, mean, and lowly styles.[71] Norbrook notes that in *Areopagitica* Milton counters Edmund Waller's charge that the "new radical London would destroy learning" by authoring one of the "most erudite and allusive political pamphlets ever composed."[72] I have argued that Milton inventoried a range of popular toleration texts before settling on the structure and styles of *Areopagitica,* thereby legitimating the democratic, allegedly ephemeral idiom of the political tract. More significantly, by inscribing onto a pamphlet his unique mythopoetic signature, Milton models the sort of text that an idealized republican might be expected to read and devises a template for the form of artifacture that a republican poetics might be expected to produce.

The University of Akron

NOTES

1. *Of Education,* in *The Complete Prose Works of John Milton,* 8 vols., gen. ed. Don M. Wolfe et al. (New Haven, 1953–1982), 2:401. All subsequent references to *Areopagitica* are to this volume, hereafter designated YP and cited parenthetically by volume and page number. Most criticism addresses Milton's argument or its ideological context. For detailed discussions of style, see Joseph Anthony Wittreich Jr., " 'The Crown of Eloquence': The Figure of the Orator in Milton's Prose Works," in *Achievements of the Left Hand: Essays on the Prose of John Milton,* ed. Michael Lieb and John T. Shawcross (Amherst, Mass., 1974), 3–54; James Egan, *The Inward Teacher: Milton's Rhetoric of Christian Liberty* (University Park, Pa., 1980), chap. 2.

2. The most authoritative treatments of Milton's relationship to the classical rhetorical tradition are J. Milton French, *The Life Records of John Milton,* 5 vols. (New Brunswick, N.J., 1949–1958); William Riley Parker, *Milton: A Biography,* 2 vols. (Oxford, 1968); Barbara K. Lewalski, *The Life of John Milton: A Critical Biography* (Malden, Mass., 2000); Wittreich, "The Crown of Eloquence."

3. On the interface of rhetoric and poetry, see especially Brian Vickers, *In Defence of Rhetoric* (Oxford, 1988), and "Rhetoric and Poetics," in *The Cambridge History of Renaissance Philosophy,* ed. Eckhard Kessler and Quentin Skinner (Cambridge, 1988), 715–45; George A. Kennedy, *Classical Rhetoric and Its Christian and Secular Tradition from Ancient to Modern Times,* 2nd ed. (Chapel Hill, 1999); Thomas O. Sloan, "The Crossing of Rhetoric and Poetry in the English Renaissance," in *The Rhetoric of Renaissance Poetry from Wyatt to Milton,* ed. Thomas O. Sloan and Raymond B. Waddington (Berkeley and Los Angeles, 1974), 212–42; Wayne A. Rebhorn, *The Emperor of Men's Minds: Literature and the Renaissance Discourse of Rhetoric* (Ithaca, N.Y., 1995).

4. Commentary on Milton's familiarity with poetry's kinship to rhetoric is extensive. See, for example, Wittreich, "The Crown of Eloquence"; O. B. Hardison Jr., "The Orator and the Poet: The Dilemma of Humanist Literature," *Journal of Medieval and Renaissance Studies* 1 (1971): 33–44; David Loewenstein, "Milton and the Poetics of Defense," in *Politics, Poetics, and Hermeneutics in Milton's Prose,* ed. David Loewenstein and James Grantham Turner (Cambridge, 1990), 176–80. That *Areopagitica's* rhetoric often approaches the poetic is a venerable critical commonplace. To appreciate the range of this commonplace, see, for example, William Haller, "Before *Areopagitica,*" *PMLA* 42 (1927): 875–900, and *Liberty and Reformation in the Puritan Revolution* (New York, 1955), as well as Juanita Whitaker, " 'The Wars of Truth': Wisdom and Strength in *Areopagitica,*" in *Milton Studies* 9, ed. James D. Simmonds (Pittsburgh, 1976), 185–201.

5. Don M. Wolfe, *Milton in the Puritan Revolution* (New York, 1941); Arthur E. Barker, *Milton and the Puritan Dilemma 1641–1660* (Toronto, 1942); Christopher Hill, *Milton and the English Revolution* (New York, 1977); Abbe Blum, "The Author's Authority: *Areopagitica* and the Labour of Licensing," in *Re-Membering Milton,* ed. Mary Nyquist and Margaret W. Ferguson (New York, 1987), 74–95; Haller, "Before *Areopagitica*"; YP 2:53–183.

6. See especially Joad Raymond, "The Literature of Controversy," in *A Companion to Milton,* ed. Thomas N. Corns (Oxford, 2001), 191–210, and *Pamphlets and Pamphleteering in Early Modern Britain* (Cambridge, 2003), as well as Elizabeth Skerpan Wheeler, "Early Political Prose," in *A Companion to Milton,* 263–78. My own studies of Milton's dialogues include " 'As His Own Rhetorick Shall Persuade Him': Refutation and Aesthetic Self-Construction in Milton's Antiprelatical Tracts," *Prose Studies* 24, no. 2 (August 2001): 41–64; "Rhetoric, Polemic, Mimetic: The Dialectic of Genres in *Tetrachordon* and *Colasterion,*" in *Milton Studies* 41, ed. Albert C. Labriola (Pittsburgh, 2002), 117–38; and "Creator-Critic: Aesthetic Subtexts in Milton's Antiprelatical and Regicide Polemics," in *Milton Studies* 30, ed. Albert C. Labriola (Pittsburgh, 1993), 45–66.

7. Barker, *Milton and the Puritan Dilemma*, 108; Hill, *Milton and the English Revolution*, 150; Wolfe, *Milton in the Puritan Revolution*, 129–30; Blum, "The Author's Authority," 80, 78 (compare Haller, "Before *Areopagitica"*—Haller first explored the pamphlets intellectually adjacent to *Areopagitica*); Michael Wilding, "Milton's *Areopagitica*: Liberty for the Sects," in *The Literature of Controversy: Polemical Strategy from Milton to Junius,* ed. Thomas N. Corns (London, 1987), 13; Quentin Skinner, "John Milton and the Politics of Slavery," in *Milton and the Terms of Liberty,* ed. Graham Perry and Joad Raymond (Cambridge, 2003), 17.

8. Haller, "Before *Areopagitica*," 876.

9. Wittreich, "The Crown of Eloquence," 30–31, and *Angel of Apocalypse: Blake's Idea of Milton* (Madison, 1975), 167–69.

10. Raymond, "The Literature of Controversy," 193–96, and Wheeler, "Early Political Prose," 270–78. See also Thomas N. Corns, "Radical Pamphleteering," in *The Cambridge Companion to Writing of the English Revolution,* ed. N. H. Keeble (Cambridge, 2001), 71–86. Compare my essays on Milton's treatment of adjacent and oppositional rhetorics in note 6.

11. Raymond, "The Literature of Controversy," 207, 196, 197, 201.

12. Ibid., 196.

13. John F. Wilson, *Pulpit in Parliament: Puritanism during the English Civil Wars 1640–1648* (Princeton, 1969), 118, 237–80.

14. Ibid., 141. See also Perry Miller, *The New England Mind: The Seventeenth Century* (New York, 1939), 332–39.

15. Wilson, *Pulpit in Parliament,* 141.

16. Ibid., 141.

17. Laura Lunger Knoppers, "Milton's *The Readie and Easie Way* and the English Jeremiad," in Loewenstein and Turner, *Politics, Poetics, and Hermeneutics in Milton's Prose,* 213–14.

18. Ibid., 214–15. See also James Egan, " 'This is a Lamentation and shall be for a Lamentation': Nathaniel Ward and the Rhetoric of the Jeremiad," *Proceedings of the American Philosophical Society,* 122, no. 6 (1978): 400–10.

19. Knoppers, "Milton's *The Readie and Easie Way,*" 214–15.

20. Henry Robinson, *Liberty of Conscience* (1644), in *Tracts on Liberty in the Puritan Revolution 1638–1647,* 3 vols., ed. William Haller (New York, 1933), 3:1–62; Robert Greville, Lord Brooke, *A Discourse Opening the Nature of . . . Episcopacie,* 2nd ed. (1642), in *Tracts on Liberty,* 2:1–118; hereafter cited in the text by page number.

21. Thomas Goodwin, Philip Nye, Sidrach Simpson, Jeremiah Burroughes, and William Bridge, *An Apologeticall Narration* (1644), in *Tracts on Liberty,* 2:30; hereafter cited in the text by page number.

22. Raymond, "The Literature of Controversy," 201.

23. Wheeler, "Early Political Prose," 273–78.

24. William Walwyn, *The Compassionate Samaritane* (1644), in *Tracts on Liberty,* 3:1–79; hereafter cited in the text by page number.

25. The literary qualities of Walwyn's prose have been frequently noted. See Haller, *Tracts on Liberty,* 1:122–23; Joseph Frank, *The Levellers: A History of the Writings of Three Seventeenth-Century Social Democrats* (New York, 1969), 30; Warren Chernaik, "Civil Liberty in Milton, the Levellers, and Winstanley," in *Winstanley and the Diggers, 1649–1999,* ed. Andrew Bradstock (Portland, Ore., 2000), 101–7. Compare Nigel Smith, "*Areopagitica*: Voicing Contexts, 1643–5," in Loewenstein and Turner, *Politics, Poetics and Hermeneutics in Milton's Prose,* 112–13. Smith contends that Milton does not borrow or condense Walwyn's arguments; in contrast, I argue that Milton draws upon Walwyn's arguments, but not upon his rhetoric or style.

26. Raymond, "The Literature of Controversy," 193, 207; Thomas N. Corns, "Milton's

Quest for Respectability," *MLR* 77 (1982): 769–79; Blum, "The Author's Authority," 75; David Loewenstein, "Milton among the Religious Radicals and Sects: Polemical Engagements and Silences," in *Milton Studies* 40, ed. Albert C. Labriola (Pittsburgh, 2001), 223, 238.

27. Wolfe, *Milton in the Puritan Revolution,* 130.

28. Blum, "The Author's Authority," 80, 75.

29. On oratorical structure, see Kennedy, *Classical Rhetoric,* 92. On oratorical structure in Milton, see Wittreich, "The Crown of Eloquence," 4–11; Wilbur E. Gilman, *Milton's Rhetoric: Studies in His Defense of Liberty* (New York, 1970). My reading of *Areopagitica's* structure merges what is sometimes referred to as the "national digression" (YP 2:551–56) into the larger framework of the oration's confirmation and refutation.

30. See Egan, "Rhetoric, Polemic, Mimetic," 117–25.

31. James Egan, "Milton and the Marprelate Tradition," in *Milton Studies* 8, ed. James D. Simmonds (Pittsburgh, 1975), 103–21.

32. For the most forceful recent argument linking *Areopagitica* to the traditions of classical humanism, see Paul M. Dowling, *Polite Wisdom: Heathen Rhetoric in Milton's "Areopagitica"* (Lanham, Md., 1995).

33. Christopher Kendrick, *Milton: A Study in Ideology and Form* (New York, 1986), 44; John Illo, "Areopagiticas Mythic and Real," *Prose Studies* 11, no. 1 (May 1988): 10.

34. Wilson, *Pulpit in Parliament,* 62, 108; H. R. Trevor-Roper, "The Fast Sermons of the Long Parliament," in *Religion, the Reformation, and Social Change* (London, 1967), 309, 342.

35. Lori Anne Ferrell, *Government by Polemic: James I, The King's Preachers, and the Rhetorics of Conformity, 1603–1625* (Stanford, 1998), 10–12; Thomas S. Nowak, "Propaganda and the Pulpit: Robert Cecil, William Barlow and the Essex and Gunpowder Plots," in *The Witness of Times: Manifestations of Ideology in Seventeenth Century England,* ed. Katherine Z. Keller and Gerald J. Schiffhorst (Pittsburgh, 1993), 35.

36. Hill, *Milton and the English Revolution,* 149; Smith, "Voicing Contexts," 104; Wheeler, "Early Political Prose," 276; Wolfe, *Milton in the Puritan Revolution,* 123–24; Egan, "Rhetoric, Polemic, Mimetic," 118–25. Milton had also grown apart from his Smectymnuan allies of 1640–1642, some of whom preached fast sermons before the Long Parliament. See Thomas Kranidas, "The *Colasterion:* Milton's Plural Adversary," *Prose Studies* 19 (December 1996): 275–81; Haller, *Liberty and Reformation,* 124.

37. Compare Wittreich, "The Crown of Eloquence," 8–47.

38. Wolfe, *Milton in the Puritan Revolution,* 136.

39. Haller, *Liberty and Reformation,* 181; Parker, *Milton,* 1:267.

40. Miller, *The New England Mind,* 349; Wilson, *Pulpit in Parliament,* 146.

41. Peter Auksi, *Christian Plain Style: The Evolution of a Spiritual Ideal* (Montreal, 1995), 53, 57, 59.

42. Egan, *The Inward Teacher,* chap. 2.

43. *Rhetorica ad Herennium,* trans. Harry Caplan, Loeb Classical Library (Cambridge, Mass., 1968), 4.8.11–10.14. Used by Cicero and once attributed to him, the treatise is now thought to have been composed by Cornificus. Compare Wittreich, "The Crown of Eloquence," 12. Wittreich observes that Milton had mastered the three styles in English in *Areopagitica,* but he does not illustrate this.

44. *Brutus and Orator,* trans. G. L. Hendrikson and H. M. Hubbell, Loeb Classical Library (Cambridge, Mass., 1952), *Orator,* 26.87.

45. *Institutio Oratoria,* trans. Donald A. Russell, Loeb Classical Library (London, 2001), vol. 2, book 4, lines 60–61. Subsequent references will be to the Loeb edition.

46. *De Partitione Oratoria,* trans. H. Rackham, Loeb Classical Library (Cambridge, Mass., 1948), 6.20.

47. *Institutio Oratoria,* vol. 5, book 12, 10.62. See also vol. 4, book 9, 2.26–44.

48. Egan, *The Inward Teacher,* 18–20. Compare Debora K. Shuger, *Sacred Rhetoric: The Christian Grand Style in the English Renaissance* (Princeton, 1988), 62–110. What I have described as the "apocalyptic high style" would be included in Shuger's description of the "Christian grand style." See also Vickers, *In Defence of Rhetoric,* 80–81.

49. Compare Shuger, *Sacred Rhetoric,* 87, 109.

50. Hardison, "The Orator and the Poet," 36; William S. Howell, *Poetic, Rhetoric, and Logic: Studies in the Basic Disciplines of Criticism* (Ithaca, N.Y., 1975), 48–49; Edward S. Le Comte, "*Areopagitica* as a Scenario for *Paradise Lost,*" in Lieb and Shawcross, *Achievements of the Left Hand,* 121; Arthur F. Kinney, "Rhetoric as Poetic: Humanist Fiction in the Renaissance," *ELH* 43 (1976): 413; Kennedy, *Classical Rhetoric,* 136.

51. Thomas Kranidas, *The Fierce Equation: A Study of Milton's Decorum* (The Hague, 1965), 13–104.

52. Of course, satire in *Areopagitica* has been noted by many. See especially Peggy Joann Curet, "The Rhetoric of Humor in Milton's *Areopagitica*" (Ph.D. diss., Southwestern Louisiana University, 1976), 89, 99, 103, 110, 115, 129. Curet inventories Milton's "humorous" devices well, though her analysis and its aim differ substantially from mine.

53. See, for example, these parallels between *Areopagitica* and Brooke's *Discourse* (page references are to YP, vol. 2): 551, 560, 565; Walwyn's *Compassionate Samaritane:* 543, 556, 563; Robinson's *Liberty of Conscience:* 545, 554, 561, 566, 569; John Goodwin's *Theomachia:* 561, 568; Roger Williams' *Queries of Highest Consideration:* 550, 562; *An Apologeticall Narration:* 553.

54. Walwyn, *The Compassionate Samaritane,* 64.

55. Compare Irene Samuel, "A Theophrastan Character in Milton," *N&Q* 203 (1958): 528–30, who argues for a Theophrastan influence on Milton's character, a point that seems plausible. However, even if Theophrastus suggested the genre blueprint and format for this character, Walwyn's *Compassionate Samaritane* likely provided its immediate occasion and historical circumstances.

56. Walwyn, *The Compassionate Samaritane,* 62–65.

57. Brooke, *A Discourse . . . of Episcopacie,* 91.

58. Keith W. Stavely, *The Politics of Milton's Prose Style* (New Haven, 1975), 71. For a position on Milton's imagery parallel to Stavely's on structure, see John X. Evans, "Imagery as Argument in Milton's *Areopagitica,*" *TSLL* 8 (1966): 204.

59. The most prominent metaphors are those of Isis and Osiris, London as the "City of refuge" (YP 2:553–58), the "noble and puissant Nation," (558), and Truth's battle with Falsehood (562–64).

60. Stephen Halliwell, "Pleasure, Understanding, and Emotion in Aristotle's *Poetics,*" in *Essays on Aristotle's Poetics,* ed. Amelie Oksenberg Rorty (Princeton, 1992), 253.

61. Haller, *Liberty and Reformation,* 182; Gerald F. Else, *Plato and Aristotle on Poetry,* ed. Peter Burian (Chapel Hill, 1986), 198.

62. John D. Boyd, S.J., *The Function of Mimesis and Its Decline* (New York, 1980), 23.

63. See, for example, Wittreich, "The Crown of Eloquence," 26–48; Stephen Halliwell, *Aristotle's Poetics* (Chapel Hill, 1986), 79–81, 106, 136; John S. Diekhoff, *Milton's "Paradise Lost": A Commentary on the Argument* (New York, 1963), 2–8; Arthur F. Kinney, "Rhetoric and Fiction in Elizabethan England," in *Renaissance Eloquence: Studies in the Theory and Practice of Renaissance Rhetoric,* ed. James J. Murphy (Berkeley and Los Angeles, 1983), 393.

64. Compare Dowling, *Polite Wisdom,* 82. Dowling believes that Milton merely "affects the excited tone and otherworldly perspective of Puritan sectaries," a position my reading challenges.

65. Le Comte, *"Areopagitica* as a Scenario," 122, 121; Joan Webber, *Milton and His Epic Tradition* (Seattle, 1979), 106, 3. See also Loewenstein, "Milton and the Poetics of Defense," 183–85; Wittreich, "The Crown of Eloquence," 8, 32, 46; Knoppers, "Milton's *The Readie and Easie Way*," 213; E. M. W. Tillyard, *The English Epic and Its Background* (New York, 1954), 4, 12; Barbara Lewalski, *"Paradise Lost" and the Rhetoric of Literary Forms* (Princeton, 1985), 4; John T. Shawcross, *With Mortal Voice: The Creation of "Paradise Lost"* (Lexington, 1982), 97; C. M. Bowra, *From Virgil to Milton* (London, 1967), 28. See also David Norbrook, *Writing the English Republic: Poetry, Rhetoric, and Politics, 1627–1660* (Cambridge, 1999), 121. Charles Martindale, *John Milton and the Transformation of Ancient Epic* (London, 1986), 223.

66. Blair Hoxby, *Mammon's Music: Literature and Economics in the Age of Milton* (New Haven, 2002), 26–52.

67. Sandra Sherman, "Printing the Mind: The Economics of Authorship in *Areopagitica*," *ELH* 60 (Summer 1993): 342, 337, 325, 332.

68. David Loewenstein, *Milton and the Drama of History: Historical Vision, Iconoclasm, and the Literary Imagination* (Cambridge, 1990), 1, 4, 39, 45–48; Loewenstein, "Milton and the Poetics of Defense," 174–87.

69. Norbrook, *Writing the English Republic*, 129–30; Janel Mueller, "Contextualizing Milton's Nascent Republicanism," in *Of Poetry and Politics: New Essays on Milton and His World*, ed. Janel Mueller (Binghamton, 1995), 265; Martin Dzelzainis, "Milton's Classical Republicanism," in *Milton and Republicanism*, ed. David Armitage, Armand Himy, and Quentin Skinner (Cambridge, 1995), 3–24.

70. Norbrook, *Writing the English Republic*, 124–30, 135, 137.

71. See Egan, *The Inward Teacher*, chap. 2. While *Areopagitica* is the best example of Milton's "Englishing" of classical styles, it should be noted that such "Englishing" was a common practice in the 1640s, from *Of Reformation* (1641), to both editions of *The Doctrine and Discipline of Divorce* (1643, 1644), to *The Tenure of Kings and Magistrates* (1649).

72. Norbrook, *Writing the English Republic*, 125.

QUID NOMINE POPULI INTELLIGI VELIMUS: DEFINING THE "PEOPLE" IN THE SECOND DEFENSE

Hugh Jenkins

I F I N T H E P E R O R A T I O N of *The Second Defense* Milton claims kinship with the epic poets, having "celebrated at least one heroic achievement of my countrymen," he begins the work more modestly. While confessing that "I can scarcely restrain myself from loftier and bolder flights than are permissible in this exordium," he admits that the "distinguished orators of ancient times undoubtedly surpass me, both in their eloquence and in their style."[1] Nonetheless, many of Milton's contemporaries praised the eloquence, grace, and power of his Latin, above even the epic political themes of the work. The often-cited praise from Andrew Marvell's letter to Milton, in which he claims to be "getting . . . [*The Second Defense*] by Heart: esteeming it . . . as the most compendious Scale, for so much, to the Height of Roman eloquence" with "its turnes and rises [and] so many figures," is mirrored in comments by Eli Bouhereau and the early biographers John Toland and Jonathan Richardson.[2] Milton's opponents, too, recognized his Latin as a vital yet vulnerable point. Hence, Alexander More in his *Fides Publica* says that when defending the English people (and not himself), Milton's language "grows weak, becomes feeble, lies more frigid than Gallic snow," while George Crantzius, in the preface of the 1654 Hague edition of *The Second Defense* (which printed Milton's work along with Alexander More's reply), claims that Milton "Fabulator est & merus Poeta, licet oratorio sit Prosaica" [Is a fabricator and a mere poet, though his style is prosaic]. Similarly, Francis Vavassor in 1672 mocked Milton for attributing to Salmasius solecisms that he himself commits.[3]

Whatever the validity of these criticisms, Milton's modesty is largely a ploy, a common rhetorical topos that Marvell and others, steeped in the classical rhetorical tradition, were sure to recognize. The topos is meant to help establish his stylistic prowess and, as such, is essential to Milton's overall strategy of ethical proof, the logic of which, as John Hale argues, posits that good Latin argues a good man; a good man, a good cause.[4] Still, in the same passage from the peroration, Milton insists that what does set him apart from his predecessors and models is the cause itself, "the grandeur of my subject and my theme": the execution of the tyrant Charles I and the establishment of the Godly English Republic (554). Most recent critics have tended to focus on that "subject and theme" from *The Second Defense*. Since that subject necessarily includes, as part of the work's ethical proof, the author himself, the long biographical passage (612–28) has been analyzed for the light it sheds on Milton's physical appearance, his psychological state (especially in relation to his blindness), and his adaptation to the events of the early 1650s.[5] Milton's comments on these events have proven equally tantalizing. Is he advocating an "aristocratic republic" in the speech, backtracking from the idealism of the 1640s, or does he keep faith with the English people and their cause through these difficult times?[6] These questions assume a particular importance given the focus of Milton's mighty peroration, Oliver Cromwell, because the ethical strategies of *The Second Defense* center on Cromwell as much as on Milton himself. The peroration raises the question of whether Milton subtly criticizes or admonishes Cromwell, as many believe, or whether, as Robert Fallon argues, it is relatively straightforward panegyric.[7] To put it in the context of Roman republicanism, whose accents Milton assumes continually in the speech, does Milton see Cromwell as a Caesar or Augustus, turning the new republic toward tyranny, or as a Cato or Cicero, saving the republic from enemies internal and external?[8]

Important as these questions are, they tend to distract attention from the true subject of *The Second Defense,* the subject that inspires Milton to equally heightened (and ambiguous) rhetoric: the English people. After all, Milton titled the speech *Pro Populo Anglicano Defensio Secunda* and linked himself with his subject (while simultaneously countering his opponents' anonymity) by adding his name and, in boldface, his nationality, above the title: Joannis Miltoni ANGLI.[9] I will argue that by returning to Milton's actual subject—the English people—and his actual language—the Latin praised by his contemporary admirers and scorned by his enemies—many of the difficulties raised by the critics cited above can be resolved.

Of course, approaching *The Second Defense* in this way raises further problems and questions. Connecting himself with his subject is not without its difficulties for Milton. In a moment of anxious candor, Milton balances the self-praise that concludes the peroration with a warning to his countrymen: "if after such brave deeds you ignobly fail, posterity will speak out and pass judgment" on them and, by extension, on Milton's work and himself (685). Thus at the core of the argument of *The Second Defense* is a paradox. The elaborate series of ethical proofs with which Milton justifies himself and the new government, in particular Cromwell, against their detractors depends as much on what they represent as on who they are. This paradox informs much of the rhetorical strategy of the speech. Yet, by writing in Latin, Milton severely curtails his English audience. His immediate readership is, ostensibly, not the English people, but rather Alexander More, who Milton mistakenly thought was responsible for *Regii sanguinis clamor ad coelum, adversus parricidas Anglicanos*, the tract that occasioned Milton's own. (The work was actually written by the Anglican divine Pierre du Moulin.)[10] Milton often addresses More directly, using the second person, shifting the tone of the speech from epideictic to forensic. This strategy has its advantages: it allows Milton to speak in the manner of Demosthenes and Cicero, thereby adding their rhetorical gravitas to his cause.[11] At the same time, though, Milton modulates his voice and enlarges his audience, investing his ethical proofs with universal significance. Central to Milton's prose tracts, as James Egan has argued, is his "narrative presence" as a regenerate Christian and its concomitant moral authority. In *The Second Defense* he goes further, often assuming the tone of a biblical prophet so that, rather than merely speaking to or for one man, he speaks "for the entire human race [*pro universo potius hominum genere*] against the foes of liberty," explicitly equating the English people and their champions with that great and godly cause (558).[12] Milton is bridging wide chasms in his argument, with an audience both domestic and foreign, a style and tone both classical and biblical, a subject both unique and universal. These raise and reiterate the importance of the central question of the work: who exactly are the English people Milton is defending?

Answering this question is the unstated but implicit challenge of *The Second Defense*. Its immediate cause arises from Salmasius's probing demand to the English regicides in his *Defensio Regia*, a demand Milton had quoted in his *Defensio:* "'We must explain,' you say, 'what we mean by people'" [*Doceamus te oportet quid nomine populi intelligi velimus*]. Salmasius implies, Milton notes, that "we mean by *people* [*nomine populi*] only the populace [*plebem*]" (471/7:390). Salmasius's demand is a dangerous one for Milton and the republic; it raises questions about the nature of the new government prompted not only by the execution of the king, but also by the abolition of the House of Lords and the Leveller agitations (as well as those by Diggers and other radical groups) of the late 1640s. Milton's reply reveals his anxiety about the charge. He shifts terms from the more benign but amorphous *populus* to the more specific *plebs*, replete with elitist political and social connotations, to bring Salmasius's implications to the fore and make his target clearer. Though Milton had at one point in the *Defensio* explicitly defended the "plebeian scum" [*de faece illa plebis*] Salmasius criticizes, here he agrees that the "dregs" [*infima plebe*] of the population are indeed "blind and brutish . . . the most fickle of men, the emptiest, the unsteadiest, and the most inconstant," while saying, in effect, it takes one to know one. Milton thus counters Salmasius's class assumptions with those of Cicero and other members of the Roman republican elite, who considered the *plebs* "depraved and untrustworthy, [their] poverty routinely being associated with crime and subversiveness," and who ensured that their de jure citizenship rights were tightly circumscribed de facto by both social and ideological restraints.[13] In essence, Milton knows that Salmasius is accusing the English republic of mob rule or anarchy. Having put a poison word in Salmasius's mouth, Milton replies with a soothing anodyne: he cites "all citizens" [*omnes ordinis cuiuscunque cives*] as the true meaning of the word "people" [*populi*] in the English republic. But Milton's new term (*cives*) raises a host of other definitional problems that he fails to address. After all, the *plebs* were citizens too, and the brevity of his definition (he quickly reverts to personal attacks on Salmasius) and its vagueness (*ordinis cuiuscunque*—of whatever order) suggest that Milton was unhappy with both the demand and his answer (471/7:390–92).

More/du Moulin presents Milton with an opportunity, in *Regii Sanguinis Clamor*, to clarify and amplify the distinctions and definition he had tentatively made in the *Defensio*. If Milton the rhetorician uses the form of oration to craft his arguments into art in his *Second Defense*, Milton the logician uses the opportunity of the oration to define the public he defends to all his audiences, home and abroad. In *The Second Defense,* he struggles for the precise vocabulary and tone with which to accomplish this task; his eventual triumph in both justifies Marvell's high praise. For, rather than letting lexical flexibility become a source of anxiety, Milton exploits it; it allows him, in the language of a Roman orator and with the tone of a biblical prophet, to celebrate and castigate at the same time his subject and its leaders. Most importantly, it allows him to posit the English people not as a fixed but rather as a developing entity, a work in progress. The ultimate paradox of *The Second Defense* is that by writing in a foreign tongue and ostensibly to a broad but elite audience, Milton is able to explore and ultimately define the subject closest to his heart during the early, troubled days of the Commonwealth, the English people themselves: who they are now and what they could and should become.[14]

I

No one would dispute that *The Second Defense* is often caustic about those it defends and at least seems far removed from the idealism about the English people that animates the earlier *Areopagitica* and *Tenure of Kings and Magistrates*. Milton justifies writing in Latin in part because of the reception given his divorce tracts: he wishes he had written those in Latin as well, "for then I would not have met with vernacular readers [*vernas lectores*], who are usually ignorant of their own good" (610/8:114). Milton, in fact, begins *The Second Defense* with a series of distinctions about his countrymen, distinctions that begin the process of answering Salmasius's demand left over from the *Defensio*. The exordium introduces his ethical argument as Milton lists the three "most weighty reasons" for the speech: the civil war and its conclusion, Salmasius's attack on the English regicides, and Milton's own response in the *Pro Populo Anglicano Defensio*. In evoking the civil war, Milton describes it as a time when "her citizens, with pre-eminent virtue and a nobility and steadfastness [*quibus civium virtus eximia*] . . . freed the state from grievous tyranny" both political and ecclesiastic. He contrasts the virtues of the "citizens" to the words of Salmasius (from the *Defensio Regia*) and the actions of the English "multitude" [*multi*] who, "in the wonted manner of a mob [*ut est fere ingenium vulgi*] venomously attacked these noble achievements." In describing his own *Defensio,* Milton claims that "he did not disappoint the hope or judgment of my countrymen [*civium meorum*] about me" (548–49/8:2]. He thus entwines all three of his reasons for writing with basic distinctions about those he is defending. The distinctions he sketches here are ones to which he will return repeatedly in *The Second Defense*.[15]

These distinctions revisit and revise those he had made in the *Defensio*. The mob (*multi, vulgi*) Milton attacks is less a discrete political entity or social class than a confused and dangerous mixture of unthinking obedience and unrestrained anarchy. While supporting Charles and the divine rights of kings, when "inflamed with the empty name of liberty," the mob's "unbridled license" also compels it to "scorn for the laws or desecration of them" (551–52). In this mob, Milton describes what Salmasius had implied in *Defensio Regia:* the dangers of "democratic" rule. Here, however, Milton replies with more precise distinctions and thus clearer definitions. By shifting the term from *plebs* to *vulgi*, Milton removes the political or social confusion of his reply in the *Defensio* to make the issue instead an ethical one. In the terms of Roman republicanism, the *vulgi* comprised the lowest orders of the poor, not the *plebs* but the *plebs sordida* or *infima* (the term Milton had used generally in the *Defensio*), excluded by their own depravity almost entirely from the political process except as "rental mobs" and, as Cicero believed, fickle and licentious even in that role.[16] Milton strategically leaves the definition of "citizen" implicit here and will spend much of *The Second Defense* fleshing it out. Still, in the initial context and in reference to Roman republicanism, the contrast is clear. The sober, steadfast *civis* manages his own affairs and thus earns the right to participate in the state's; he combines, that is, the ethical and political virtues a republic needs to avoid sliding into mob rule.[17] With the new distinction Milton thus turns on its head Salmasius's charge against the English republic: he, like Cicero in his great orations against Catiline and Antony, defends not only the policies, but in particular the virtues of republicanism. These virtues stand fast against, rather than yield to, the whims of the multitude. The ethical proof thus encompasses the entire nation or, more precisely, the parts of it that make up its citizenship.

As such, these initial distinctions would appear to indicate the often-perceived elitism of *The Second Defense,* the "aristocratic republic" that Barbara Lewalski sees Milton rhetorically constructing in the speech.[18] But in a kind of progressive political revelation, Milton continually repeats and elaborates on this distinction, further narrowing it in some instances but expanding it in others. Almost immediately, he redefines the "mob" by adding a necessary religious dimension to his ethical distinctions. Andrew Barnaby has noted how "for Milton in the 1650s, ancient Rome is a compelling figure for his political agenda . . . because its imperial orientation can so easily be assimilated into Christianity's as well as England's own imperial [and republican] ideologies."[19] For Milton, "Christianity" means Protestantism, and its enemies—papal Rome and the Stuart monarchy—mean tyranny. So in praising his nation and its actions, he compares the English to "those illustrious Greeks and Romans whom we particularly admire[, who] expelled the tyrants from their cities without other virtues than the zeal for freedom." This, Milton continues, was a time before tyranny had become "a sacred institution" and before tyrants could hide themselves "behind the blind superstition of the mob" [*caeca vulgi superstitione*] (550/8:6). Salmasius's arguments for monarchy had appealed only to "the deep-rooted prejudice (or rather it should be called superstition) of the mob" [*inveterate vulgi opinione, sive superstitio*] (603/8:100). Milton again contrasts the "mob" to the English "people" who, though "a multitude in numbers" [*cum numero populus sane magnus*], never became a "mob" [*vulgus*] by reason of their better instruction and divine inspiration (552/8:8). Milton must have particularly enjoyed reinforcing the distinction between the learned citizens and the superstitious vulgar with the irony of attacking his enemies' "blindness," which was one of the charges they had hurled against him. More importantly, Milton would expect his readers to equate "superstition" with Catholicism and both, in turn, with spiritual as well as mental blindness—an equation he had exploited in the *Defensio.*[20]

Milton returns to this point and hammers it home in the peroration, which he directs largely to the English people. He emphasizes that citizens become worthy of their liberty only by overcoming those vices that make the mob a slave to its own superstitions and passions. To be free, Milton asserts again, is an ethical condition before it is a political state; it is "precisely the same as to be pious, wise, just and temperate, careful of one's property, aloof from another's, and thus finally to be magnanimous and brave" (684). Those "citizens" [*omnes . . . cives*] who maintain such virtues "have an equal right to freedom in the state" (680/8:234). To be otherwise is to be a "slave" [*servum*] (684/8:250). In delineating the vices of a slave, Milton returns again and again to superstition [*superstitio*], the basis of the speech's initial distinction between citizens and the mob. He appeals to his "fellow citizens" [*vos, o cives*][21] to "drive from your minds the superstitions [*superstitiones*] that are sprung from ignorance of real and genuine religion," lest those you have ostensibly defeated "reap rich reward from your ignorance and superstition [*superstitione*]" (680/8:240), and he lists "superstitions" [*superstitionibus*] along with "hatred . . . injustices, lusts, and rapine" as the vices threatening the self-rule of true citizens (684/8:250). By using superstition (Catholicism) rather than class as the basis of his distinction between the "mob" and the true citizens of the republic, Milton effectively identifies classical republican virtues with Protestant theology. This identification marks the climax of his defense of the English people themselves, linking exordium and peroration into a neat lexical frame around the more personal battle with Salmasius and More that constitutes the central portion of his speech. As Barnaby argues, "Milton reduc[es] the issue to its simplest terms": a choice between "God's purposes for history" and "a kind of political idolatry"—Stuart and papal tyranny.[22]

The distinction between the virtues of Protestant citizenship and the Catholic "superstition" that characterizes the *vulgi* is the firmest one Milton will make in *The Second Defense*. Flexibility and ambiguity are essential to the way Milton defines other aspects of citizenship in his speech.[23] These can be seen even when he personifies Protestant virtues in his portraits of the leaders of the new republic, in many ways the most elitist—and controversial —part of his argument. In praising and defending Bradshaw, Fairfax, Fleet-wood, and the rest (see, in particular, 674–78), Milton employs the same terms he had used to define the real English people: "these men come not from the off-scourings of the mob" [*colluvione vulgi*] but are "most of them citizens of the better stamp" [*meliores plerique notae cives*] (674/8:230), even the "most illustrious men and honored citizens" [*ornatissimis viris & spec-tatissimis civibus*] (678/8:234). Foremost among them is, of course, Oliver Cromwell, to whose praise (or admonition) Milton devotes the bulk of his peroration. Milton lauds Cromwell for his command not only over his armies, but also over himself, for he has defeated in himself those vices that charac-terize the mob: "vain hopes, fears, desires"—all the elements that allow "su-perstition" to triumph (667–68).[24] His virtues make him "the man most fit to rule" and earn him the title of *pater patriae*, father of his country, the title awarded to Cicero after his defeat of Catiline, the symbol of mob rule's threat to republican virtues.[25] Milton again returns to the distinctions of the exordium as he notes that Cromwell has rejected more regal titles, "which seem so great in the opinion of the mob" [*vulgi licet opinione magnus*] (672/8:224).

Such patriarchal metaphors seem to solidify the speech's elitism and support Fallon's contention that *The Second Defense* reveals "Milton's admiration for Cromwell at the time and his clear preference for the Protectorate over the bungling governments that preceded it." Though Fallon argues that one can find criticism of Cromwell only by "mining scattered words" in the text, close attention to Milton's Latin demonstrates that these "scattered words" actually form a pattern, though one of studied ambiguity.[26] Much as he had done in his earlier distinctions between the mob and the citizens, so too Milton employs the language of Roman republicanism to create distinctions more flexible than they initially seem. The praise Milton bestows on Cromwell with the title *pater patriae* is certainly double-edged in this context. The same Roman senate that gave the title to Cicero would soon thereafter bestow it upon Caesar and Augustus when they assumed imperial rule. The phrase could thus equate Cromwell with absolutist antirepublicanism as much as with republican virtues. Indeed, in the *Defensio* Milton had forcefully rejected the phrase, pointing out to Salmasius that the metaphor *pater patriae* hardly constitutes a persuasive case for equating paternal and royal authority (326/7:44).[27]

The ambiguity in Milton's republican praise of Cromwell implies that his ethical distinctions between the citizens and the mob could work in another way as well. The greatest tribute Milton gives Cromwell contains within it the direst warning: that in surrendering to the lack of moral restraint that characterizes the "mob," Cromwell could become a tyrant. Milton is careful throughout the peroration to balance praise of Cromwell's republican ethical, political, and Christian virtues (in particular, religious tolerance) with their opposites. Each of Cromwell's celebrated virtues, Milton implies, is a notch on a yardstick to measure his future political performance. Cromwell is being tried by providential history, and "these trials . . . require a man supported by divine help" (674): that is, supported by the true Father, not by some metaphor.[28] In this context, Milton's praise of the same virtues in other leaders of the revolution like Bradshaw and Overton, who had opposed Cromwell's dissolution of the Rump, becomes potentially double-edged as well. Noticeably, he singles out Fairfax, who, emulating that other great hero of Roman republicanism, Cato, had "defeated . . . ambition" and in doing so displayed the Christian virtues of "supreme modesty and supreme holiness," showing his "divine favor" [*divinus favor*] (669/8:216).[29] Yet it is not merely God's aid that Cromwell needs; Milton concludes this section of the speech by warning him that "you yourself cannot be free without us [*sine nobis*]," so he exhorts Cromwell to "restore to us [*nobis*] our liberty unharmed and even enhanced" as a first step in remaking the "people [*nos*]" in his image (673–74/8:226–28).

The pronouns Milton employs at this crucial moment reflect a significant shift both within the text and from the *Defensio*. They rephrase the conclusion of the *Defensio*, which addresses the English people as "you" [*vos quoque, o cives*] (535/7:550), as the more inclusive "we" [*nos*]. "We," moreover, lacks a clear antecedent. Does it refer solely to the *cives* who Milton had previously argued are the basis of the new state? Or does it suggest a broader formulation of the "English people"? The closest nouns do not clarify much. In beginning his exhortations, Milton thrice refers to the nation or country, twice using the broad, even geographical Latin term *patria* (673/8:224) and once the general (though with tribal or clannish connotations) *gens* (673/8:226). But Milton uses a more intriguing word toward the end of this section of the speech when he reminds Cromwell that he must "rule with wisdom three powerful nations [and] lead their peoples [*populos*] from base customs to a better standard of morality and discipline than before" (674/8:228). *Populus* introduces a new concept into the discussion, or rather reintroduces it, for it is the same term Salmasius had challenged the English revolutionaries to define in his *Defensio Regia*. The term, which replaces the one Milton had used for the people in the *Defensio*, *plebs*, seems strongly linked with "we" [*nos*], and thus suggests a third possibility, a more flexible category between the ethical and political rectitude of the *cives*, on the one hand, and the moral and religious depravity of the *vulgi*, on the other.[30]

The Latin of the Roman republicanism from which Milton draws supports this suggestion. In that lexicon, *populus* has the connotation both of the people composing the governing structures of the state, the patricians and the *cives*, and of the masses, the *plebs* and the *vulgi*. As used by orators like Cicero, it signified a rhetorical and ideological construct as much as a discrete political entity; it allowed for exclusiveness and inclusiveness, elitism and populism at once. The *populus* as a whole were a safe rhetorical bastion, as they would always be in the right, regardless of the meanness or depravity of their constituent groups.[31] Milton takes full advantage of this nominal flexibility in the Latin title of the work (*pro Populo Anglicano*) but does so especially in the central sections of his argument, where he tussles with More over the nature of the English republic. There he eschews (with just a few notable exceptions) the distinctions of the exordium and peroration and instead interchanges or uses both the delineating terms (*populo, Anglicano*) of his title, particularly in crucial, heightened rhetorical moments. For example, when employing the modesty *topos* and turning on its head More's contempt that only "a certain

John Milton" was found to respond to Salmasius, Milton says he "regrets" that "I alone was found to defend the cause of the people of England [*populi Anglicani*]" (607/8:110; see also 611/8:118). Later, he will joust with More about what constitutes the national character of the "English" [*Angli*] (629/8: 140), and he uses *populus* and *Anglus* interchangeably when contrasting the Scottish desire to retain the monarchy and the "English" [*Angli*] desire to do away with it because the state has faith in the judgment of the "people" [*populo*] (642–43/8:166). Perhaps most crucially, when praising Bradshaw and his courage in presiding over the trial of Charles, Milton notes that his "loyalty, sobriety, dignity, and presence of mind" in conducting himself and overseeing the trial symbolize divine providence for this "task, which God . . . had long since ordained was to be performed among this people [*in hoc populo*]" (638/8:156). In all these instances, the virtues of the broadly construed "people" merge with those of their spokesmen or leaders, whether Milton, Parliament, Bradshaw, or even God.

At times, Milton must sharpen his distinctions. God's task and the people's will and resolution regarding the execution of the king are at the core of Milton's argument against *Clamor* and the man Milton believed was its author. The defining moment comes at the people's reaction to the regicide. More, like Salmasius before him, attacks the dissolution of the House of Lords and the episcopacy, hinting at the leveling tendencies of the former and giving the latter the tint of "Anabaptist doctrine." Milton briefly defends both acts against the charges of radicalism, saying "equality in the state is not Anabaptist doctrine; it is democracy [*Democratia*], a much more ancient thing" (632–33/8:146). Yet Milton almost immediately begins qualifying this bold assertion as he seeks to define his terminology. First, he claims the "people" [*populus*] urged Parliament to hasten the execution. But almost immediately he asks whether Parliament should "have waited for the consent of the people [*populi nutus*], as if the outcome of such great counsels depended on that consent?" The next sentence conflates the two positions: he asks whether Parliament, summoned by "the people as a whole" [*ab universo populo*], is obliged to "defer to the commands of the people [*iussa populi*]" and throw itself "into the snares of the tyrant, if he chanced to be acquitted by the people [*a populo*]?" (634/8:150).

Attempting to define democracy in *The Second Defense* seems to have caused Milton the same sort of trouble that he experienced in defining the people in the *Defensio*. The result is either a troubling distinction (some people are more equal than others) or complete confusion.[32] To clarify matters, the passage must, of course, be put into the broader context of the speech and the questions it raises about the nature of the people it claims to defend. Milton continues to refine the distinction. He asks whether Parliament, having received "supreme powers," should be forced continually to refer questions "beyond the capacity of the masses [*vulgi captum*]" back not to the "people, but to the mob" [*non dico ad populum, sed ad multitudinem*]? Milton reverts, that is, to the distinction that begins and ends his speech, only with a difference: it is now not between citizens and the mob, but between the people and the mob. In just a few sentences, Milton seems to have traveled a long way from *Democratia*.

The huge ideological but short textual distance Milton's distinction traverses suggests ambiguity, or an alloy of irony, in Milton's Latin. Certainly contrasting the "people" and the "mob" enlarges the former category while further restricting the latter, particularly when the "mob" is linked with "superstition" or Catholicism. And Milton proceeds to balance his reconception of the "people" to the exclusion of the masses with redefinitions of his earlier key terms as well. Only twice does the term *cives* occur in the central portion of *The Second Defense*. In the first, Milton explains his return home from Italy as occasioned by his "fellow citizens [*mei cives*] . . . fighting for their liberty" (619/8:124). This reference is balanced by the only instance in which Milton uses *cives* in a pejorative sense in the speech, when he defends the regicides against the popular revulsion at the King's execution by asking "who denies that times may often come when a majority of the citizens [*civium major numerus*] are wanton, preferring to follow Catiline or Antony rather than the sounder party of the Senate?" Milton contrasts their actions with those of the "upright citizens" [*boni cives*], who have "regard rather for their duty than for their small number" (648/8:176). By replacing the *cives* and *vulgi* distinction with one between two forms of *cives* at this crucial moment in the speech, Milton appears to make a stunning admission about the deterioration of the virtues of the citizens whom his speech posits as the backbone of the new republic. The reference to Catiline is particularly notable, as it sets up Milton's appropriation of the term *pater patriae* for Cromwell, which promotes the ambiguities Milton exploits.

Milton is clearly asking for some fine distinctions within his broad definition of the English people as he replies to their detractors. But Milton would not be Milton if he did not prepare his readers to make precisely such distinctions. Thus, he balances his redefinition of *cives* with redefinitions of *vulgi* as well. At the very beginning of the exordium, he had exploited the class connotations of the term *vulgi* to link it contemptuously with "superstition" or Catholicism, identified as the true ethical markers of the internal enemies of the English people. Now he reverses the connotations to condemn the external enemies of the English. When countering More's praise of Salmasius and recounting his own (mock) trepidation before attempting the *Defensio*, Milton deflates Salmasius's pretensions to learning by mocking him

as a mere schoolteacher [*grammaticus*] and by noting his "great many books
. . . not indeed especially useful, but concerned with most obscure subjects
and crammed with quotations from important authors. There is nothing
calculated more quickly to win the admiration of the reading public" (602).
The Latin phrase Milton uses, with pointed irony, for Salmasius's audience is
literatorum vulgus, which Burnett and Hadas translate more accurately as
the "literary vulgar" (8:100–102). Milton reinforces the irony just a few lines
later by noting Salmasius's appeal (cited previously) to "the deep-rooted
prejudice (or rather it should be called superstition) of the mob [*inveterate
vulgi opinio, sive superstitio*]" (603/8:100). That is, there can be a learned,
elite "mob" as well, exemplified in one sense by people like Salmasius who,
"swollen and complacent with his empty grammarian's conceit," attack the
republic "in the wonted manner of the mob" [*ut est fere ingenium vulgi*].
Significantly, the Latin Milton initially uses for the learned mob exemplified
by Salmasius, *multi,* is cognate to the *multitudinem* he later contrasts with the
true "people" [*populus*] of England (549/8:2–4). Those whose learning is
only a pretense, Milton suggests, are as incapable of the ethical demands of
citizenship as those who lack learning altogether.

Milton emphasizes this point by contrasting authors who are parodies of
learning with true poets (that is, himself). The distinction thus becomes part
of the argument's central ethical struggle, embracing Milton and his assumed
protagonist. A "poetaster," the title Milton gives to More for his praise of
Salmasius, is to an authentic poet as the genuine "people" are to the "multitude." While true poets "are bitterly hostile to tyrants," they (poetasters)
display the same qualities Milton attributes to the mob: "nothing could be
more foolish, more idle, more corrupt, or more false than such as they" (592–
93). Milton continues in this personal vein when he identifies a third Hydra's
head of this "learned mob," his old enemies the censors. He defends his
Areopagitica with a witty Latin paradox; he condemns censors as "a few men
[*paucos*] (and these mostly ignorant and of vulgar discernment [*indoctos, &
vulgaris judicii homines*])" (626/8:134), conflating and at the same time in-
verting the prior contrast between the ethical qualities of the few and the
qualities of the many. The ethical basis of the *vulgi,* like that of the people,
lies neither in numbers nor in social class but rather, as Milton's close distinctions continually emphasize, on obedience to God's wishes and the best use
of the talents granted by God.[33]

Nonetheless, teacher, poet/orator, and censor were all offices Milton
took up in service of the people and the republic. It is little wonder that he
continually emphasizes such fine distinctions when his opponents aspire to
these very offices. There is a sense in which his opponents have correlatives
in *The Second Defense,* in which Milton matches them with the categories he

has proposed: the mob, the citizens, and the people. The censor keeps the affairs of the state out of the hands and minds of the giddy vulgar; the poet/orator addresses the elite audience of the learned citizens, praising their heroic deeds in confronting tyrants; the teacher educates the people on their long journey toward responsible, pious citizenship. In these correlations Milton's strategy of ethical proof reaches its height as he invites his readers to ponder the effect of the pedantic Salmasius, the salacious More, or their English equivalents in any of these roles. *The Second Defense*, in its broad definitions and sharp distinctions, suggests that a people shaped by such would never reach the heights of citizenship and would soon degenerate into the mob Milton fears.

II

Of course, there is elitism in Milton's distinctions, elitism of the sort many see as central to his political (and cultural) ideology. Milton puts himself in a moral and intellectual vanguard. In *The Second Defense,* this means pledging allegiance to Cromwell despite many misgivings. But the central problem of deducing Milton's definition of the people he defends can easily be side-tracked by such concerns. In drawing on the terms and strategies of the Roman orators of the republic, Milton is able to play both sides: he can be inclusive in his definition of the people to his opponents, while restricting its definition when he addresses the actual power structures of the English republic. By linking these definitions to God's providential history (and England's special place within it), Milton can go beyond his classical models and assume the mantle of a biblical prophet and teacher, a modern Saint Paul able to praise and criticize the institutions he defends.[34] Yet there is a sense in which Milton's definitions are more than rhetorical, for they transcend the strategies of his Roman predecessors to fulfill the promises of his biblical ones. By combining ethical proofs with flexible social and political categories, Milton suggests a kind of political and ethical flexibility that his Roman models could not have imagined.[35] The people in this conception are less a vague, general abstraction than a vital, developing entity: a work in progress, rather than a static (if amorphous) mass to be used or manipulated. In this sense, Sharon Achinstein is right: Milton "never gave up on the English people," largely because he refused to define them in any fixed way.[36] The question this flexibility raises, though, is how—and by whom—the people can and should be molded into something worthy of a more fixed definition.

Milton's attacks on More and Salmasius as teachers, poets, and censors clarify who should *not* be given such a task. The conclusion of *The Second Defense* seems to imply that it is Cromwell's job to mold the English "people" in his image. But the ambiguities of Milton's praise of the Protector have already been noted; as always, Milton eschews easy answers. But I would argue that he does weave strong suggestions into the intricate design of *The Second Defense*. Milton singles out for particular praise not just the leaders of the New Model Army, but the army itself. The central portion of Milton's praise comes at a key moment of his argument, as he defends the revolution against charges of "heresy" and just after he has distinguished between the actions of the "wanton" and "upright" citizens concerning the regicide (see above). To fight More's charges and the anxieties they have raised, Milton makes the army a microcosm of the "people" he defends, positing similar distinctions for it as he has for the larger category. He admits that some "common soldiers" [*gregarios milites*] can be undisciplined and that these "behaved rather insolently" at Charles's execution (644/8:168–70). Such soldiers parallel the "wanton citizens," or the *vulgi*, whom Milton has cited previously as supporting the king. Milton, however, praises those "better disciplined" parts of the army that have continued to support Cromwell and the "cause," like the *cives* of the exordium and peroration of the speech. These soldiers and their leader indeed are "welcomed and cherished by their fellow citizens" [*civibus gratum atque dilectum*] (668–69/8:216).

Equating the New Model Army with the ideals of citizenship would seem an authoritarian answer to the problems of the early English republic. The discipline Milton praises is not just blind, military obedience, however. In fact, its central elements are scarcely military at all. As he counters More's attack on the army and in particular his depiction of it as "a Lernean swamp of all heresies," Milton distinguishes between other armies, full of "lusts, rapine, gaming, swearing, and perjuring," and "our army" [*exercitum nostrum*], in which "what leisure is available is spent in the search for truth, in careful reading of the Scripture, nor does anyone think it more glorious to smite the foe than to instruct himself and others in the knowledge of heavenly things, or think it more noble to practice warlike rather than evangelical combat" (648/8:170). That is, Milton praises in the soldiers the same sort of self-discipline he praises—and later questions—in Cromwell himself. Disciplined reading and rational discourse overcome the "superstitions" and factions that are the inevitable results of freedom of conscience. Thus, the New Model Army exemplifies to the English people how to become free by themselves, how to become a genuine "people" worthy of the name.

The praise of the army as a self-disciplined spiritual as well as military force may be one of Milton's strongest admonitions to Cromwell in *The Second Defense*. Fear of spiritual even more than political tyranny animates almost all of Milton's revolutionary writings, and by emphasizing the ability of common soldiers to become spiritual warriors Milton hopefully posits a strong check on any tyrannical impulses the republic's leaders may be nurturing. So he closes his admonitions to Cromwell with fervent pleas for religious liberty, moral education, and free inquiry: such are the means by which a nation can fashion itself into a true people (678–79). He forcefully posits the opposite as well, particularly in showing how a ruler can easily become a tyrant. Throughout *The Second Defense,* as in the *Defensio,* Milton is careful to demonstrate that he opposes not monarchy per se, but rather monarchy that devolves into tyranny. Milton even goes so far as to praise a female ruler to illustrate this distinction. His encomium on Queen Christina of Sweden has puzzled readers accustomed to Milton's contemptuous dismissal of other female rulers (Boadicea in *History of Britain,* for example) and often of the gender as a whole. More would characterize it as "a fawning digression."[37] But what exactly makes for the distinction and what makes Milton overcome his inveterate prejudices? As More suggests, vanity certainly plays a part, as Milton was pleased by the queen's enthusiastic response to the *Defensio.* He believes Christina has seen through Salmasius and thus has seen Milton himself correctly, proving her "keen judgment" and setting herself above the *vulgus literatorum* (602–3/8:100). For Milton, she is the kind of reader his text requires: a ruler parallel to the readers in the New Model Army. But as a ruler, Christina must do more than read; she assumes the task of schoolmistress to her people as well. Thus, when Milton praises her relationship to her "people" [*tui populi*], he links her judgment with theirs. What is her greatest accomplishment? Building them a library: "it is not for nothing that you collected from every source so many costly books, so many works of literature, not as if they could teach you anything, but so that from them your fellow-citizens [*tui cives*] could learn to know you and contemplate the excellence of your virtue and wisdom." Hence, the "calm judgment" [*tam nihil turbatam . . . judicantem*] and proper rights of the virtuous ruler come to accord with those of "her people" [*tui populi*] even in times of crisis (605/8: 104–6). While negating the "disorder" [*turbatam*] of the mind that characterizes the mob [*turba,* "mob"] and tyrants, the lexical movement between *populus* and *cives* traces the path Milton's distinctions seek to blaze for the English people and their leaders throughout *The Second Defense.*

Perhaps only in his true epic poem, *Paradise Lost,* has Milton exploited the precision and flexibilities of language with such art. The very looseness of Milton's definition(s) of the people becomes their true defense: they are what they can make themselves as well as what they can be made into. If the conclusion of *The Second Defense* with its dire warnings is darker than that of, say, *Areopagitica,* it remains based on the same ideals, and those ideals— Protestant liberty of conscience and free inquiry—are what the English people will rise or fall by. The same applies to their rulers, who, lest they become tyrants, must ensure those ideals and actively promote them in order to renew their legitimacy. Because of the broad, flexible distinctions that Milton develops about the subject that his tract defends, he is able to transcend petty, personal invective and moderate strident elitism. His answer to Salmasius's question comes late, comes in a foreign language, and comes with immense complexities; yet all these, paradoxically, in the end prove the greatest compliments Milton pays to the people he defends.

Union College

NOTES

I would like to thank Al Labriola for his patient help in shaping and polishing this essay and Dean Christie Sorum (1944–2005) of Union College for her unfailing support of my studies in Milton's Latin. *Interque felices perennis / Elysio spatiere campo.*

1. John Milton, *Second Defense of the English People*, in *The Complete Prose Works of John Milton*, 8 vols., ed. Don M. Wolfe et al. (New Haven, 1953–1982), 4.1:685, 554. All English citations of Milton's prose are, unless otherwise indicated, to this volume and will hereafter be cited parenthetically by page number. Citations of other volumes of the *Complete Prose* will be hereafter designated YP and cited parenthetically by volume and page number.

2. The citation of Marvell's letter comes from H. M. Margoliouth, *The Poems and Letters of Andrew Marvell*, 2 vols. (Oxford, 1952), 2:293. Bouhereau says of Milton's work, "he is everywhere brilliant and he says insults with so beautiful grace that . . . you won't stop being diverted with it." Cited and translated from the French by J. Milton French in *The Life Records of John Milton*, 5 vols. (New York, 1966), 5:44–45. Toland says little of *The Second Defense*, not wishing to "rake into the Ashes of the Dead," and contents himself with citing two passages that demonstrate "*Milton's* wit." Richardson cites *The Second Defense* extensively, largely for biographical purposes, but also to show Milton's "Manly eloquence." I take these citations from Helen Darbishire, *The Early Lives of Milton* (London, 1932), 163, 252.

3. See *Fides Publica*, in YP 2:1106; French, *Life Records*, 3:422; William Riley Parker, *Milton: A Biography*, 2 vols., 2nd ed., rev. and ed. Gordon Campbell (Oxford, 1996), 1:622.

4. John Hale, "Neo-Latin Polemic in the 1650s: Milton versus Salmasius and Others," *Classical and Modern Literature* 21, no. 1 (2001): 22. Hale's essay contains a good discussion of Milton's use of the ethical proof.

5. The early biographers, along with Parker and, more recently, John Shawcross, *John Milton: The Self and the World* (Lexington, Ky., 1993), mine the work for such biographical details throughout. Willliam Kerrigan examines the psychological dimensions of Milton's blindness, using passages from *The Second Defense*, in *The Sacred Complex: On the Psychogenesis of "Paradise Lost"* (Cambridge, Mass., 1983). On Milton's adaptations to the politics of the 1650s, see, for example, A. N. Wilson, *The Life of John Milton* (Oxford, 1983), 177–79, and Christopher Hill, *Milton and the English Revolution* (New York, 1977). Hill discusses *The Second Defense* only briefly (chap. 13), and largely to set up his next chapter, "Losing Hope."

6. For the first position, see Barbara Lewalski, *The Life of John Milton* (Oxford, 2000), 310; for the second, see Sharon Achinstein, *Milton and the Revolutionary Reader* (Princeton, 1994), 14.

7. Robert Fallon, "A *Second Defense*: Milton's Critique of Cromwell?" in *Milton Studies* 39, ed. Albert C. Labriola (Pittsburgh, 2000), 168–69. See footnote 27, below, for critics arguing that Milton admonishes Cromwell.

8. On the influence of Roman Republicanism on *The Second Defense,* see, for example, David Norbrook, *Writing the English Republic: Poetry, Rhetoric and Politics 1627–1660* (Cambridge, 1999), 331. Andrew Barnaby, "'Another Rome in the West?': Milton and the Imperial Republic, 1654–1670," in *Milton Studies* 30, ed. Albert C. Labriola (Pittsburgh, 1993), 67–108, argues that Milton links the imperial and republican ambitions of Protestant England through the Virgilian epic tradition; here, I focus on the classical rhetorical tradition.

9. As David Loewenstein, *Milton and the Drama of History: Historical Vision, Iconoclasm, and the Literary Imagination* (Cambridge, 1990), argues, "the dramas of nation and self are . . . never far apart in Milton's polemic" (78).

10. Roberts succinctly summarizes Milton's mistakes about the authorship of *Regii Sanguinis Clamor;* see YP 4.1:542–43. For simplicity's sake, I will retain Milton's error and refer to his opponent as More throughout.

11. On Milton's use of Cicero and Demosthenes, see Roberts, YP 4.1:539, and Lewalski, *The Life of John Milton,* 307–8.

12. Latin citations of Milton's work are from *The Works of John Milton,* 18 vols. in 21, ed. Frank A. Patterson et al. (New York, 1931–1938), 8:18, hereafter designated as CM. Milton's Latin will hereafter be cited by volume and page number following the page citation to the English of YP. On Egan's notion of "narrative presence," see *The Inward Teacher: Milton's Rhetoric of Christian Liberty* (University Park, Pa., 1980), 8–9. Egan does not, unfortunately, treat Milton's Latin tracts. On Milton's prophetic voice in *The Second Defense,* see Joseph Wittreich, "'The Crown of Eloquence': The Figure of the Orator in Milton's Prose Works," in *Achievements of the Left Hand: Essays on the Prose of John Milton,* ed. Michael Lieb and John Shawcross (Amherst, Mass., 1974), 3–54; and Reuben Sanchez, *Persona and Decorum in Milton's Prose* (Cranbury, N.J., 1997), 127–42.

13. Henrik Mouritsen, *Plebs and Politics in the Late Roman Republic* (Cambridge, 2001), 139–40, details the complexities of Roman political life in the republic thoroughly, and my essay is indebted to his research. It is obviously beyond the scope of this essay, however, to delineate the complex realities of Roman republicanism; rather, I am interested in how an educated European of the seventeenth century would have used and responded to its terminology. Throughout the *Defensio* Milton uses the traditional terms of Roman class division, *plebs* and *nobiles/optimates,* to describe English society (see, for example, 309/7:24, 316–17/7:28, 394/7:198, 424/7:274, 432/7:290), adding *rex*—a term odious to Romans—to emphasize Charles's tyranny.

14. Milton uses this term on the title pages of both his *Defenses.* Milton also sought to define the English in, for instance, his *History of Britain;* see my own "Shrugging Off the Norman Yoke: Milton's *History of Britain* and the Levellers," *ELR* 29 (1999): 306–25.

15. I would like to thank Hans-Friedrich Mueller of the Union College classics department for his help with translating Milton's Latin, though the ultimate responsibility for the accuracy of the translations is my own.

16. On the *plebs sordida,* see Mouritsen, *Plebs and Politics,* 76. Cicero says in *Pro Murena* that "nothing is more fickle than the masses [*vulgo*]" (cited by Mouritsen, 98). Milton does use *plebs* once in the exordium (551/8:6) to refer to the "common people," but it is an isolated use and lacks the patterning into which I will argue Milton shapes the other terms (*cives, vulgi, populi*) he employs. Martin Dzelzainis, "Milton's Classical Republicanism," in *Milton and Republicanism,* ed. David Armitage et al. (Cambridge, 1995), 3–24, examines Cicero's influence on Milton's republican thinking, though he does not treat *The Second Defense* in his article. Of

course, classical republicanism is not the only source for Milton's ideas about self-governance; Elizabeth Tuttle has examined biblical images in the *Defenses* in her "Biblical References in the Political Pamphlets" in the same volume; see especially 80–81.

17. Sherwin White, *The Roman Citizenship*, 2nd ed. (Oxford, 1973), 264. Definitions are from the *Oxford Latin Dictionary (OLD)*.

18. Lewalski, *Life*, 310, 314.

19. Barnaby, "'Another Rome in the West,'" 69.

20. Milton cites some of the attacks on his blindness on 582–92. He explicitly connects the pope's rule with "superstition" and "tyranny" in the *Defensio:* "He [the pope] . . . became the worst of tyrants . . . by persuading the people, whose minds he had long controlled by the bonds of superstition [*superstitione*], that even the worst of kings could not be deposed unless the pope had himself released them from their oath of allegiance" (396/7:202). He links Charles I's tyranny with Catholicism as well, noting that he had introduced "superstitious practices" [*superstitiosos cultus*] from the "depths of popery" (522/7:518). Milton also uses "superstition" synonymously with Catholicism in, for instance, *Of Reformation,* where he notes that "quick-sighted Protestants" cleared their eyes "from the mist of Superstition" (YP 1:592) and famously in *Areopagitica*, where he denies free speech to "Popery, and open superstition" (YP 2:565). See also *Paradise Lost* 12, where Michael tells Adam that in the Church, "Wolves shall succeed for teachers / . . . and the truth / With superstitions and traditions taint" (508–12).

21. North, the translator of the *Second Defense* in YP, renders *cives* here as "fellow countrymen," missing, I believe, the distinction Milton is making. Burnett's translation in CM (revised by Moses Hadas) uses "citizens" here.

22. Barnaby, "'Another Rome in the West?'" 67–68.

23. Here my argument intersects with those made (provocatively) by Stanley Fish in *How Milton Works* (Cambridge, Mass., 2001). Fish argues that Milton's works are essentially static and univocal, seeking to voice the demands "of an omniscient God whose will must be obeyed" (10) against those of a mutable and fluid world. In the sense that Protestantism is one of these demands and the essential qualification for citizenship in *The Second Defense,* my argument agrees with Fish's. But Fish rejects the possibility of the sort of lexical fluidity I argue is essential to Milton's project of defining the English people; here Milton seems to embrace at least part of the "centrifugal forces" of flux and ambiguity that Fish argues Milton's works seek to "rein in, as an omniscient and pervasive power either routs . . . or expels [them] . . . or reveals their plans to be a subset of his" (7). It is telling that Fish does not examine the *Defenses* at all in his book; nor does he look at the other predominately political tracts (*The Tenure of Kings and Magistrates, Eikonoklastes, The Readie and Easie Way*) in any detail.

24. Loewenstein, "Milton and the Poetics of Defense," links Milton's praise of Cromwell here with his own self-presentation as a champion of the people (187).

25. See Roberts, YP 4.1:672 n. 508. Thomas Corns, "Milton and the Characteristic of a Free Commonwealth," in Armitage et al., *Milton and Republicanism,* sees this as part of deliberate praise of Cromwell "as a godly monarch who transcends the achievement of kings" (36), an assessment that misses the ambiguities and ironies I will cite later.

26. Fallon, "Milton's Critique of Cromwell?" 180. Recent critics discussing the ambiguity of Milton's praise of Cromwell include David Armitage, "John Milton: Poet Against Empire," *Milton and Republicanism,* 206–25, who argues that "Milton put[s] the Protector and his regime on probation" in the conclusion of the *Second Defense* (214); Loewenstein, "Milton and the Poetics of Defense," who says it shows "Milton's keen political realism" (188–89); and Blair Worden, "Milton and Marchamont Needham," in Armitage et al., *Milton and Republicanism,* 156–80, who notes that the warnings to Cromwell "went beyond [the] conventions" of Renaissance praise that mix glorification with edification and admonishment (176). Lewalski, *Life,* sees

the panegyric to Cromwell as filled with instructions and urgings, but sees the warnings to "his fellow citizens" as the strongest (315–18). More in the *Fides Publica* claims that Milton "would appear more lofty than the very exalted Cromwell . . . whom you advise under the guise of praising, for whom you dictate laws, set aside titles, and prescribe duties" (YP 4.2:1109).

27. The distinction is even stronger in the Latin: "At hercle etiam in tenebris es, qui jus patrium a regio non distinguis: et cum reges Patriae Patres nominaveris, ea statim metaphora persuasisse credis, ut quicquid de patre non negaverim, id continuo de rege verum esse concedam" (7:44). *Hercle* is an interjection "used to express strong feeling" and reserved almost exclusively for male speakers or writers (*OLD*). Milton rejects the *pater patriae* metaphor again in the *Defensio* on 472/7:394. Roberts's footnote (43), YP 4.1:473, succinctly sums up "the sharp polemical difference" here between Milton and Salmasius over the phrase. Many recent critics, though alert to the ambiguities of Milton's relationship with Cromwell, fail to see it here. Loewenstein, "Milton and the Poetics of Defense," for instance, argues that "As *pater patriae,* Cromwell resembles a classical leader who embodies the political ideals of his nation" (187). See also Corns, "Milton and the Characteristic of a Free Commonwealth," 36.

28. See Loewenstein, *Milton and the Drama of History,* 78.

29. On the political significance of the other leaders Milton praises, see Austin Woolrych, "Milton and Cromwell: A Short and Scandalous Night of Interruption," in Lieb and Shawcross, *Achievements of the Left Hand,* 192–94, and Parker, *Milton,* 1:441, 444–45.

30. As Hale, "Neo-Latin Polemic," notes, Milton even modifies the republican formula *SPQR* (*Senatus Populusque Romanus*), describing Parliament as *Senatus Populusque Anglicanus* (13 n. 22). Milton does use *populus* (as well as *civis*) in the *Defensio,* but no apparent pattern emerges because he is restrained by the need to respond to Salmasius's terminology.

31. See Mouritsen's analysis of the workings of the Roman *contio* (a nonlegislative public meeting), in *Plebs and Politics,* chap. 3. As he summarizes later, "the profound respect for a notional *populus Romanus,* professed by all Roman politicians, went hand in hand with a disdain for the actual people, highlighting . . . the ambiguous nature of this concept in Roman politics" (141). He cites Wood's description of uses of the term as "rhetorical genuflexions" in *Cicero's Social and Political Thought* (Berkeley and Los Angeles, 1988), 96.

32. Roberts, for instance, calls Milton's reasoning here "sophistical" (YP 4.1:635 n. 370).

33. The most telling instances of this would, of course, be the Lady in *Comus,* Abdiel in *Paradise Lost,* and Christ in *Paradise Regained.* Again, see Fish, *How Milton Works,* for the argument for this as the inflexible dogma informing all of Milton's work.

34. Again, see Reuben Sanchez, *Persona and Decorum in Milton's Prose,* especially 130–31, and Wittreich, "Crown of Eloquence," especially 8–10.

35. Mouritsen, *Plebs and Politics,* rebuts recent scholarship, suggesting a more "democratic" Roman republic, concluding that "the people of Rome never became fully integrated into the political process" (144).

36. Achinstein, *Milton and the Revolutionary Reader,* 14.

37. *Fides Publica,* in YP 4.2:1106. The *Defensio,* for example, contains some of his most strident statements on women as Milton derides Salmasius's masculinity, claiming he is "used to suffer so slavishly a woman's tyranny at home" (380; see also 471).